Mobil ★★★★★

Travel Guide®

GREAT PLAINS

ACKNOWLEDGEMENTS

We gratefully acknowledge the help of our representatives for their efficient and perceptive inspections of the lodging and dining establishments listed, the establishments' proprietors for their cooperation in showing their facilities and providing information about them, and the many users of previous editions who have taken the time to share their experiences. Mobil Travel Guide is also grateful to all the talented writers who contributed entries to this book.

Maps: ©GeoNova. This product contains proprietary property of GeoNova. Unauthorized use, including copying, of this product is expressly prohibited.

Front cover photos:
Iowa Corn Field: U.S. Landmarks and Travel/Getty Images
Des Moines Skyline: U.S. Landmarks and Travel/Getty Images
White Barn: © Julia Brabec
St. Louis Arch at Sunset: © Barry Howe/ Corbis

ISBN: 0-8416-0310-3 or 978-0-8416-0310-3
Manufactured in the Canada.
10 9 8 7 6 5 4 3 2 1

CONTENTS

MAPS

GREAT PLAINS

mobiltravelguide.com

CELEBRATING 50 YEARS

Because time is precious and the travel industry is ever-changing, having accurate, reliable travel information at your has fingertips is essential. Mobil Travel Guide provided invaluable insight to travelers for 50 years, and we are committed to continuing this service into the future.

The Mobil Corporation (known as Exxon Mobil Corporation since a 1999 merger) began producing the Mobil Travel Guide books in 1958 following the introduction of the U.S.-interstate highway system in 1956. The first edition covered only five Southwestern states. Since then, our books have become the premier travel guides in North America, covering all 50 states and Canada.

Since its founding, Mobil Travel Guide has served as an advocate for travelers seeking knowledge about hotels, restaurants and places to visit. Based on an objective process, we make recommendations to our customers that we believe will enhance the quality and value of their travel experiences. Our trusted Mobil One- to Five-Star rating system is the oldest and most respected lodging and restaurant inspection and rating program in North America. Most hoteliers, restaurateurs and industry observers favorably regard the rigor of our inspection program and understand the prestige and benefits that come with receiving a Mobil Star rating.

The Mobil Travel Guide process of rating each establishment includes:
★ Unannouced facility inspections
★ Incognito service evaluations for
★ A review of unsolicited comments from the general public
★ Senior management oversight

For each property, more than 450 attributes, including cleanliness, physical facilities and employee attitude and courtesy, are measured and evaluated to produce a mathematically derived score, which is then blended with the other elements to form an overall score. These scores form the basis that we use to assign our Mobil One- to Five-Star ratings.

This process focuses on guest expectations, guest experience and consistency of service, not just physical facilities and amenities. It's fundamentally a rating system that rewards those properties that continually strive for and achieve excellence each year. The very best properties are consistently raising the bar for those that wish to compete with them.

Only facilities that meet Mobil Travel Guide's standards earn the privilege of being listed in the guide. Deteriorating, poorly managed establishments are deleted. A Mobil Travel Guide listing constitutes a positive quality recommendation. Every listing is an accolade, a recognition of achievement.

★★★★★The Mobil Five-Star Award indicates that a property is one of the very best in the country and consistently provides gracious and courteous service, superlative quality in its facility and a unique ambience. The lodgings and restaurants at the Mobil

iv

Five-Star level consistently continues their commitment to excellence, doing so with grace and perseverance.

★★★★The Mobil Four-Star Award honors properties for outstanding achievement in overall facility and for providing very strong service levels in all areas. These award winners provide a distinctive experience for the ever-demanding and sophisticated consumer.

★★★The Mobil Three-Star Award recognizes an excellent property that provides full services and amenities. This category ranges from exceptional hotels with limited services to elegant restaurants with a less-formal atmosphere.

★★The Mobil Two-Star property is a clean and comfortable establishment that has expanded amenities or a distinctive environment. These properties are an excellent place to stay or dine.

★The Mobil One-Star property is limited in its amenities and services but provides a value experience while meeting travelers' expectations. Expect the properties to be clean, comfortable and convenient.

We do not charge establishments for inclusion in our guides. We have no relationship with any of the businesses and attractions we list and act only as a consumer advocate. We do the investigative legwork so that you won't have to.

Restaurants and hotels—particularly small chains and stand-alone establishments—change management or even go out of business with surprising quickness. Although we make every effort to update continuously information, we recommend that you call ahead to make sure the place you've selected is still open.

We hope that your travels are enjoyable and relaxing and that our books help you get the most out of every trip you take. If any aspect of your accommodation, dining, spa or sightseeing experience motivates you to comment, please contact us. Mobil Travel Guide, 200 W. Madison St., Suite 3950, Chicago, IL 60611, or send an e-mail to info@mobiltravelguide.com.
Happy travels.

HOW TO USE THIS BOOK

The Mobil Travel Guide Regional Travel Planners are designed for convenience. Each state has its own chapter, beginning with a general introduction that provides a geographical and historical orientation to the state and gives basic statewide tourist information. The remainder of each chapter is devoted to travel destinations within the state—mainly cities and towns, but also national parks and tourist areas—which, like the states, are arranged in alphabetical order.

THE STAR RATINGS
MOBIL RATED HOTELS

Travelers have different needs when it comes to accommodations. To help you pinpoint properties that meet your particular needs, Mobil Travel Guide classifies each lodging by type according to the following characteristics.

★★★★★The Mobil Five-Star hotel provides consistently superlative service in an exceptionally distinctive luxury environment,

© GeoNova

with expanded services. Attention to detail is evident throughout the hotel, resort or inn, from bed linens to staff uniforms.

★★★★The Mobil Four-Star hotel provides a luxury experience with expanded amenities in a distinctive environment. Services may include automatic turndown service, 24-hour room service and valet parking.

★★★The Mobil Three-Star hotel is well appointed, with a full-service restaurant and expanded amenities, such as a fitness center, golf course, tennis courts, 24-hour room service and optional turndown service.

★★The Mobil Two-Star hotel is considered a clean, comfortable and reliable establishment that has expanded amenities, such as a full-service restaurant on the premises.

★The Mobil One-Star lodging is a limited-service hotel, motel or inn that is considered a clean, comfortable and reliable establishment For every property, we also provide pricing information. The pricing categories break down as follows:

★   **$** = Up to $150
★   **$$** = $151-$250
★   **$$$** = $251-$350
★   **$$$$** = $351 and up

All prices quoted are accurate at the time of publication, however prices cannot be guaranteed. In some locations, special events, holidays or seasons can affect prices. Some resorts have complicated rate structures that vary with the time of year, so confirm rates when making your plans.

SPECIALITY LODGINGS

A Speciality Lodging is a unique inn, bed and breakfast or guest ranch with limited service, but appealing, attractive facilities that make the property worth a visit.

MOBIL RATED RESTAURANTS

All Mobil Star-rated dining establishments listed in this book have a full kitchen and most offer table service.

★★★★★The Mobil Five-Star restaurant offers one of few flawless dining experiences in the country. These establishments consistently provide exceptional food, service and décor.

★★★★The Mobil Four-Star restaurant provides professional service, distinctive presentations and wonderful food.

★★★The Mobil Three-Star restaurant has good food, warm and skillful service and enjoyable décor.

★★The Mobil Two-Star restaurant serves fresh food in a clean setting with efficient service. Value is considered in this category, as is family friendliness.

★The Mobil One-Star restaurant provides a distinctive experience through culinary specialty, local flair or individual atmosphere. The pricing categories are defined as follows, per diner, and assume that you order an appetizer or dessert, an entrée and one drink:

★   **$** = $15 and under
★   **$$** = $16-$35
★   **$$$** = $36-$85
★   **$$$$** = $86 and up

All prices quoted are accurate at the time of publication, but prices cannot be guaranteed.

MOBIL RATED SPAS

Mobil Travel Guide is pleased to announce its newest category, hotel and resort spas. Until now, these spas have not been formally rated or inspected by any organization. Every spa selected for inclusion in this book underwent a rigorous inspection process similar to the one Mobil Travel Guide has applied to lodgings and restaurants for five decades. After researching more than 300 spas and performing exhaustive incognito inspections of more than 200 properties, we narrowed our list to the best spas in the United States and Canada.

★★★★★The Mobil Five-Star spa provides consistently superlative service in an exceptionally distinctive luxury environment with extensive amenities. The staff at a Mobil Five-Star spa provides extraordinary service beyond the traditional spa experience, allowing guests to achieve the highest level of relaxation and pampering.

★★★★The Mobil Four-Star spa provides a luxurious experience with expanded amenities in an elegant and serene environment. Throughout the spa facility, guests experience personalized service. Amenities might include, but are not limited to, single-sex relaxation rooms where guests wait for their treatments, plunge pools and whirlpools in both men's and women's locker rooms, and an array of treatments, including at a minimum a selection of massages, body therapies, facials, and a variety of salon services.

★★★The Mobil Three-Star spa is physically well appointed and has a full complement of staff.

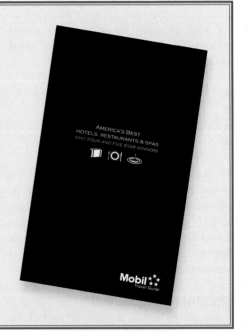

★ CELEBRATING ★
50 YEARS OF MOBIL TRAVEL GUIDE

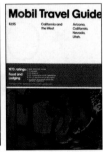

├─ **1962** ──── **1964** ──── **1968** ──── **1971** ──── **1973** →

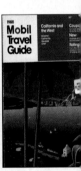

├─ **1976** ──────── **1978** ──── **1979** ──── **1986** ──── **1988**

├─ **1989** ──── **1992** ──── **1994** ──── **1997** ──── **2003**

IOWA

PROBABLY MORE THAN ANY OTHER HEARTLAND STATE, IOWA CONJURES UP IMAGES OF table-top-flat cornfields dotted with silos and farmhouses. And while in some parts of the state you will indeed find yourself driving through a sea of corn that stretches to the horizon (Iowa grows more of it than any state but Illinois), with a bit of exploring, you'll find ski slopes, towering bluffs above the Mississippi River, six wildlife refuges—one harboring wetlands and fields that teem with birds during migration season, another that showcases Iowa's prairie heritage, with native grasses and wild flowers and the chance to encounter buffalo and elk, and another where you can climb up and down hills left untouched by the glaciers that chiseled and flattened the land elsewhere thousands of years ago.

The Sioux called Iowa the "Beautiful Land" and it's a name that fits. Every region of the state has a loop of Scenic Byways, well-marked routes that reveal the beauty of the countryside. Iowa has miles of bike trails, many built on the gentle grades of old railroad lines. Hikers can retreat into the tranquility of nature preserve trails that retrace such historical journeys as those of Louis and Clark or the Mormons as they moved west.

History abounds in Iowa. This is the birthplace of Buffalo Bill Cody, John Wayne and Herbert Hoover. In Des Moines, visitors to the State Historical Museum are greeted by a 16,000-year-old Hebior mammoth, while airplanes "buzz" overhead in the atrium. To the northeast, in Dubuque, freshwater creatures and habitats get their due, in the recently opened National River Museum and Aquarium. Down the road, in Eldon, see the house that inspired the background for Iowa native Grant Wood's most famous painting, "American Gothic." And in the southeast, the Amana colonies—seven historic villages formed by German immigrants as a religious communal society—offer attractions than can easily fill a day, or even a week.

You won't need a guidebook to discover Iowa's essential charm, the friendly character of people who are by heritage tied to the land and the value of work. To find this, sit down in a local cafe in a small town at lunchtime. Or, in the summer, make your way to one of the fairs held in each of the 99 counties. Buy yourself a corn dog and head to the agricultural barn where kids display their meticulously groomed cows, pigs and sheep. From the dedication and pride you'll see in these young people's faces, you'll learn what Iowa is about.

1

IOWA

★ SPOTLIGHT

★ Iowa's nickname, the Hawkeye state, is said to be a tribute to Chief Black Hawk, a Native American warrior in the War of 1812.

★ Iowa holds the first presidential caucus in January every election year, making it the benchmark for presidential races.

★ The state produces more ethanol that any other in the country.

★ Famous Iowans include John Wayne, Ashton Kutcher, Elijah Wood and Herbert Hoover.

FROM THE BRIDGES OF MADISON COUNTY TO THE LOESS HILLS

Surrounded by wooded hills, Winterset, originally a Quaker settlement, is the hub of several short side trips to the six covered bridges made famous by the Robert Wallers novel *The Bridges of Madison County*. If you want to make the full circuit, pick up a free brochure and map to all the bridges from local businesses (most are on remote county roads). If you don't have time for the full tour, one of the bridges is now preserved in Winterset's city park. The Madison County Historical Complex is an 18-acre park with a number of historic buildings, including a limestone barn and the old Winterset train depot.

Quaker-founded Winterset was a station along the Underground Railroad. A painted brick house, now in the Winterset Art Center, served as a temporary home for hundreds of displaced slaves during the 1850s and 1860s, including scholar George Washington Carver, who lived here after experiencing discrimination elsewhere in the Midwest. Winterset is also the birthplace of actor John Wayne, who was born Marion Robert Morrison. His family home is open to visitors.

Drive south on Highway 169 and turn west on Highway 34 to Creston, an old railroading center with an impressive core of late Victorian homes and storefronts. The town's McKinley Park houses the Union County Historical Museum, with remnants of Creston's heyday in the 1880s. Continue on Highway 34 to the village of Corning, once home to the Icarian Colony, the longest operating nonreligious utopian community in the United States. Founded in 1850, the 80-member community disbanded in 1900 after establishing vineyards, lilac hedges and stands of rhubarb in the area. (Rhubarb pie is still a favorite in local cafes.)

Follow Highway 34 across the prairies to Red Oak and then go south on Highway 59 to Shenandoah, originally a Mormon settlement. From Shenandoah, turn west on Highway 2 toward Sidney, a village in Iowa's famous Loess Hills. These green, heavily eroded hills were formed at the end of the last Ice Age. The Missouri River brought silt-rich waters from the north, where massive glaciers were busy grinding rock into till. As the silt deposits dried, winds blew the fine sand into dunes hundreds of feet high. Now covered with virgin prairie grasslands and upland forests, the Loess Hills are home to wildlife such as coyotes, deer, bald eagles and prairie dogs, and were considered for national park status during the Clinton administration.

While in Sidney, be sure to stop at the Penn Drug Store. Built in 1865, the store is still operated by the Penn family; it is the oldest family-owned business in the state-and features an old-fashioned soda fountain. From Sidney, two scenic back roads, the Pleasant Overview Loop and the Spring Valley Loop, wind into the Loess Hills. Approximately 205 miles

2

IOWA

ALGONA

Originally known as Call's Grove, this town later chose its present name, a shortened form of Algonquin. In its early days, a fort enclosed the town hall. After frontier hostilities subsided, this fort was torn down and the wood was used for a plank road.

Information: Chamber of Commerce, 123 E. State St., 515-295-7201; www.algona.org

WHAT TO SEE AND DO

Ambrose A. Call State Park
2007 Call Park Dr., Algona,
515-295-3669;
www.state.ia.us/dnr/organiza/ppd/
ambrose.htm
These 130 acres of rolling, timbered hills include hiking trails, a Frisbee golf course, picnic areas, a playground, 16 campsites and a log cabin lodge. Daily 4 a.m.-10:30 p.m.

Smith Lake Park
2407 Hwy. 169, Algona,
515-295-2138
The 124 acres of this park include Smith Lake. Swimming, fishing, boating (electric motors only), picnicking, playgrounds, a hiking trail, camping and tree garden. Daily during daylight hours.

HOTELS

★Burr Oak Motel
Hwy. 169 S., Algona,
515-295-7213; 877-745-6315;
www.burroakmotel.com
40 rooms. Pets accepted; fee. Complimentary continental breakfast. **$**

RESTAURANTS

★★Sister Sarah's
Hwy. 18, Algona, 515-295-7757
American menu. Lunch, dinner. Closed Sunday-Monday, holidays. Bar. Children's menu. Outdoor seating. **$**

3

AMANA COLONIES

The history of this religious community goes back to the 1714 founding in Germany of the Inspirationists, a Lutheran separatist group. Members migrated to America and settled near Buffalo, New York. Later they bought 25,000 acres of prairie land in Iowa and moved west. Their first Iowa village was called Amana, a Biblical name meaning "remain faithful." Five more villages were built (West, High, Middle, East and South Amana). The village of Homestead was purchased outright so that the towns could use its railroad terminal.

At first, the members of the Amana Colonies lived a simple, communal life. Families were assigned living quarters with common kitchen and dining facilities and everything was shared equally. Farming was (and still is) a mainstay of the group. In 1932, common property was dissolved and redistributed on a stock basis. The new corporation, encouraging individual skills and vigor, prospered mostly because of the quality work of its artisans. Today, nearly every family owns its own house.

Information: Amana Colonies Convention and Visitors Bureau, 39-38th Ave., Amana, 319-622-7622, 800-579-2294; www.amanacolonies.com

WHAT TO SEE AND DO

Amana Heritage Sites
Hwy. 151 and Hwy. 220, Amana, 319-622-3567; www.amanaheritage.org
This community has a furniture factory that offers tours of the production area; a woolen mill with salesroom; woodworking shops, meat shop, general store, brewery, wineries, restaurants and shops. The residence of the late Christian Metz, former leader of Amana Colonies, is here.

Amana Heritage Museum

4310 220th Trail, Amana, 319-622-3567
Exhibits include a schoolhouse, crafts, lithographs and documents. An audiovisual presentation explains the history of the Amanas. April-November: Monday-Saturday 10 a.m.-5 p.m., Sunday noon-5 p.m.

Old Creamery Theatre Company

Price Creek Stage, 39 38th Ave., Amana, 319-622-6194, 800-352-6262; www.oldcreamery.com
Professional theater company performs a variety of productions. April-mid-December: Wednesday-Sunday.

HOTELS

★★Holiday Inn

2211 U. Ave., Williamsburg, 319-668-1175, 800-633-9244; www.holiday-inn.com
155 rooms. Pets accepted. Restaurant, bar. Fitness room. Indoor pool, children's pool, whirlpool. Little Amana complex is adjacent with an old-time general store and winery. **$**

★Super 8

1708 N. Highland St., Williamsburg, 319-668-9718
33 rooms. Pets accepted, some restrictions; fee. Complimentary continental breakfast. Fitness room. Indoor pool, outdoor pool, whirlpool. **$**

RESTAURANTS

★★Brick Haus

728 47th Ave., Amana, 319-622-3278
German, American menu. Breakfast, lunch, dinner. Closed holidays. Children's menu. Valet parking. Photos on the wall detail the history of village. **$$**

★★Ox Yoke Inn

4420 220th Trail, Amana, 319-622-3441; www.oxyokeinn.com
German, American menu. Lunch, dinner, Sunday brunch. Bar. Children's menu. **$$**

★★Ronneburg

4408 220th Trail, Amana, 319-622-3641; www.ronneburgrestaurant.com
German, American menu. Breakfast, lunch, dinner, brunch. Bar. **$$**

★★Zuber's

2206 45th Ave., Amana Colonies, 319-622-3911
American menu. Lunch, dinner, Sunday brunch. Children's menu. Restored century-old inn. Baseball memorabilia. **$$**

AMES

Located near the geographical center of the state, Ames beats to the pulse of Iowa State University. The town is named in honor of a Massachusetts congressman, Oakes Ames, who was financially interested in a local railroad project.
Information: Convention and Visitors Bureau, 1601 Golden Aspen Dr., 515-232-4032, 800-288-7470; www.ames.ia.us

WHAT TO SEE AND DO

Iowa Arboretum

1875 Peach Ave., Madrid, 515-795-3216; www.iowaarboretum.org
This arboretum includes 340 acres of trees, shrubs and gardens. Trails, horticultural plantings, scenic overlooks, ravines, streams. Guided and self-guided tours; educational programs. Daily.

Iowa State University

117 Beardshear Hall, Ames, 515-294-4777; www.iastate.edu
One of the oldest land-grant universities in the United States, founded in 1858, ISU is known for its spacious, green central campus with sculptures and fountains by artist Christian Petersen and for its many historic buildings. The school is also the birthplace of the electronic digital computer, built by

John V. Atanasoff in the basement of the Physics Building in the late 1930s.

Farm House
290 Farm House Lane, Ames,
515-294-3342
This 1860 house is a restored original residence on the Iowa State Agricultural College farm; period furnishings. September-May.

Grant Wood Murals
Parks Library, Morrill Rd., Ames
Considered among the best works of this Iowa artist, the nine murals began as a Works Projects Administration project during the Great Depression. They depict various academic divisions of the school as well as the breaking of sod by pioneer farmers.

Mamie Doud Eisenhower Birthplace
709 Carroll St., Boone, 515-432-1896
This one-story frame house includes such period furnishings as the bed in which Mamie Eisenhower was born. Summer kitchen, library, museum. June-October: daily; April-May: Tuesday-Sunday afternoons; also by appointment.

HOTELS
★Baymont Inn
2500 Elwood Dr., Ames,
515-296-2500, 866-999-1111;
www.baymontinns.com
89 rooms. Pets accepted. Complimentary continental breakfast. Indoor pool, whirlpool. $

★★The Hotel At Gateway Center
2100 Green Hills Dr., Ames,
515-292-8600, 800-367-2637;
www.thegatewayames.com
188 rooms. Pets accepted. Restaurant, bar. Fitness room. Indoor pool, whirlpool. Airport transportation available. Business center. $

RESTAURANTS
★★Broiler Restaurant and Lounge
6008 W. Lincoln Way, Ames,
515-292-2516;
www.thebroilerrestaurant.com
Steak menu. Dinner. Bar. Children's menu. $$$

★Hickory Park
1404 S. Duss, Ames, 515-232-8940;
www.hickorypark-bbq.com
American menu. Lunch, dinner. Children's menu. $$

★Lucullans
400 Main St., Ames, 515-232-8484;
www.lucullans.com
Italian menu. Lunch, dinner. Bar. Children's menu. $$

5

IOWA

ATLANTIC
This small southwestern Iowa town has several preserved buildings, including the historic Rock Island Depot, which houses the Chamber of Commerce.
Information: Chamber of Commerce, 614 Chestnut St., 712-243-3017, 877-283-2124; www.atlanticiowa.com

WHAT TO SEE AND DO
Danish Windmill
4038 Main St., Elk Horn, 712-764-7472
Built in Denmark (1848), this 60-foot-high working windmill was dismantled and shipped to Elk Horn where it was reassembled by community volunteers. Daily.

HOTELS
★Super 8
1902 E. Seventh St., Atlantic,
712-243-4723, 888-243-2378;
www.super8.com
59 rooms. Complimentary continental breakfast. $

SPECIALTY LODGINGS
Chestnut Charm Bed & Breakfast
1409 Chestnut St., Atlantic, 712-243-5652;
www.chestnutcharm.org

At this Victorian inn, built in 1898, there are guest rooms as well as cozy carriage houses.
9 rooms. No children allowed. Complimentary full breakfast. **$**

BETTENDORF
Bettendorf began as a quiet rural village called Gilbert. In 1903, the town's future changed with the arrival of the Bettendorf Axle and Wagon Company, which became the largest manufacturer of railroad cars west of the Mississippi. The growing city changed its name in honor of the company. Today Bettendorf, on the Mississippi River, is part of the Quad Cities metropolitan area.
Information: Quad Cities Convention and Visitors Bureau, 102 S. Harrison St., Davenport, 563-322-3911, 800-747-7800; www.quadcities.com

WHAT TO SEE AND DO
Buffalo Bill Cody Homestead
28050 230th Ave., Princeton,
563-225-2981; www.scottcountyiowa.com
Restored boyhood home of Buffalo Bill Cody, built by his father in 1847. Buffalo are on the grounds. April-October: daily.

Family Museum of Arts & Science
2900 Learning Campus Dr., Bettendorf,
563-344-4106; www.familymuseum.org
This museum features hands-on exhibits as well as a traveling exhibit gallery. Daily.

Isle of Capri Casino
1777 Isle Pkwy., Bettendorf,
563-359-7280, 800-724-5825;
www.isleofcapricasino.com
Casino gambling, restaurant, gift shop, lodging. Valet parking.

HOTELS
★★Holiday Inn
909 Middle Rd., Bettendorf,
563-355-4761, 800-626-0780;
www.holiday-inn.com
150 rooms. Restaurant, bar. Fitness room. Indoor pool. Airport transportation available. **$**

★Ramada Bettendorf/Davenport
3020 Utica Ridge Rd., Bettendorf,
563-355-7575; www.ramada.com

119 rooms. Complimentary full breakfast. Fitness room. Outdoor pool. Airport transportation available. Business center. **$**

★★The Lodge
900 Spruce Hills Dr., Bettendorf,
563-359-7141, 800-285-8637;
www.lodgehotel.com
210 rooms. Pets accepted, some restrictions; fee. Restaurant, bar. Fitness room. Indoor pool, outdoor pool, whirlpool. Airport transportation available. **$**

SPECIALTY LODGINGS
Abbey Hotel
1401 Central Ave., Bettendorf,
563-355-0291, 800-438-7535;
www.theabbeyhotel.com
This Romanesque hotel, once a monastery, overlooks the Mississippi River and is surrounded by gardens and landscaping.
19 rooms. Complimentary full breakfast. Bar. Fitness room. Outdoor pool. Airport transportation available. **$**

RESTAURANTS
★★★The Faithful Pilot Café
117 N. Cody Rd., Le Claire,
563-289-4156; www.faithfulpilotcafe.com
This restaurant features progressive American cuisine served in an elegant, modern dining room. Menu highlights include rack of lamb over minted wild rice, and grilled beef tenderloin with rosemary potatoes. American menu. Dinner. **$$**

★★★The Lodge Restaurant
900 Spruce Hills Dr., Bettendorf,
563-359-1607; www.lodgehotel.com
This restaurant features an American and German menu. Specialties include regensburg goulash, chicken von jumer and rack of lamb.

American, German menu. Lunch, dinner. Bar. Children's menu. **$$**

★★Stubbs Eddy Restaurant/Pub
1716 State St., Bettendorf, 563-355-0073
American menu. Breakfast, lunch, dinner, late-night. Bar. Children's menu. **$$$**

BURLINGTON

Burlington, a river port, is a shopping, industrial and farm center. It traces its history back to the days when it was called Flint Hills by Native Americans and served as neutral ground where tribes hunted flint for implements. Zebulon Pike raised the Stars and Stripes here in 1805, and a trading post was built in 1808. The city became capital of the Wisconsin Territory in 1837, then capital of the Iowa Territory from 1838 to 1840.
Information: Convention and Tourism Bureau, 807 Jefferson St., 319-752-6365, 800-827-4837; www.visit.burlington.ia.us

WHAT TO SEE AND DO
Apple Trees Historical Museum
Perkins Park, 1616 Dill St., Burlington, 319-753-2449
The museum, a remaining wing of railroad magnate Charles E. Perkins's mansion, contains Victorian furnishings, antique tools, costumes, dolls, toys, buttons, glass and china. The museum is maintained by the Des Moines County Historical Society. Guided tours, May-October: weekends 1:30-4:30 p.m.; by appointment Monday-Friday.

Hawkeye Log Cabin
2915 S. Main St., Burlington, 319-753-2449
Replica (1910) of a pioneer cabin with antique furnishings and tools. Guided tours, May-September, by appointment Monday-Friday; Saturday-Sunday 1:30-4:30 p.m.

Phelps House
521 Columbia St., Burlington, 319-753-2449
This mansard-roofed, Italianate Victorian mansion has original furnishings used by three generations of the Phelps family. Also inside is an extensive collection of rare china and family portraits. Guided tours, May-October, by appointment Monday-Friday; Saturday-Sunday 1:30-4:30 p.m.

Heritage Hill National Historic District
Washington and High Streets, Burlington
This 29-square-block area contains churches, mansions and houses in a wide variety of architectural styles, including a full range of Victorian buildings from the 1870s to the turn of the century. Walking tours and brochures available. Contact the Convention & Tourism Bureau.

Snake Alley
Sixth St., Burlington
The zigzagging brick-paved street, built in 1894, is, according to *Ripley's Believe It or Not*, the "crookedest street in the world."

SPECIAL EVENTS
Burlington Steamboat Days and the American Music Festival
200 N. Front St., Burlington, 319-754-4334; www.steamboatdays.com
Athletic competitions, fireworks, midway, parade, name entertainment. Mid-June.

HOTELS
★★Best Western Pzazz Motor Inn
3001 Winegard Dr., Burlington, 319-753-2223, 800-373-1223; www.bestwestern.com
151 rooms. Pets accepted. Restaurant, bar. Fitness room. Indoor pool, whirlpool. Airport transportation available. **$**

7

IOWA

★Quality Inn
3051 Kirkwood, Burlington, 319-753-0000

52 rooms. Pets accepted, some restrictions; fee. Complimentary continental breakfast. Outdoor pool. **$**

CARROLL

This town is named for Charles Carroll, a signer of the Declaration of Independence.
Information: Chamber of Commerce, 223 W. Fifth St., 712-792-4383, 866-586-4383; www.carrolliowa.com

WHAT TO SEE AND DO
Black Hawk State Park
227 S. Blossom St., Lake View,
712-657-8712
This park consists of 86 acres along 925-acre Black Hawk Lake. Swimming, fishing, boating, snowmobiling, picnicking, camping. Standard hours, fees.

War Memorial Monuments
E. First St., Carroll

Located here is a monument for each war beginning with the Civil War and ending with Desert Storm.

HOTELS
★★Carrollton Inn
1730 N. U.S. Hwy. 71, Carroll,
712-792-5600, 877-798-3535;
www.carrolltoninn.com
86 rooms. Restaurant, bar. Indoor pool, whirlpool. **$**

CEDAR FALLS

Once one of the most important milling centers in the state, today Cedar Falls is a university town, home to the University of Nothern Iowa.
Information: Tourism and Visitors Bureau, 10 Main St., 319-268-4266, 800-845-1955; www.cedarfallstourism.org

★
★
★
☆
☆

WHAT TO SEE AND DO
Cedar Falls Historical Society Victorian Home Museum
308 W. Third, Cedar Falls, 319-266-5149;
www.cedarfallshistorical.org
This Victorian house is furnished in period style. The Carriage House Museum contains a library, archives, fashions, Lenoir train exhibit and memorabilia of the first permanent settlement in Black Hawk County. Wednesday-Saturday 10 a.m.-4 p.m., Sunday 1-4 p.m.

George Wyth House
303 Franklin St., Cedar Falls,
319-266-5149
The residence of George Wyth, founder of the Viking Pump Company, was built in 1907. It's now furnished in the Art Deco style of the 1920s and includes pieces by Gilbert Rhode. The Viking Pump Company museum is housed on the third floor. Tours,

May-September: Sunday afternoons; also by appointment.

Little Red School
First and Clay Streets, Cedar Falls,
319-266-5149.
This country school (1909) has been authentically furnished to reflect turn-of-the-century education. May-October, Wednesday and Saturday-Sunday afternoons.

University of Northern Iowa
1222 W. 27th St., Cedar Falls, 319-273-2311;
www.uni.edu
This campus of 14,000 students, founded in 1876, features a campanile built in Italian Renaissance style that chimes daily. Also on campus is a museum with exhibits on geology and natural history.

SPECIAL EVENTS
Cedar Falls Municipal Band

Overman Park, Second and Franklin Streets, Cedar Falls, 319-266-1253; www.cedarnet.org/cfband
The Cedar Falls Municipal Band, the oldest concert band in the state, entertains crowds each summer outdoors at a modern band shell. Bring a lawn chair or blanket and relax as these 45 musicians perform. Tuesday evenings, June-August.

HOTELS
★★Holiday Inn
5826 University Ave., Cedar Falls, 319-277-2230; www.holiday-inn.com

181 rooms. High-speed Internet access. Restaurant, bar. Fitness room. Indoor pool, outdoor pool, whirlpool. Airport transportation available. **$**

RESTAURANTS
★★Olde Broom Factory
125 W. First St., Cedar Falls, 319-268-0877; www.thebroomfactory.com
American menu. Lunch, dinner, Sun brunch. Bar. Children's menu. Structure built in 1862. Valet parking. **$$**

CEDAR RAPIDS
Cedar Rapids, located at the rapids of the Cedar River, is the industrial leader of the state.
Information: Cedar Rapids Area Convention and Visitors Bureau, 119 First Ave. S.E., 319-398-5009, 800-735-5557; www.cedar-rapids.com

WHAT TO SEE AND DO
Brucemore
2160 Linden Dr. S.E., Cedar Rapids, 319-362-7375; www.brucemore.org
A Queen Anne-style 21-room mansion built in 1886, this house includes a visitor center, gift and flower shops, formal gardens, lawns, orchard and pond. The sunroom was decorated by native artist Grant Wood. The estate serves as a community cultural center. February-December: Tuesday-Saturday 10 a.m.-3 p.m.; Sunday noon-3 p.m.

Cedar Rapids Museum of Art
410 Third Ave. S.E., Cedar Rapids, 319-366-7503; www.crma.org
Housed here is an extensive collection of works by Grant Wood, Marvin Cone and Mauricio Lasansky. Children 7 and under free. Tuesday-Sunday.

Czech Village
48 16th Ave. S.W., Cedar Rapids, 319-362-2846
A bakery, meat market, gift shops, restaurants and historic structures preserving Czech heritage are featured here.

National Czech and Slovak Museum and Library
30 16th Ave. S.W., Cedar Rapids, 319-362-8500; www.ncsml.org
This museum houses a large collection of folk costumes. Permanent and changing exhibits; museum grounds include restored immigrant home. Tours. Daily.

Indian Creek Nature Center

6665 Otis Rd. S.E., Cedar Rapids, 319-362-0664; www.indiancreeknaturecenter.org
On this 210-acre nature preserve is an observatory and museum offering changing exhibits in a remodeled dairy barn. Hiking trails. Monday-Friday; closed holidays.

Masonic Library

813 First Ave. S.E., Cedar Rapids, 319-365-1438
This library houses the most complete Masonic collection in the United States. The building is a Vermont-marble structure with bas-relief decoration and stained-glass windows. Tours. Monday-Friday.

Palisades-Kepler State Park

Hwy. 30, Cedar Rapids, 319-895-6039.
This 970-acre park includes limestone palisades that rise 75 feet above the Cedar River; timbered valleys, wildflowers. Fishing, boating; nature and hiking trails, snowmobiling; picnicking, lodge, camping, cabins. Standard hours.

Paramount Theatre

123 Third Ave. S.E., Cedar Rapids, 319-398-5211; www.uscellularcenter.com
A restored theater built in the 1920s, the Parmount hosts stage productions, films, Broadway series and is the home of the Cedar Rapids Symphony.

Science Station

427 First St. S.E., Cedar Rapids, 319-366-0968; www.sciencestation.org
Science and technology museum features unusual hands-on exhibits including a working hot air balloon and giant kaleidoscope. Tuesday-Sunday.

US Cellular Center

370 First Ave. N.E., Cedar Rapids, 319-398-5211; www.uscellularcenter.com
This 10,000-seat entertainment center features sports events, concerts, exhibits, rodeos, ice shows and more.

SPECIAL EVENTS

Freedom Festival

226 Second St. S.E., Cedar Rapids, 319-365-8313
Eighty events for all ages are held citywide, topped off by a large fireworks display. Two weeks preceding and including July 4.

Houby Days

Czech Village, 48 16th Ave. S.W., Cedar Rapids, 319-362-8500
Features Czech fine arts, folk arts and customs, music, dancing, food; mushroom hunt contests, races. Weekend after Mother's Day.

HOTELS

★★Best Western Cooper's Mill Hotel

100 F Ave. N.W., Cedar Rapids, 319-366-5323, 800-858-5511; www.bestwestern.com
86 rooms. Pets accepted; fee. Restaurant, bar. $

★Comfort Inn

5055 Rockwell Dr., Cedar Rapids, 319-393-8247, 800-228-5150; www.comfortinn.com
59 rooms. Pets accepted, some restrictions. Complimentary continental breakfast. $

★Comfort Inn

390 33rd Ave. S.W., Cedar Rapids, 319-363-7934, 800-228-5150; www.comfortinn.com
60 rooms. Pets accepted, some restrictions. Complimentary continental breakfast. $

★★★Crowne Plaza

350 First Ave. N.E., Cedar Rapids, 319-363-8161, 800-227-6963; www.crowneplaza.com
Located in downtown Cedar Rapids, this hotel is near shopping, restaurants, and entertainment
275 rooms. Restaurant, bar. Fitness room. Indoor pool, whirlpool. Airport transportation available. Business center. $

★Hampton Inn

3265 Sixth St. S.W., Cedar Rapids,

10

IOWA

319-364-8144, 800-426-7866; www.hamptoninn.com
106 rooms. Complimentary continental breakfast. Bar. Fitness room. Indoor pool, whirlpool. **$**

★★Marriott Cedar Rapids
1200 Collins Rd. N.E., Cedar Rapids, 319-393-6600; www.marriott.com
221 rooms. Restaurant, bar. Fitness room. Indoor pool, whirlpool. Airport transportation available. Business center. **$**

CHEROKEE

Center of one of the heaviest cattle feeding and hog raising areas of Iowa, Cherokee is home to many processing and manufacturing plants. The Cherokee Community Center houses a symphony orchestra and an active community theater.
Information: Chamber of Commerce, 228 W. Main St., 712-225-6414; www.cherokeeiowa.net

WHAT TO SEE AND DO

Sanford Museum and Planetarium

117 E. Willow St., Cherokee, 712-225-3922; www.sanfordmuseum.org
Natural history, science, and changing exhibits. Classes (by appointment); planetarium programs (last Sunday of month; also by appointment). Daily.

SPECIAL EVENTS

Cherokee County Fair

Cherokee County Fairgrounds, Cherokee, 712-225-6414
Features a demolition derby and team dance competition. Early July.

Cherokee Rodeo

228 W. Main, Cherokee, 721-225-6414
Professional Rodeo Cowboys Assocation sanctioned. Weekend after Memorial Day weekend.

HOTELS

★★Best Western La Grande Hacienda

1401 N. Second St., Cherokee, 712-225-5701, 800-924-3765; www.bestwestern.com
55 rooms. Complimentary full breakfast. Restaurant. Indoor pool, whirlpool. **$**

CLARINDA

Clarinda is the birthplace of Big Band-era legend Glenn Miller. It's also where, at the turn of the century, rural school teacher Jessie Field Shambaugh started the Boys' Corn Clubs and Girls' Home Clubs, which later became the 4-H movement.
Information: Chamber of Commerce, 200 S. 15th St., 712-542-2166; www.clarinda.org

WHAT TO SEE AND DO

Lake of Three Fires State Park

2303 Hwy. 49, Bedford, 712-523-2700
This park has 691 acres with a 97-acre lake. Swimming, fishing, electric boating; hiking, bridle trails, snowmobiling; picnicking, camping, cabins. Standard hours, fees.

Nodaway Valley Historical Museum

1600 S. 16th St., Clarinda, 712-542-3073
Featured here are exhibits on the history of the Nodaway River area including agricultural displays, artifacts from the early

days of the 4-H movement and Glenn Miller memorabilia. Visits to the nearby Glenn Miller Birthplace Home (by appointment only; additional fee) can be arranged through the museum. Tuesday-Sunday afternoons.

SPECIAL EVENTS

Glenn Miller Festival

122 W. Garfield, Clarinda, 712-542-2461
This event honor's Glen Miller and his music. Second weekend in June.

RESTAURANTS
★★J Bruner's
1100 E. Washington St., Clarinda,
712-542-3364
Steak menu. Dinner. Closed Sunday-Monday. Bar. Children's menu. $$$

CLEAR LAKE
Scene of a Native American uprising in 1854, Clear Lake challenged Mason City for honors as the county seat, but lost out because it was not in the geographic center of the area. Taking its name from the nearby lake, this is an ancient Native American fishing and hunting ground and a popular resort town.
Information: Chamber of Commerce, 205 Main Ave., 641-357-2159, 800-285-5338; www.clearlakeiowa.com

WHAT TO SEE AND DO
Clear Lake State Park
2730 S. Lakeview Dr., Clear Lake, 641-357-4212
Swimming, fishing, boating, snowmobiling, picnicking, camping are all available at this park.

Surf Ballroom
460 North Shore Dr., Clear Lake, 641-357-6151
This was the site of Buddy Holly's last concert before Holly, Ritchie Valens and J. P. Richardson (the Big Bopper) died in a plane crash nearby on February 2, 1959. The ballroom features entertainment on weekends and a museum of musical history. Tours available.

SPECIAL EVENT
Buddy Holly Tribute
Surf Ballroom, 460 North Shore Dr., Clear Lake, 641-357-6151
An event to commemorate Holly's last concert, this tribute features local and national entertainers. First weekend in February.

HOTELS
★★Best Western Holiday Lodge
2023 Seventh Ave. N., Clear Lake, 641-357-5253, 800-606-3552; www.bestwestern.com
138 rooms. Pets accepted, some restrictions; fee. Complimentary full breakfast. Restaurant. Indoor pool, whirlpool. Airport transportation available. $

★
★
★
★
★

CLINTON
Agriculture, industry and business are blended in this city of wide streets and modern buildings on the Mississippi River. First called New York, it was later renamed after DeWitt Clinton, former governor of New York. Once the largest lumber-producing city in the world, Clinton today is famous for its prime beef production.
Information: Clinton Area Chamber of Commerce, 333 Fourth Ave. S., 563-242-5702, 800-828-5702; www.clintonia.com

WHAT TO SEE AND DO
Eagle Point Park
N. Third St. and Stockwell Lane, Clinton, 563-243-1260
This park featuers flower gardens, picnicking shelters, a lodge, playground, observation tower, children's nature center and petting zoo. Mid-April-late October, daily.

Mississippi Belle II
Showboat Landing, 311 Riverview Dr., Clinton, 563-243-9000; 800-457-9975
Year-round gambling along the Mississippi River is available at this casion boat.

Lillian Russell Theatre
311 Riverview Dr., Clinton, 563-242-6760

This theater is located aboard the paddlewheel showboat the *City of Clinton*. Musicals and comedies. June-August.

SPECIAL EVENTS
Civil War Reenactment
Eagle Point Park, 1401 11th Ave. N.,
Clinton, 563-243-5368
See actors in period costume reenact the battle for Burnside Bridge. May.

Riverboat Days
115 Fourth Ave. S., Clinton, 800-395-7277
Pageant, events, tractor pulls, entertainment, shows, carnival. July 4 weekend.

HOTELS
★★Best Western Frontier Motor Inn
2300 Lincoln Way St., Clinton,
563-242-7112, 800-728-7112;
www.bestwestern.com
113 rooms. Pets accepted, some restrictions; fee. Complimentary full breakfast. High-speed Internet access. Restaurant, bar. Fitness room. Indoor pool, whirlpool. Airport transportation available. **$$**

★Country Inn & Suites
2224 Lincoln Way, Clinton,
563-244-9922, 888-201-1746;
www.countryinns.com
63 rooms. Pets accepted; fee. Complimentary continental breakfast. High-speed Internet access. Indoor pool, whirlpool. Airport transportation available. **$**

COUNCIL BLUFFS
The Lewis and Clark expedition stopped in Council Bluffs in 1804 to rest and hold their first "council bluff" with local Native American tribes. Council Bluffs was settled in 1846 by Mormons fleeing religious persecution. They called the town Kanesville, but the city officially took the name Council Bluffs in 1853. The town subsequently became a booming hub of commerce as the nation's fifth-largest rail center. Today the Loess Hills Scenic Byway passes through the area.
Information: Convention and Visitors Bureau, 7 N. Sixth St., 712-325-1000, 800-228-6878; www.councilbluffsiowa.com

13

IOWA

★
★
★
★
★

WHAT TO SEE AND DO
Golden Spike Monument
S. 21st St. and Ninth Ave., Council Bluffs
Erected in 1939, this 56-foot golden concrete spike commemorates the junction of the Union Pacific and Central Pacific railroads in Council Bluffs.

Historic General Dodge House
605 Third St., Council Bluffs,
712-322-2406
Guided tours are given of this restored Victorian housee built by Grenville M. Dodge, chief construction engineer for the Union Pacific Railroad and a general in the Civil War. Tuesday-Sunday; also January.

Historic Pottawattamie County Jail
226 Pearl St., Council Bluffs,
712-323-2509

This unique three-story rotary jail is sometimes referred to as the "human squirrel cage" or "lazy Susan jail." May and September: weekends; June-August: Wednesday-Sunday, or by appointment.

Lewis and Clark Monument
19962 Monument Rd., Council Bluffs,
712-328-4650
A shaft of native stone on the bluffs depicts Lewis and Clark holding council with the Oto and Missouri tribes.

Lincoln Monument
323 Lafayette Ave., Council Bluffs
This granite shaft marks the spot from which Lincoln designated the town as the eastern terminus of the Union Pacific Railroad. Erected in 1911.

Mormon Trail Memorial
Bayliss Park, Council Bluffs
A huge boulder marks the passage of Mormons out of the city on the trek to Utah.

RailsWest Railroad Museum
16th Ave. and S. Main St.,
Council Bluffs, 712-323-5182
The historic Rock Island depot was built in 1899. Displayed here are railroad memorabilia and HO gauge model trains. March-December: Wednesday-Monday.

Western Historic Trails Center
3434 Richard Downing Ave.,
Council Bluffs, 712-366-4900.
Explore preserved and restored sites along the Lewis and Clark, Mormon Pioneer, California and Oregon trails. Discover the history of Native American tribes and trails heritage in the region. Guided group tours. Daily; closed holidays.

HOTELS
★★Ameristar Casino
2200 River Rd., Council Bluffs,
712-328-8888, 877-462-7827;
www.ameristarcasinos.com
160 rooms. Restaurant, bar. Fitness room. Indoor pool, whirlpool. Gaming. $

★Fairfield Inn
520 30th Ave., Council Bluffs,
712-366-1330, 800-228-2800;
www.fairfieldinn.com
62 rooms. Complimentary continental breakfast. Indoor pool, whirlpool. $

★Heartland Inn Council Bluffs
1000 Woodbury Ave., Council Bluffs,
712-322-8400, 800-334-3277;
www.heartlandinns.com
87 rooms. Pets accepted, some restrictions; fee. Complimentary continental breakfast. High-speed Internet access. Indoor pool. Business center. $

RESTAURANTS
★Christy Crème
2853 N. Broadway, Council Bluffs,
712-322-2778; www.christycreme.com
American menu. Lunch, dinner. Closed December-January. Children's menu. Outdoor seating. $

★Pink Poodle Steakhouse
633 N. Old Lincoln Hwy.,
Crescent, 712-545-3744;
www.pinkpoodlesteakhouse.com
American menu. Dinner. Closed Monday. $

14

IOWA

★
★
★
★
★

★ DAVENPORT
Stretching five miles along the Mississippi River, Davenport is part of the Quad Cities metropolitan area. Davenport's Palmer College of Chiropractic is the fountainhead of that practice in the United States. The city is named for its founder, a former U.S. Army officer who explored this bank of the river while stationed on Rock Island. The state's first railroad came here when tracks were put across the Mississippi at this point in 1854. In pre-Civil War days, Dred Scott claimed the town as his home, and John Brown camped here before his attack on Harpers Ferry.
Information: Quad Cities Convention and Visitors Bureau, 102 S. Harrison St., 563-322-3911, 800-747-7800; www.quadcities.com

WHAT TO SEE AND DO
Dan Nagle Walnut Grove Pioneer Village
18817 290th St., Long Grove, 563-328-3283; www.scottcountyiowa.com
This three-acre walk-through site contains 18 historic buildings moved from various locations in the county. Visitors can explore a blacksmith shop, schoolhouse, pioneer family home; also St. Anne's Church. April-October: daily.

Figge Art Museum
1737 W. 12th St., Davenport,
563-326-7804; www.figgeartmuseum.org
Rotating displays from a permanent collection of 19th- and 20th-century paintings,

Mexican Colonial, Asian and native Haitian art are displayed here, as well as works by regional artists Grant Wood and Thomas Hart Benton. Tuesday-Sunday.

Putnam Museum of History & Natural Science
1717 W. 12th St., Davenport,
563-324-1933; www.putnam.org
Permanent and changing exhibits of regional history, natural science, and world cultures. Daily.

Scott County Park
19251 290th St., Long Grove,
563-285-9656
More than 1,000 acres with a pioneer village and nature center. Swimming, fishing, ball fields, 18-hole golf, skiing, tobogganing, ice skating, picnicking, camping and trailer sites. Daily.

SPECIAL EVENT
Bix Beiderbecke Memorial Jazz Festival
LeClaire Park, 311 N. Ripley St.,
Davenport, 563-324-7170;

A WALK THROUGH DAVENPORT

Davenport is one of the Quad Cities, a four-city metropolitan area that straddles the Mississippi and includes Moline and Rock Island in Illinois, plus Bettendorf, just upriver from Davenport. Begin this walk on Credit Island Park, the site of a turn-of-the-century amusement park. Scenic trails loop around the island, and number of public art pieces are found here, part of the Quad Cities Art in the Park project. Cross over to the Iowa mainland from the east end of Credit Island Park and walk along the Mississippi through two more riverside parks. Centennial Park features riverside walkways past sports fields and stadiums. Atop the bluff on Division Street is Museum Hill, home of the Putnam Museum of Science and Natural History (1717 W. 12th St.) and the Davenport Museum of Art (1737 W. 12th St.). The Putnam houses two permanent exhibits about the Mississippi River. The art museum's permanent collection includes works by Midwestern painters, including Thomas Hart Benton and Grant Wood, an Iowa native famous for his painting, American Gothic. Just to the east is LeClaire Park, home to summer outdoor events and concerts.

The Davenport Downtown Levee includes a riverboat casino, restaurants, nightclubs and the renovated Union Station railroad depot, which houses the Quad Cities Convention and Visitors Center. A local Farmers' Market is also held here on Wednesday and Saturday mornings from May through October.

Just downstream from the historic Government Bridge, Dam 15 provides a navigational pool for commercial shipping on the Mississippi. Lock 15 allows boats to transfer between the rivers pools. Cross Government Bridge to Arsenal Island, which was acquired by the U.S. Government in 1804 under a treaty with the Sauk and Fox Indians. Fort Armstrong was established in 1816 on the tip of the island, where a replica now stands. Manufacturing began on the island in 1840, and in 1869 it became home to the Rock Island Arsenal, a major military manufacturing facility. The island contains a number of historic homes and structures, including the Rock Island Arsenal Museum; the restored Colonel George Davenport Mansion, filled with furnishings from the mid-1800s; and the Mississippi River Visitors Center, with exhibits about the history of navigation on the river. A Confederate Soldiers Cemetery and National Military Cemetery date back to the 1800s. Hikers and bikers can enjoy a five-mile trail around the island.

15

IOWA

★
★
★
★
★

www.bixsociety.org
Join the crowd at a jazz festival to honor the Davenport-born musician. Mid-July.

HOTELS
★Hampton Inn
3330 E. Kimberly Rd., Davenport,
563-359-3921; www.hamptoninn.com
132 rooms. Pets accepted, some restrictions; fee. Complimentary continental breakfast. Fitness room. Indoor pool. Airport transportation available. **$**

★★Presidents Casino Blackhawk
200 E. Third St., Davenport,
319-328-6000, 800-553-1173
189 rooms. Restaurant, bar. Fitness room. Airport transportation available. **$**

★Super 8
410 E. 65th St., Davenport,
563-388-9810, 800-800-8000;
www.super8.com
61 rooms. Pets accepted; fee. Complimentary continental breakfast. **$**

RESTAURANTS
★Iowa Machine Shed
7250 N.W. Blvd., Davenport,
563-391-2427; www.machineshed.com
American menu. Breakfast, lunch, dinner. Bar. Children's menu. **$$**

★★Thunder Bay Grille
6511 Brady St., Davenport,
563-386-2722; www.thunderbaygrille.com
American menu. Lunch, dinner. Bar. Children's menu. Bilevel dining. **$$**

DECORAH
A center of Norwegian culture in the United States, Decorah is the seat of Winneshiek County and located in one of the state's most picturesque areas. Within a short distance are Siewers and Twin Springs and towering spires of limestone along the Upper Iowa River. The town is named for a Native American chief who aided settlers during the Black Hawk War.

Information: Decorah Area Chamber of Commerce, 300 W. Water, 563-382-3990, 800-463-4692; www.decorah-iowa.com

WHAT TO SEE AND DO
Bily Clocks
323 N. Main St. Spillville, 563-562-3569
Collection of elaborately carved musical clocks with moving figures, some nine feet tall. May-October: daily.

Fort Atkinson State Preserve
Hwy. 24, Decorah, 563-425-4161
Fort built in 1840 as federal protection for the Winnebago from the Sac, Fox, and Sioux. Restored buildings include barracks, a blockhouse and magazine. Museum exhibits Native American and pioneer relics. Mid-May-mid-October, daily.

Seed Savers Heritage Farm
3094 N. Winn Rd., Decorah,
563-382-5990; www.seedsavers.org
This 173-acre farm features displays of endangered vegetables, apples, grapes and ancient White Park cattle. Preservation Gardens house 15,000 rare vegetable varieties; Cultural History Garden displays old-time flowers and vegetables. Historic Orchard has 650 19th-century apples and 160 hardy grapes. Daily.

Vesterheim Norwegian-American Museum
523 W. Water St., Decorah,
563-382-9681; www.vesterheim.org
Extensive exhibits relate history of Norwegians in America and Norway. Pioneer objects, handicrafts, ship gallery, arts displayed in a complex of 13 historic buildings with a restored mill. Daily.

SPECIAL EVENTS
Nordic Fest
300 W. Water St., Decorah, 800-382-3378

Parades, dancing, pioneer tool display; demonstrations of cooking, needlework, and rosemaling. Last full weekend in July.

HOTELS

★Super 8
810 Hwy. 9 E., Decorah,
563-382-8771, 800-800-8000;
www.super8.com
60 rooms. Pets accepted. Complimentary continental breakfast. Fitness room. Whirlpool. **$**

★★★Hotel Winneshiek
104 E. Water St., Decorah, 563-382-4164;
www.hotelwinn.com
The Hotel Winneshiek is a gem: an elegantly restored 1905 hotel in the heart of downtown. Guests are greeted at a concierge desk in an entryway decorated with fresh flowers and displays of antique glassware and porcelain figurines. The lobby has an octagonal three-story atrium, set under a large stained-glass skylight. Rooms are simple but decoarted with antique reproductions.

31 rooms. Complimentary continental breakfast. Restaurant, bar. **$**

SPECIALTY LODGINGS

Thornton House
371 Diagonal St., Lansing,
563-538-3373; www.thorntonhouse.net
This brick mansion has more than 3,300 square feet of living space with a two-story enclosed deck.
4 rooms. **$$$$**

RESTAURANTS

★Milty's
200 Main St., Lansing, 563-538-4585
American menu. Lunch, dinner. Closed Monday. **$**

★★Stone Hearth Inn
811 Commerce Dr., Decorah,
563-382-4614
American menu. Lunch, dinner. Closed Sunday. Bar. Children's menu. **$$**

DENISON

J. W. Denison, an agent for the Providence Western Land Company and a Baptist minister, came to this area in 1855 and gave the new town its name. In 1933, Denison farmers nearly rioted during land foreclosures triggered by the Great Depression. Denison is the seat of Crawford County.
Information: Chamber of Commerce, 109 N. 14th St., 712-263-5621; www.denisonia.com

WHAT TO SEE AND DO

Yellow Smoke Park
2237 Yellow Smoke Rd., Denison,
712-263-2070
A 320-acre recreation area with a swimming beach, this park offers fishing, boating, hiking and camping.

SPECIAL EVENT

Donna Reed Festival for the Performing Arts
1305 Broadway, Denison, 712-263-3334
Special workshops in the performing arts conducted by professionals from around the nation. Parade. Golf tourney. 10K run. Saturday night gala. Street fair. Third full week in June.

HOTELS

★Super 8
502 Boyer Valley Rd., Denison,
712-263-5081, 800-800-8000;
www.super8.com
40 rooms. Pets accepted, some restrictions; fee. Complimentary continental breakfast. **$**

RESTAURANT

★Cronk's
812 Fourth Ave. S., Denison,
712-263-4191
Steak menu. Breakfast, lunch, dinner, late-night, Sunday brunch. Bar. **$**

DES MOINES

Des Moines is the capital of Iowa and largest city in the state. This city is the industrial, retail, financial and political hub of Iowa. A military garrison established Fort Des Moines at a point on the Raccoon and Des Moines rivers in 1843. Two years later the territory was opened to settlers and the town of Fort Des Moines was chosen as the county seat. The word "fort" was abandoned when the community became a city in 1857; the next year it became the state capital. Today more than 60 insurance companies have their home offices here, as does media giant Meredith Corporation, publishers of *Better Homes & Gardens* and *Ladies' Home Journal.*

Information: Greater Des Moines Convention and Visitors Bureau, 405 Sixth Ave., 515-286-4960, 800-451-2625; www.desmoinesia.com

SPOT★ LIGHT

★ DES MOINES WAS ALMOST NAMED FORT RACCOON.

★ *BETTER HOMES AND GARDENS MAGAZINE* WAS LAUNCHED IN DES MOINES IN 1922.

WHAT TO SEE AND DO

Adventureland Park
305 34th Ave. N.W., Altoona,
515-266-2121;
www.adventureland-usa.com
This amusement park has more than 100 rides, shows and attractions. June-late August: daily; May and September, weekends.

Blank Park Zoo
7401 S.W. Ninth St., Des Moines,
515-285-4722; www.blankparkzoo.com
The animal and bird habitats at this zoo are designed for close viewing. Includes Australian and African walk-through displays, a farm animal contact area, camel rides and an Old West train ride. Daily.

Des Moines Art Center
4700 Grand Ave., Des Moines,
515-277-4405;
www.desmoinesartcenter.org
Exhibits of 19th- and 20th-century paintings and sculptures are displayed in a contemporary building designed by Eliel Saarinen, with additions by Richard Meier and I.M. Pei. Tuesday-Sunday.

Des Moines Botanical Center
909 Robert D. Ray Dr.,
Des Moines, 515-323-6290;
www.botanicalcenter.com
Displays of nearly 1,500 species from around the world; seasonal floral displays. Daily.

Drake University
2507 University Ave., Des Moines,

515-271-2011; www.drake.edu

This small private university has many buildings designed by distinguished architects, including Eliel and Eero Saarinen, Harry Weese and Associates, Borg and Skiles and Ludwig Mies van der Rohe.

Heritage Village
State Fairgrounds,
E. 30th and University Ave.,
Des Moines, 515-262-3111
Featured here are a century-old barn, exposition hall with displays of early farm machinery, an authentically furnished country school and replicas of an 1834 church. Tours mid-April-mid-October, by appointment.

Hoyt Sherman Place
1501 Woodland Ave., Des Moines,
515-244-0507; www.hoytsherman.org
This 1877 house was once the home of General William Tecumseh Sherman's brother. It now features the city's oldest art gallery, including artifacts, antique furniture and art collection. Tours by appointment. Theater (1,200 seats) added in 1922. Monday-Friday.

Iowa Historical Building
Capitol Complex, 600 E. Locust,
Des Moines, 515-281-5111
Modern cultural center houses state historical museum. Displays portray Iowa history and heritage. Library contains county, state and family history materials; rare books and manuscripts about Iowa; census records; and newspapers. Museum.

Living History Farms
2600 111th St., Urbandale, 515-278-5286;
www.lhf.org
This complex has four farms and a town set on 600 acres. A Native American settlement includes gardens, shelters and crafts of the Ioway tribe. The pioneer farm of 1850 features a log cabin and outbuildings. The horse-powered farm of 1900 depicts farm and household chores typical of period.

The 1875 town of Walnut Hill includes a Victorian mansion, schoolhouse, pottery, blacksmith and carpentry shops, veterinary infirmary, church, bank, newspaper, doctor's offices and a general store. May-mid-October: daily.

Prairie Meadows Racetrack and Casino
1 Prairie Meadows Dr., Altoona,
800-325-9015; www.prairiemeadows.com
Live Thoroughbred, quarter horse and harness racing (late April-October); simulcasts of Thoroughbred and greyhound racing; 24-hour casino with more than 1,500 slots, poker room and video poker machines. Daily.

Science Center of Iowa
4500 Grand Ave., Des Moines,
515-274-4138; www.sciowa.org
Natural and physical science exhibits are the draw at this center, as are live demonstrations, Digistar planetarium shows and laser shows. Daily.

State Capitol
1005 Grand Ave., Des Moines,
515-281-5591
The towering central dome of this 1871 building is covered with 23-carat gold leaf; four smaller domes have golden seam marks. State offices, Supreme Court, House and Senate chamber, law library. Paintings, mosaics, collection of war flags. Daily.

Terrace Hill
2300 Grand Ave., Des Moines,
515-281-3604; www.terracehill.org
This extravagant Italianate/Second Empire mansion, now the residence of Iowa governors, is situated on a commanding knoll above downtown. The restored house is an outstanding example of Victorian residential architecture. Tours include first and second floors, carriage house and gardens. March-December: Tuesday-Saturday 10 a.m.-1:30 p.m..

19

IOWA

THE DES MOINES RIVER VALLEY

This route travels through picture-perfect farming communities founded by European settlers, then along the lower Des Moines River, where historic towns have changed little since the riverboat era. From Des Moines, drive east on Highway 163 toward Pella. Founded in 1847 by Dutch settlers who came to this valley to escape religious persecution in Holland, Pella retains a sense of Dutch orderliness and is filled with trim historic homes and tulip-filled public parks.

East on Highway 163 through rolling hills is Oskaloosa, a farming town settled by Quakers. The town's past is retold at Nelson Pioneer Farm and Craft Museum, which preserves a farm community from the 1850s. From Oskaloosa, follow Highway 163 to Ottumwa, a busy industrial center.

Continuing on, turn east on Highway 34, and then turn south on Highway 16, which closely follows the Des Moines River. One of the earliest settled regions of Iowa, this section of the Des Moines valley is lined with tiny towns founded in the 1830s when the river was the only avenue for travel. Bypassed by the rail lines and the freeway system, these towns were forgotten by the forward rush of time. Today, they have handsome period architecture, newly refurbished small hotels and inns, historical museums and antique stores.

The town of Eldon contains one of the most archetypal structures in the Midwest: at the corner of Gothic and Burton Streets is the house painted by Grant Wood as the backdrop to his famous portrait "American Gothic." The rustic couple in the painting were the painter's sister and his dentist. Keosauqua is home to the oldest courthouse in the state, as well as the imposing Manning Hotel, 150 years old and still in operation. Farther downstream, the entire village of Bentonsport, once a sizable river port, is a National Historic District. The Mason House Hotel, built by Mormon craftsmen in the 1840s, is open for tours and for paying guests. At the town of Bonaparte, the original grist and woolen mills have been preserved.

From Bonaparte, follow Highway 81 south to Farmington, with the oldest Congregational Church west of the Mississippi River (1848) and a stone carriage factory. Continue east to Highway 218 and turn south to Keokuk, at the confluence of the Des Moines and Mississippi rivers. Keokuk was head of steamboat navigation on the Mississippi before Lock Number 19, the largest on the river system, was built in 1913. The lock is part of Keokuk Dam, which was the world's largest hydroelectric dam until the 1930s. Approximately 185 miles.

SPECIAL EVENTS

Drake Relays

Drake University, 2507 University Ave., Des Moines, 515-271-3647

One of the most prestigious intercollegiate track and field events in the country; more than 5,000 athletes compete. Last week in April.

Iowa State Fair

Fairgrounds, E. 30th and University Ave., Des Moines, 515-262-3111; www.iowastatefair.com

One of the oldest and largest fairs in the country, it includes 20 acres of farm machinery, fine arts, a giant midway, grandstand stage and track events, free entertainment and contests. August.

HOTELS

★★Adventureland Inn

3200 Adventureland Dr., Altoona, 515-265-7321; 800-910-5382; www.adventureland-usa.com

130 rooms. Restaurant, bar. Indoor pool. **$**

★Best Inn
5050 Merle Hay Rd., Johnston,
515-270-1111; 800-237-8466;
www.bestinn.com
91 rooms. Pets accepted; fee. Complimentary continental breakfast. Indoor pool, whirlpool. **$**

★★Embassy Suites
101 E. Locust St., Des Moines,
515-244-1700, 800-362-2779;
www.embassysuites.com
234 rooms, all suites. Complimentary full breakfast. Restaurant, bar. Fitness room. Indoor pool, whirlpool. Airport transportation available. **$$**

★★Four Points by Sheraton
1810 Army Post Rd., Des Moines,
515-287-6464, 800-368-7764;
www.fourpoints.com
141 rooms. Complimentary continental breakfast. Restaurant, bar. Indoor pool. Airport transportation available. **$**

★Hampton Inn
5001 Fleur Dr., Des Moines,
515-287-7300, 800-426-7866;
www.hampton-inn.com
122 rooms. Complimentary continental breakfast. Fitness room. Outdoor pool. Airport transportation available. **$**

★Heartland Inn Des Moines West
11414 Forest Ave., Clive,
515-226-0414, 800-334-3277;
www.heartlandinns.com
85 rooms. Pets accepted, some restrictions; fee. Complimentary continental breakfast. High-speed Internet access. Whirlpool. Business center. **$**

★★Holiday Inn
6111 Fleur Dr., Des Moines,
515-287-2400, 800-248-4013;
www.holiday-inn.com
227 rooms. Check-out noon. Restaurant, bar. Fitness room. Indoor pool, whirlpool. Airport transportation available. Business center. **$**

★★Hotel Fort Des Moines
1000 Walnut St., Des Moines,
515-243-1161, 800-532-1466;
www.hotelfortdesmoines.com
242 rooms. Pets accepted. Restaurant, bar. Fitness room. Indoor pool, whirlpool. Airport transportation available. **$**

★★★Des Moines Marriott Downtown
700 Grand Ave., Des Moines,
515-245-5500, 800-228-9290;
www.marriott.com
Connected to the Iowa Events Center by skywalk, this downtown hotel is close to the city's top shopping and restaurants. Rooms have been updated with the chain's luxury bedding, including down duvets and pillow-top mattresses.
415 rooms. Pets accepted, some restrictions. Restaurant,

★Wildwood Lodge
11431 Forest Ave., Clive,
515-222-9876, 800-728-1223;
www.thewildwoodlodge.com
100 rooms. Complimentary continental breakfast. Bar. Fitness room. Indoor pool, whirlpool. **$**

RESTAURANTS
★★★Christopher's
2816 Beaver Ave., Des Moines,
515-274-3694
Italian-American food, including pastas, steaks and seafood, and a casual atmosphere, have made this dining room a local favorite for many years.
American, Italian menu. Dinner. Closed Sunday. Bar. Children's menu. **$$**

★★★Greenbrier
5810 Merle Hay Rd., Johnston,
515-253-0124
The menu at this main-street restaurant offers a broad selection of seafood, chicken, pasta and specialty prime rib.
American menu. Lunch, dinner. Closed Sunday. Children's menu. Outdoor seating. **$$**

IOWA

★
★
★
★
★

★House of Hunan
6810 Douglas Ave., Des Moines,
515-276-5556
Chinese menu. Lunch, dinner. Bar. $

★Jesse's Embers
3301 Ingersoll, Des Moines,
515-255-6011; www.jessesembers.com
Seafood, steak menu. Lunch, dinner. Closed
Sunday. Bar. $$$

★The Machine Shed
11151 Hickman Rd., Urbandale,
515-270-6818
American menu. Breakfast, lunch, dinner.
Bar. Children's menu. $$

★Maxie's
1311 Grand Ave., West Des Moines,
515-223-1463

Steak menu. Lunch, dinner. Closed Sunday.
Bar. Children's menu. $$

★Ohana Steakhouse
2900 University Ave.,
West Des Moines, 515-225-3325;
www.ohanasteakhouse.com
Japanese menu. Dinner. Closed Monday;
holidays. Bar. Children's menu. $$

★Spaghetti Works
300 Court Ave., Des Moines,
515-243-2195
American, Italian menu. Dinner. Bar. Chil-
dren's menu. Outdoor seating. $$

★Waterfront Seafood Market
2900 University Ave.,
West Des Moines, 515-223-5106
Seafood menu. Lunch, dinner. Closed Sun-
day. Bar. Children's menu. $$

DUBUQUE

Facing both Wisconsin and Illinois across the broad Mississippi River, Dubuque became
the first known European settlement in Iowa when Julien Dubuque, a French Canadian,
came from Quebec in 1788 and leased land from the Native Americans to mine lead. After
his death, Native Americans barred settlement until 1833 when the territory was opened
under a treaty with Chief Black Hawk. Once a boisterous river and mining town, Dubuque
had the first bank and newspaper in what is now Iowa. Its downtown has been extensively
rejuvenated in recent years, with a number of restaurants opening in restored buildings.
Information: Convention and Visitors Bureau, 300 Main St., 563-557-9200, 800-798-8844;
www.traveldubuque.com

WHAT TO SEE AND DO

Field of Dreams Movie Site
28963 Lansing Rd., Dyersville,
563-875-8404
Background set of the movie *Field of Dreams*
including the baseball diamond on visitors
can actually play ball. Daily.

Spirit of Dubuque
400 E. 3rd St., Dubuque,
563-583-8093, 800-747-8093; www.
spiritofdubque.com
Sightseeing and dinner cruises (1 1/2-hour)
on the Mississippi River aboard this paddle-
wheeler. May-October.

Bellevue State Park
24668 Hwy. 52, Dubuque, 563-872-3243
Approximately 540 acres on a high bluff
above the Mississipi. Native American
mounds, rugged woodlands, hiking trails,
snowmobiling, picnicking, camping, nature
center. Standard hours, fees.

Cathedral Square
Second and Bluff Streets, Dubuque,
563-582-7646
Surrounding the square are stylized figures
of a lead miner, farmer, farmer's wife,
priest and river hand. Opposite the square
is the architecturally and historically
significant St. Raphael's Cathedral.

Crystal Lake Cave
7699 Crystal Lake Cave Dr., Dubuque,
563-556-6451
A network of passageways carved by underground streams surrounds a lake with glittering stalactites and stalagmites, with water that really is crystal-clear. Guided tours. Memorial Day-late October: daily; May: weekends.

Diamond Jo Casino
Ice Harbor, 400 E. Third St., Dubuque,
563-583-7005, 800-582-5956;
www.diamondjo.com
Casino gambling on the river.

Dubuque Arboretum and Botanical Gardens
3800 Arboretum Dr., Dubuque,
563-556-2100;
www.dubuquearboretum.com
Features annual and perennial gardens, rose, water, formal gardens; ornamental trees, woodland and prairie wildflower walk. Daily.

Dubuque County Courthouse
720 Central Ave., Dubuque, 563-589-4445
This gold-domed courthouse is on the National Historic Register of Places. Monday-Friday.

Dubuque Museum of Art/Old County Jail
701 Locust St., Dubuque, 563-557-1851
This museum is housed in a brand-new facility. The gallery is an example of Egyptian Revival architecture. Tuesday-Friday, weekend afternoons.

Eagle Point Park
2200 Bunker Hill Rd., Dubuque,
563-589-4263
On a high bluff above the Mississippi, this 164-acre park overlooks three states. A Works Proress Administration project, the park's Prairie School pavilions and naturalistic landscaping were designed by Alfred Caldwell, who studied under Frank Lloyd Wright. From the bluff, see a view of barges moving through the lock-and-dam on the river below. Mid-May-mid-October, daily.

Fenelon Place Elevator
512 Fenelon Place, Dubuque,
563-582-6496
In operation since 1882, one of the world's shortest, steepest incline railways connects Fenelon Place with Fourth Street, providing a three-state view. Accepts bicycles. April-November: daily 8 a.m.-10 p.m.

Five Flags Theater
405 Main St., Dubuque,
563-589-4254; www.fiveflagscenter.com
Designed by Rapp and Rapp, premier theater architects of their day, the Five Flags was modeled after Parisian music halls. Tours by appointment.

General Zebulon Pike Lock and Dam
3000 Lock and Dam Road,
Dubuque, 563-582-1204
A steady stream of barges and other river traffic moves through lock.

Grand Opera House
135 Eighth St., Dubuque, 563-588-1305
This century-old opera house was recently restored, and offers a variety of entertainment throughout the year.

Heritage Trail
13606 Swiss Valley Rd., Dubuque,
563-556-6745
This trail provides 26 miles of scenic hiking, biking and cross-country skiing on an old railroad along rugged Little Maquoketa River valley. Level, surfaced trails cross from wooded, hilly, "driftless" areas to rolling prairie near Dyersville. Self-guided tour identifies railroad landmarks, includes water-powered mill sites. Daily.

Julien Dubuque Monument
Grandview Ave. and Julien Dubuque Dr.,
Dubuque, 563-556-0620
Tower built in 1897 at the site of Julien Dubuque's mine and the spot where Native Americans buried him in 1810. Provides an excellent view of the Mississippi River.

Mathias Ham House Historic Site
2241 Lincoln Ave., Dubuque, 563-583-2812

IOWA

An 1857 Italianate/Victorian mansion with a cupola, this house has spectacular views of the Mississippi River. Built by lead miner Mathias Ham. Also Iowa's oldest log cabin and one-room schoolhouse. June-October: daily; May: weekends only.

National Mississippi River Museum and Aquarium

350 E. Third St., Dubuque, 563-557-9545; www.missiissippirivermusem.com

Complex of six Dubuque County Historical Society museums, all emphasizing the city's river history. Daily.

Woodward Discovery Center

350 E. Third St., Ice Harbor, Dubuque, 563-557-9545; www.mississippirivermuseum.org

Dramatizes 300 years of Mississippi River history: Native Americans, explorers, lead miners, boat builders and steamboat captains; lead mines; pilothouse and log raft displays. The aquarium may be the nation's most significant display of river and freshwater creatures, with five huge tanks and live-animal exhibits. This is one of the region's outstanding attractions.

Sundown Mountain Ski Area

16991 Asbury Rd., Dubuque, 563-556-6676, 888-786-3696; www.sundownmtn.com

Skiing in Iowa? Yep. And at this spot, the lodge is at the top of the run. Five chairlifts, tow rope, patrol, school, rentals, snowmaking. Twenty-one runs; longest run 1/2 mile; vertical drop 475 feet. Late November-mid-March: daily.

SPECIAL EVENTS

Dubuque County Fair

Dubuque County Fairgrounds, 14569 Olde Hwy. Rd., Dubuque, 563-588-1406

Recently the fair has had a knack for booking country and contemporary rock acts just as they are hitting it big. Late July.

HOTELS

★★Best Western Midway Hotel

3100 Dodge St., Dubuque, 563-557-8000, 800-336-4392; www.midwayhoteldubuque.com

148 rooms. Pets accepted, some restrictions. Complimentary full breakfast. High-speed Internet access. Restaurant, bar. Children's activity center. Fitness room. Indoor pool, whirlpool. Airport transportation available. $

★Comfort Inn

4055 McDonald Dr., Dubuque, 563-556-3006, 800-228-5150; www.choicehotels.com

52 rooms. Pets accepted, some restrictions; fee. Complimentary continental breakfast. Indoor pool, whirlpool. Airport transportation available. $

★★Days Inn

1111 Dodge St., Dubuque, 563-583-3297, 800-772-3297; www.daysinn.com

155 rooms. Pets accepted; fee. Complimentary continental breakfast. Restaurant, bar. Fitness room. Outdoor pool.

★Heartland Inn Dubuque West

4025 McDonald Dr., Dubuque, 563-582-3752, 800-334-3277; www.heartlandinns.com

85 rooms. Pets accepted, some restrictions; fee. Complimentary continental breakfast. Indoor pool. Airport transportation available. $

★★Holiday Inn

450 Main St., Dubuque, 563-556-2000, 800-465-4329; www.holiday-inn.com

193 rooms. Pets accepted, some restrictions; fee. High-speed Internet access, wireless Internet access. Restaurant, bar. Fitness room. Indoor pool, whirlpool. Airport transportation available. Business center. $

★★Julien Inn

200 Main St., Dubuque, 563-556-4200, 800-798-7098; www.julieninn.com

137 rooms. Restaurant, bar. Fitness room. Airport transportation available. **$**

★★The Grand Harbor Resort and WaterPark
350 Bell St., Dubuque,
563-690-4000, 888-690-4006;
www.grandharborresort.com
193 rooms. Restaurant, bar. Children's activity center. Fitness room. Indoor pool, outdoor pool, children's pool, whirlpool. Airport transportation available. **$$**

★★Timmerman's Hotel & Resort
7777 Timmerman Dr.,
East Dubuque, Illinois,
815-747-3181, 800-336-3181;
www.timmermanhotel.com
74 rooms. Pets accepted, some restrictions; fee. Complimentary continental breakfast. Restaurant, bar. Indoor pool, whirlpool. **$**

SPECIALTY LODGINGS
The Landing
703 S. River Park Dr., Guttenberg,
563-252-1615; www.thelanding615.com
This limestone structure was erected in the late 1800s and features great views of the Mississippi River.

5 rooms. Pets accepted, some restrictions. **$$**

The Redstone Inn
504 Bluff St., Dubuque, 563-582-1894;
www.theredstoneinn.com
This restored 1890s Victorian mansion was built by a prominent Dubuque industrialist as a wedding gift for his daughter.
14 rooms. Pets accepted. Complimentary full breakfast. High-speed wireless Internet access. **$$$**

RESTAURANTS
★★Cafe Mississippi
431 S. River Park Dr., Guttenberg,
563-252-4405
American menu. Lunch, dinner. **$$**

★★Mario's
1298 Main St., Dubuque, 563-556-9424
Italian, American menu. Lunch, dinner. Closed Sunday. Bar. **$$**

★Yen Ching
926 Main St., Dubuque, 563-556-2574
Chinese menu. Lunch, dinner. Closed Sunday. **$**

FORT DODGE
Fort Dodge was established to protect settlers. Its commander, Major William Williams, was given a large tract of land as part of his compensation, and here the town was laid out. Fort Dodge was an innocent party to a scientific hoax when a huge slab of gypsum cut here was freighted to Chicago and carved into the celebrated Cardiff Giant, falsely claimed to be a petrified prehistoric man (now at the Farmer's Museum in Cooperstown, New York).
Information: Chamber of Commerce, 1406 Central Ave., 515-955-5500, 800-765-1438; www.fortdodgechamber.com

WHAT TO SEE AND DO
Fort Dodge Historical Foundation, Fort Museum and Frontier Village
South Kenyon and Museum Rd.,
Fort Dodge, 515-573-4231
A replica of an 1862 fort, this park houses a museum, trading post, blacksmith shop, general store, log home, drugstore, cabinet shop, newspaper office, church, jail and one-room school. May-October: daily; rest of year: by appointment.

Kalsow Prairie
Manson, 15 miles W. on Hwy. 7 to Manson, then 2 miles N. on county road
Approximately 160 acres preserving untouched Iowa prairie.

HOTEL
★★Quality Inn
2001 Hwy. 169 S., Fort Dodge,
515-955-3621; www.qualityinn.com

102 rooms. Pets accepted. High-speed Internet access. Restaurant, bar. Fitness room. Indoor pool, children's pool. **$**

GRINNELL

When Horace Greeley said, "Go west, young man, go west and grow up with the country!" he was talking to Josiah Bushnell Grinnell, who took the advice, went west to a bit of prairie between the Iowa and Skunk rivers, and established the town of Grinnell. Today, Grinnell is a thriving college town.

Information: Chamber of Commerce, 833 Fourth Ave., 641-236-6555; www.grinnellchamber.org

WHAT TO SEE AND DO

Grinnell College

1121 Park St., Grinnell, 641-269-3400; www.grinnell.edu

Considered one of the top liberal arts colleges in the United States, this school was founded in 1846 and has les than 1,500 students. Tours by appointment.

Grinnell Historical Museum

1125 Broad St., Grinnell

Historical furnishings; relics, documents of J. B. Grinnell and aviator Billy Robinson housed in a late Victorian house. June-August: Tuesday-Sunday afternoons; rest of year: Saturday afternoons or by appointment.

Wells Fargo Bank of Iowa—Poweshiek County

Grinnell, downtown, on corner opposite town square

The second in the series of "jewel box" banks that architect Louis Henri Sullivan designed late in his career, this building was constructed in 1914. This unique structure, one of the more important designs in the series, has been restored within the confines of a working bank environment. Monday-Friday

HOTELS

★Super 8

2111 West St. S., Grinnell, 641-236-7888, 800-800-8000; www.super8.com

53 rooms. Pets accepted, some restrictions; fee. Complimentary continental breakfast. **$**

HAMPTON

Information: Chamber of Commerce, 5 First St. S.W. 614-456-5668; www.hamptoniowa.org

WHAT TO SEE AND DO

Beed's Lake State Park

1422 165th St., Hampton, 641-456-2047

Park of 319 acres; dam creates 100-acre lake. Swimming, beach, fishing, boating (ramps); hiking, snowmobiling, picnicking, camping (electricity, dump station). Standard hours, fees.

IOWA CITY

Referred to as "the river city," Iowa City is the home of the University of Iowa and the state's first capital. In its early days, Iowa City boomed as a backwoods metropolis, with the Territorial Legislative Assembly meeting here for the first time in 1841. A Doric stone capitol was erected, but with the shift of population, the legislators moved to Des Moines in 1857. As a conciliatory gesture to Iowa City, they selected it as the site of the new university, the University of Iowa. The city has a small-town feel accented by the kind of cultural amenities and adventurous restaurants that a university presence delivers. In the fall, the town is mesmerized by football when the Hawkeyes are playing at home on Saturdays.
Information: Iowa City/Coralville Convention and Visitors Bureau, 408 First Ave., Riverview Square, Coralville, 319-337-6592, 800-283-6592; www.iowacitycoralville.org

WHAT TO SEE AND DO
Coralville Lake
2850 Prairie du Chien Rd., Iowa City, 319-338-3543
This 5,400-acre lake offers swimming, boating and fishing. Flooding that occurred during the summer of 1993 eroded a 15-foot-deep channel exposing the underlying bedrock. Now called Devonian Fossil Gorge, it offers a rare opportunity to view Iowa's geological past. The site is an Army Corps of Engineers project. Daily.

Herbert Hoover National Historic Site
110 Parkside Dr., West Branch, 319-643-2541
The 187-acre park includes the restored house in which President Hoover was born, the Quaker meeting house where he worshipped as a boy, a school, a blacksmith shop and the graves of President and Lou Henry Hoover. Daily.

Herbert Hoover Presidential Library-Museum
210 Parkside Dr., West Branch, 319-643-5301; www.hoover.nara.gov
Administered by the National Archives and Records Administration. Features a museum with re-created historic settings in China, Belgium, Washington and other places prominent in Hoover's 50 years of public service. Research library by appointment. Daily; closed holidays.

Iowa Children's Museum
1451 Coral Ridge Ave., Coralville, 319-625-5500; www.theicm.org
Interactive exhibits for kids. Tuesday-Sunday.

Kalona Historical Village
411 Ninth St., Kalona, 319-656-2519; www.kalonaiowa.org
Amish traditions and lifestyle are preserved in this village containing the Wahl Museum, the Mennonite Museum and Archives, and an implement building; restored 110-year-old depot, log house (1842), one-room school, country store, outdoor bake oven, Victorian house, working windmill, post office (1880), and church (1869). Monday-Saturday.

Plum Grove
1030 Carroll St., Iowa City, 319-337-6846
The 1844 residence of the territory's first governor, Robert Lucas has been restored and furnished with period furniture. Memorial Day-October: Wednesday-Sunday 1-5 p.m.

University of Iowa
IMU Madison and Jefferson Streets, Iowa City, 319-335-0557; www.uiowa.edu
This major state university has more than 28,000 students, 100 major buildings on 1,900 acres, 11 colleges, six schools and 82 departments. Big Ten basketball is played at the Carver-Hawkeye Arena, and Hawkeye football is an annual Iowa City obsession.

SPECIAL EVENTS
Iowa Arts Festival
408 S. 1st Ave., Iowa City, 319-337-7944
Celebration of the arts. Mid-June.

27

IOWA

★
★
★
★

HOTELS

★★Hampton Inn
1200 First Ave., Coralville,
319-351-6600, 800-426-7666;
www.hamptoninn.com
115 rooms. Complimentary continental breakfast. Restaurant. Fitness room. Indoor pool, whirlpool. Airport transportation available. Business center. **$**

★★Holiday Inn
1220 First Ave., Coralville, 319-351-5049,
800-252-7466; www.holiday-inn.com
96 rooms. Complimentary continental breakfast. Restaurant. Fitness room. Indoor pool. **$**

★★★Sheraton Iowa City Hotel
210 S. Dubuque St., Iowa City,
319-337-4058, 800-848-1335;
www.sheraton.com
Located one block from the University of Iowa, rooms at this hotel have been updated with the chain's signature luxury beds and soaking tubs.
236 rooms. Pets accepted, some restrictions. Restaurant, bar. Fitness room. Indoor pool, whirlpool. Airport transportation available. **$$**

MARQUETTE

First known as North McGregor, this town was later renamed for Father Jacques Marquette. He and Louis Jolliet were the first to see Iowa territory from the mouth of the Wisconsin River in 1673. Within a 15-mile radius of the town are hundreds of effigy mounds, fortifications and earthworks.
Information: McGregor/Marquette Chamber of Commerce, 146 Main St., 563-873-2186, 800-895-0910; www.2chambers.com/marquette, _iowa.htm

WHAT TO SEE AND DO

Effigy Mounds National Monument
151 Hwy. 76, Harpers Ferry, 563-873-3491
Preserves traces of indigenous civilization from 2,500 years ago. Mounds built in shapes of animals, birds and other forms. Area divided by Yellow River; Great Bear Mound is the largest known bear effigy in the state, 70 feet across the shoulders, 137 feet long and five feet high. Footpath leads from headquarters to Fire Point Mound Group, to scenic viewpoints overlooking the Mississippi and Yellow rivers. Daily.

Pikes Peak State Park
15316 Great River Rd., McGregor,
563-873-2341
Park of 970 acres on bluffs overlooking the Mississippi River. Native American mounds, colored sandstone outcroppings,

woods and wildflowers. A trail leads across rugged terrain to Bridal Veil Falls. Standard hours.

Spook Cave and Campground
13299 Spook Cave Rd., McGregor,
563-873-2144
Guided 35-minute tour of underground cavern via power boat. Campground has swimming beach, lake fishing, hiking trails and picnic areas. May-October: daily.

HOTELS

★Holiday Shores
110 Front St., McGregor,
563-873-3449
33 rooms. Indoor pool, whirlpool. Overlooks the Mississippi River. **$**

MARSHALLTOWN

The business center of Marshall County prides itself on its historic courthouse, parks and numerous churches. Perhaps its most famous son is "Cap" Anson, son of the founder, who is celebrated at the Baseball Hall of Fame in Cooperstown, New York.

Information: Convention & Visitors Bureau, 709 S. Center St., 641-753-6645, 800-697-3155; www.marshalltown.org

WHAT TO SEE AND DO

Fisher Community Center Art Gallery

709 S. Center St., Marshalltown, 641-753-9013

Art collection including paintings by Sisley, Utrillo and Cassatt. Daily; closed holidays.

HOTELS

★★Best Western Regency Inn

3303 S. Center St., Marshalltown, 641-752-6321, 800-780-7234; www.bestwestern.com

105 rooms. Restaurant, bar. Indoor pool, whirlpool. $

MUSCATINE

This city produces the famous Muscatine cantaloupes and watermelons. Samuel Clemens, who once lived here, declared Muscatine's summer sunsets unsurpassed.

Information: Convention and Visitors Bureau, 319 E. Second St., 563-263-8895, 800-257-3275; www.muscatine.com

WHAT TO SEE AND DO

Meredith Willson Footbridge

Second St. S.E., Mason City

Formerly called the Willow Creek Bridge, the name was inspired by the creator of *The Music Man.*

Frank Lloyd Wright Stockman House

530 First St. N.E., Mason City, 641-421-3666

The only Prairie School house in Iowa designed by Frank Lloyd Wright, this 1908 structure is one of the few houses built by Wright during this period to address middle-class housing needs. Tours. June-August: Thursday-Sunday; September-October weekends.

Kinney Pioneer Museum

Hwy. 18 W., Mason City, 641-423-1258

Local history, pioneer, military exhibits; antique cars; original log cabin (circa 1854); one-room schoolhouse; old farm machinery, railroad caboose; artifacts, fossils. May-September: Tuesday-Sunday.

Meredith Willson Boyhood Home

314 S. Pennsylvania Ave., Mason City, 641-423-3534

Birthplace of the author of *The Music Man.* May-October: daily; November-April: weekends

HOTELS

★Comfort Inn

410 Fifth St. S.W., Mason City, 641-423-4444, 800-228-5150; www.comfortinn.com

60 rooms. Complimentary continental breakfast. Indoor pool, whirlpool. $

MASON CITY

A Native American uprising slowed growth of the city after the first settlement, but pioneers, many of whom were Masons, gradually returned. The town was first known as Shibboleth, later as Masonic Grove. This is the seat of Cerro Gordo County and was the inspiration for the classic musical *The Music Man.*

Information: Convention & Visitors Bureau, 15 W. State St., P.O. Box 1128, 50402-1128. 641-422-1663; 800-423-5724. www.masoncityia.com

WHAT TO SEE AND DO

Mark Twain Overlook
Lombard and Second Streets,
Muscatine
Three acres with a panoramic view of Mississippi River Valley and downtown Muscatine; picnicking.

Muscatine Art Center
1314 Mulberry Ave., Muscatine,
563-263-8282
Consists of the Laura Musser Museum and the Stanley Gallery. The museum is housed in an Edwardian mansion; changing art exhibits, special events, Estey player pipe organ with 731 pipes, antiques and historical displays; Oriental carpets, furniture, paintings, drawings, prints, sculpture, graphics in permanent collection. Tuesday-Sunday.

HOTELS

★★Holiday Inn
2915 N. Hwy. 61, Muscatine,
563-264-5550, 800-465-4329;
www.holiday-inn.com
112 rooms. Pets accepted; fee. Restaurant, bar. Fitness room. Indoor pool, children's pool, whirlpool. Business center. **$**

NEWTON

The washing machine industry was born here in 1898, and for years the Maytag Company was the dominant business in the city.
Information: Convention and Visitors Bureau, 113 First Ave. W. 641-792-0299, 800-798-0299; www.visitnewton.com

WHAT TO SEE AND DO

Fred Maytag Park
301 S. 11th Ave. W., Newton,
641-792-1470
Donated by the founder of the Maytag Company. Tennis, picnicking, playground, amphitheater, log cabin. Pool and water slide. June-August: daily. Park: daily.

Jasper County Historical Museum
1700 S. 15th Ave. W., Newton,
641-792-9118
Local historical displays include a bas-relief sculpture of the natural history of the county, Victorian home, schoolroom, chapel, tool and farm equipment collections. There's also a Maytag historical display of washing machines. May-September: afternoons.

HOTELS

★★★La Corsette Maison Inn
629 First Ave. E., Newton,
641-792-6833; www.lacorsette.com
This historic 1909 mission-style mansion is decorated with stained glass and oak. Guest suites have French furnishings and wood-burning fireplaces.
9 rooms. Complimentary full breakfast. Restaurant. **$$**

★Super 8
1635 S. 12th Ave. W., Newton,
641-792-8868, 800-800-8000;
www.super8.com
43 rooms. Complimentary continental breakfast. **$**

RESTAURANT

★★★La Corsette Maison Inn
629 First Ave. E., Newton,
641-792-6833; www.lacorsette.com
Located inside La Corsette Maison Inn, guests are served by tuxedoed waiters and entertained with music from the baby grand piano. Entrees include creations such as roasted pork loin with prune chutney, or orange roughy with walnut cream sauce. American menu, French. Lunch, dinner. Reservations recommended. **$$$**

OKOBOJI

Lake Okoboji and the surrounding area are among the most popular resort areas in Iowa.
Information: Tourism, 243 W. Broadway, 712-332-2209, 800-270-2574; www.vacationokoboji.com

WHAT TO SEE AND DO

Okoboji Queen II
37 Lake St., Arnolds Park, 712-332-5159
Several steamship cruises on West Okoboji Lake are offered in the summer, with a more limited schedule the rest of the year.

Arnolds Park Amusement Park
37 Lake St., Arnolds Park, 712-332-2183
Century-old amusement park with classic old rides and newer favorites, plus entertainment and games. Mid-June-mid-August: daily; May-mid-June and late August: weekends; hours vary.

Gull Point State Park
1500 Harpen St., Wahpeton, 712-337-3211
On 165 acres on West Okoboji Lake, this park has swimming, fishing, boating, snowmobiling, hiking trails, picnicking and camping.

SPECIAL EVENT

Okoboji Summer Theater
Hwy. 71, Okoboji, 712-332-7773
This theater has a new play each week and is operated by Stephens College of Columbia, Missouri. Mid-June-mid-August: Tuesday-Sunday.

HOTELS

★★Inn at Okoboji
3301 Lake Shore Dr., Okoboji, 712-332-2113; www.theinnatokoboji.com
152 rooms. Closed October-April. Restaurant, bar. Children's activity center. Indoor pool, outdoor pool. Golf. Tennis. $

★★★Arrowwood Resort And Conference Center By Clubhouse
1405 Hwy. 71 N., Okoboji, 712-332-2161; www.arrowwood-okoboji.com
This spacious resort and conference center provides guests with a relaxed environment and a host of activities to choose from, including tennis, swimming or simply taking in the beautiful scenery.
99 rooms. Pets accepted. Restaurant, bar. Fitness room. Two outdoor pools, whirlpool. Golf. Tennis. $

Ottumwa Park
105 E. Third St., Ottumwa, 641-682-1307
This 365-acre recreation area in the center of the city includes camping, fishing, tennis, volleyball, basketball courts, baseball diamond, horseshoes, bocce. April-mid-October: daily.

SIOUX CITY

At the heart of a tri-state region bordered by the Sioux and Missouri rivers, Sioux City has historically been a hub for shipping, transportation and agriculture. The Lewis and Clark expedition followed the Missouri River; the only fatality of that historic trek is commemorated here with the Sergeant Floyd Monument, the first registered historic landmark in the United States.

Today, the Missouri River is important to the city from a recreational standpoint, with a developed riverfront with parks, a dance pavilion and a riverboat casino. Sioux City also has many theaters, parks, an art center, nature center, historical attractions and festivals and events throughout the year.
Information: Sioux City Convention Center/Tourism Bureau, 801 Fourth St., 712-279-4800, 800-593-2228; www.siouxcitytourismconvention.com

WHAT TO SEE AND DO

Argosy Casino
100 Larsen Park Rd., Sioux City, 800-424-0080; www.argosy.com/siouxcity
Tri-level riverboat casino. May-October: daily.

Sergeant Floyd Monument
Glenn Ave. and Hwy. 75, Sioux City
This was the first registered national historic landmark in the United States. The 100-foot obelisk marks the burial place of Sergeant Charles Floyd, the only casualty of the Lewis and Clark expedition.

Sioux City Art Center
225 Nebraska St., Sioux City, 712-279-6272; www.siouxcityartcenter.org
Contemporary traveling exhibits and permanent collection. Three-story glass atrium. Special programs. Tuesday-Saturday, Sunday afternoon.

Sioux City Public Museum
2901 Jackson, Sioux City, 712-279-6174; www.siouxcitymuseum.org
Exhibits show Sioux City history and life in pioneer days; geological, archaeological, and Native American materials. Located in a Romanesque 23-room mansion. Tuesday-Sunday; holidays.

Stone State Park
500 Talbot Rd., Sioux City, 712-255-4698
On 1,069 acres. The park overlooks the Missouri and Big Sioux river valleys and offers views of three states from Dakota Point Lookout near Big Sioux River. Ten-acre Dorothy Pecant Nature Center, Tuesday-Sunday; closed holidays.

Woodbury County Courthouse
620 Douglas St., Sioux City, 712-279-6624
This courthouse was the largest structure ever completed in the architectural style of Chicago's Prairie School. Designed by Purcell and Elmslie, long-time associates of Louis Sullivan, the city-block-long building was constructed in 1918 of Roman brick and ornamented with massive pieces of terra-cotta, stained glass and relief sculpture by Alfonso Ianelli, who also worked with Frank Lloyd Wright. Both the exterior and highly detailed interior are in near-pristine condition. Courtrooms still contain original architect-designed furniture and lighting fixtures. Monday-Friday.

HOTELS

★Best Western City Centre
130 Nebraska St., Sioux City, 712-277-1550, 800-780-7234; www.bestwestern.com
114 rooms. Pets accepted, some restrictions; fee. Bar. Outdoor pool. Airport transportation available. $

★★Clarion Hotel and Conference Center
707 Fourth St., Sioux City, 712-277-4101, 800-593-0555
193 rooms. Pets accepted, some restrictions; fee. Restaurant, bar. Fitness room. Indoor pool. Airport transportation available. $

★Super 8
4307 Stone Ave., Sioux City,

32

IOWA

712-274-1520, 800-800-8000;
www.super8.com
60 rooms. Pets accepted, some restrictions; fee. **$**

RESTAURANT
★Green Gables
1800 Pierce St., Sioux City,
712-258-4246
Steak menu. Lunch, dinner, late-night. Children's menu. **$$**

WATERLOO
On both banks of the wide Cedar River, Waterloo has established park and picnic areas, docks and boating facilities along the shoreline. One of the largest tractor production facilities in the world is located here.
Information: Convention and Visitors Bureau, 215 E. Fourth St., 319-233-8350, 800-728-8431; www.waterloocvb.org

WHAT TO SEE AND DO
George Wyth Memorial State Park
2659 Wyth Rd., Waterloo, 319-232-5505
The 1200-acre park includes several lakes. Swimming, fishing, boating, nature, hiking and bicycle trails, snowmobiling, picnicking, camping. Standard hours.

Grout Museum of History and Science
503 South St., Waterloo, 319-234-6357;
www.groutmuseumdistrict.org
Permanent and changing exhibits on regional history and science. Discovery Zone offers many hands-on activities. Pioneer Hall, photo history area, industrial hall; genealogy library. Planetarium shows. Tuesday-Saturday.

Waterloo Community Playhouse
224 Commercial St., Waterloo,
319-235-0367; www.wcpbhct.org
Open since 1916, this theater offers seven productions yearly including comedies, dramas, mysteries and classics.

Waterloo Museum of Art
225 Commercial St., Waterloo,
319-291-4490;
www.waterloocenterforthearts.org
Permanent collections include Haitian, American and regional art plus Grant Wood drawings. Changing exhibits. Gift shop offers works by Midwest artists. Tuesday-Sunday.

SPECIAL EVENT
My Waterloo Days Festival
215 E. Fourth St., Waterloo, 319-233-8431
Citywide festival features air show, balloon rallies, parade, laser and fireworks show, music, renaissance fair, food. Four days beginning the Thursday after Memorial Day.

HOTELS
★★Best Western Starlite Village
214 Washington St., Waterloo,
319-235-0321, 800-903-0009;
www.bestwestern.com
219 rooms. Pets accepted; fee. Restaurant, bar. Indoor pool. Airport transportation available. **$**

★Heartland Inn Waterloo Crossroads
1809 LaPorte Rd., Waterloo,
319-235-4461, 800-334-3277;
www.heartlandinns.com
113 rooms. Pets accepted, some restrictions; fee. Complimentary continental breakfast. High-speed Internet access. Fitness room. Indoor pool. Business center. **$**

★Heartland Inn Waterloo Greyhound Park
3052 Marnie Ave., Waterloo,
319-232-7467, 800-334-3277
www.heartlandinns.com
54 rooms. Pets accepted, some restrictions; fee. Complimentary continental breakfast. High-speed Internet access. Indoor pool, whirlpool. Business center. **$**

33

IOWA

★
★
★
★
★

WILLIAMSBURG

This small town, located in the central-eastern half of the state, grew in the 1880s when the railroad passed through town. Today, Interstate 80 also runs through the area, drawing visitors to this Welsh, Scottish and German farming community.
Information: www.williamsburgiowa.org

RESTAURANT

★★Colony Village
2224 U Ave., Williamsburg, 319-668-1223;
www.colonyvillage.com
American, German menu. Breakfast, lunch, dinner. Bar. Children's menu. $$

KANSAS

IN THE MOVIE *THE WIZARD OF OZ*, KANSAS IS A DUSTY, EMPTY LANDSCAPE IN BLACK-AND-white. In real life, no one will deny Kansas has plenty of open space (the state has been using the slogan "As Big As You Think" to promote itself), but the curious visitor will find that Kansas is full of interesting places and natural attractions. And yes, it's in color: the gold and black of sunflowers growing by the thousands in a field, the green of vast swaths of native prairie grass (dappled with splashes of brightly colored wildflowers) and of course, the amber waves of grain—wheat—that is grown on so much of Kansas's ground.

You'll find colors of another kind at the annual Wah-Shun-Gah Days powwow in a Santa Fe Trail town, where tribal dancers in native costumes dip and sway to drums. Or if you like your colors loud and your timing is right, you can catch the spectacle of car racing at the NASCAR track in Kansas City.

Native Americans inhabited Kansas thousands of years before Spanish conquistador Francisco Vasquez de Coronado explored the territory in 1541. Other early explorers of Kansas were Meriwether Lewis and William Clark. Army Captain Zebulon Pike also explored the area, continuing westward to discover what is now Pikes Peak in Colorado.

By the 1840s, traders and immigrants had established the Santa Fe and Chisholm Trails across the region. Kansas's pre-Civil War activities included the exploits of John Brown, who operated part of the Underground Railroad for slaves escaping through Kansas. Many clashes occurred between antislavery and pro-slavery forces as Kansas was being admitted to the Union. The Abolitionists were determined that Kansas be a "free" state. As railroads expanded westward, the era of cattle drives made such towns as Abilene, Hays, Wichita and Dodge City centers of the legendary Old West, as did such men as Bat Masterson, Wyatt Earp, "Wild Bill" Hickok and the Dalton Gang.

Eastern Kansas is green, fertile and hilly, with woods, streams and lakes. Western Kansas is a part of the Great Plains, once the grass-covered haunt of the buffalo. In 1874, Mennonite immigrants from Russia introduced their Turkey Red wheat seed to Kansas soil, helping to establish Kansas as the breadbasket of the nation.

When you wish to rub elbows with civilization, Topeka, the state's largest city with a 600,000 metro-area population, has galleries and museums. Its historic Delano District, once known for its brothels and saloons, is a place to find martini lounges and jazz. For the laid-back vibe of a college town, head to Lawrence, home of the University of Kansas. While it's now a place of coffeehouses, brewpubs and great ethnic restaurants, Lawrence was where the Abolitionists and pro-slavery forces clashed. More than 150 citizens were killed in the fiery Quantrill's Raiders attack. Finally, at the state's eastern edge, the Kansas City metro area is a bustling cluster of suburbs (including Overland

KANSAS

 SPOTLIGHT

★The world's largest ball of twine, located in Cawker City, is more than 40 feet in circumference, weighs more than 17,000 pounds and is still growing.

★ At one time it was against the law to serve ice cream on cherry pie in Kansas.

Park, Shawnee, Bonner Springs, Lenexa, Olathe and Leawood) spilling over from the bigger K.C. on the Missouri side of the border. It's a place full of shopping malls and outlet stores, and restaurants ranging from barbecue to gourmet.

ABILENE

Once famous as a Kansas "cow town," Abilene in 1867 was the terminal point of the Kansas Pacific (later Union Pacific) Railroad and the nearest railhead for the shipment of cattle brought north over the Chisholm Trail. The number of cattle shipped east from here between 1867 and 1871 has been estimated at more than a million, and often 500 cowboys were paid off at a time. City marshals Tom Smith and "Wild Bill" Hickok brought in law and order in the 1870s. Today, Abilene is a wheat center, perhaps best known as the boyhood home of Dwight D. Eisenhower.

Information: Convention and Visitors Bureau, 201 N.W. Second St., 785-263-2231, 800-569-5915; www.abileneks.com

WHAT TO SEE AND DO

Abilene Smoky Valley Excursion Train
200 S. Fifth, Abilene, 785-263-1077; www.asvrr.org
This 100-hundred-year-old wooden diner coach makes trips through the historic countryside. Memorial Day-Labor Day: Tuesday-Sunday.

Dickinson County Historical Museum
412 S. Campbell St., Abilene, 785-263-2681; www.heritagecenterdk.com
Exhibits at this museum depict life in early pioneer days and include antique toys and household items used at the turn of the century. Also on site is a Heritage Center, carousel and log cabin. Daily.

Eisenhower Center
200 S.E. Fourth St., Abilene, 785-263-4751; www.dwighteisenhower.com
President Dwight D. Eisenhower's birthplace is also the location of his presidential library. Visitors can tour the 1887 house where Eisenhower was raised; the interior and most furnishings are original. The museum houses changing exhibits of mementos, souvenirs and gifts received during Eisenhower's career. The library contains presidential papers. President and Mrs. Eisenhower are buried in the Meditation Chapel. Daily.

Lebold Mansion
106 N. Vine, Abilene, 785-263-4356
A restored Victorian mansion with period furnishings, this house was built in 1880 by C. H. Lebold. Tours: Tuesday-Sunday 10 a.m.-4 p.m.

Seelye Mansion and Museum
1105 N. Buckeye, Abilene, 785-263-1084
This 25-room Georgian mansion is listed on the National Register of Historic Places. It was built in 1905 by A. B. Seelye, a patent medicine entrepreneur. The museum depicts a turn-of-the-century medicine business. Daily.

HOTELS

★Super 8
2207 N. Buckeye Ave., Abilene, 785-263-4545, 800-800-8000; www.super8.com
62 rooms. Pets accepted; fee. $

RESTAURANTS

★★ Brookville Hotel Dining Room
105 E. Lafayette, Abilene, 785-263-2244; www.brookvillehotel.com
American menu. Dinner. Closed Monday. $$$

★★★ Kirby House
205 N.E. Third St., Abilene, 785-263-7336; www.kirby-house.com
Built as a home in 1885, this Victorian-style restaurant has a friendly atmosphere popu-

36

KANSAS

★
★
★
★
★
★

lar with large groups and anyone celebrating a special occasion. The menu features American classics like country fried steak.

American menu. Lunch, dinner, Sunday brunch. Bar. Children's menu. **$$**

COLBY

This town is the hub of northwest Kansas, with cultural, shopping, and hospitality facilities. Agri-business drives the economy.

Information: Convention and Visitors Bureau, 350 S. Range, 785-462-7643, 800-611-8835; www.colbychamber.com

WHAT TO SEE AND DO
Prairie Museum of Art & History
1905 S. Franklin St., Colby, 785-460-4590; www.prairiemuseum.org

This museum features rare bisque and china dolls, glass and crystal, Chinese and Japanese artifacts, textiles and furniture. On the museum site are a sod house, restored 1930s farmstead, one-room schoolhouse, a country church and one of the largest barns in Kansas. Daily.

HOTELS
★★Quality Inn
1950 S. Range Ave., Colby, 785-462-3933, 800-228-5151; www.qualityinn.com

117 rooms. Restaurant. Bar. Indoor pool. **$**

COUNCIL GROVE

As the last outfitting place on the Santa Fe Trail between the Missouri River and Santa Fe, Council Grove, now a National Historic Landmark, holds historic significance in the development of the West. The town grew up around a Native American campground in a grove of oaks near the Neosho River and has many turn-of-the-century buildings, several parks and two lakes.

Information: Convention and Visitors Bureau, 212 W. Main St., 316-767-5882, 800-732-9211; www.councilgrove.com

WHAT TO SEE AND DO
Council Oak Shrine
313 E. Main St., Council Grove

The treaty of 1825 was signed here between U.S. government commissioners and the Osage.

Custer's Elm Shrine
S. Neosho St., Council Grove

This elm trunk stands as a shrine to a tree that was 100 feet tall, 16 feet in circumference and reputedly sheltered the camp of General George Custer in 1867 when he was leading an expedition to western Kansas.

Madonna of the Trail Monument
Union and Main Streets, Council Grove

One of 12 statues erected in each of the states through which the National Old Trails Roads passed. The Madonna pays tribute to pioneer mothers and commemorates the trails that opened the West.

Post Office Oak
E. Main and Union Streets, Council Grove.

This mammoth oak tree with a cache at its base served as an unofficial post office for pack trains and caravans on the Santa Fe Trail from 1825 to 1847.

A WALK THROUGH THE OLD WEST

If you're looking for an authentic Old West town, journey to Council Grove, a once busy trading center on the Sante Fe Trail during the 1840s and 1850s. Council Grove contains some of the best-preserved frontier-era architecture in Kansas, and many of the buildings are still used for their original commercial purpose.

Begin your tour at the Kaw Mission State Historic Site (500 N. Mission St.). Methodist missionaries built this school for native Kaw children in 1851. Today the structure contains a museum dedicated to the Kaw, the Sante Fe Trail and early Council Grove. From here, walk south on Mission Street to Main Street, which follows the route of the Santa Fe Trail through town. The Cottage House Hotel (25 N. Neosho) is a beautifully maintained Victorian hotel still in operation with wraparound porches and striking Queen Anne turrets and gazebos. Across Main Street, the Farmers and Drovers Bank (201 W. Main), is a handsome landmark of redbrick and limestone, with eclectic architectural features like Romanesque arches, stained-glass windows and a Byzantine dome.

One block east on Main Street is another historic structure, which is still in operation. The Hays House Restaurant (112 W. Main) is the oldest continuously operating restaurant west of the Mississippi. Since it was constructed in 1857, the restaurant has served the likes of General George Custer and Jesse James. The ambience is frontier-era, and peach pie is among the favorite offerings. Also on this block of Main Street is the stone Last Chance Store (also in operation since 1857) and the Council Grove National Bank Building.

Before crossing the Neosho River Bridge, turn south two blocks to the Seth Hays Home. Built in 1867, this home has been preserved and is open to visitors on Sundays and by appointment. Cross the Neosho River on Main Street. In a shelter along the riverbank is the remains of the Council Oak, a once-vast oak tree under which representatives of the United States and the Osage tribe signed a treaty in 1825 that guaranteed settlers safe passage across Indian territory. On the north corner of Main and Union Streets is a small park containing the Madonna of the Trail, a statue of a pioneer mother and children erected in 1925 by the Daughters of the American Revolution. Along with a museum of frontier history, the park is home to the Post Office Oak, a 300-year-old burr oak that served as an unofficial post depository for travelers along the Sante Fe Trail. Continue east on Main to Durland Park (at Fifth St.) where Council Grove's first jail, constructed in 1849, still stands. Also in Durland Park are two 19th-century train depots.

KANSAS

SPECIAL EVENTS

Wah-Shun-Gah Days
212 W. Main St., Council Grove,
620-767-5041
This event is the Kaw Intertribal Powwow and includes a Santa Fe Trail ride and supper, antique tractor pull and street dance. Third weekend in June.

RESTAURANTS

★★ **Hays House Historic Restaurant and Tavern**
112 W. Main St., Council Grove,
620-767-5911; www.hayshouse.com
American menu. Breakfast, lunch, dinner, Sunday brunch. Bar. Children's menu. National Register of Historic Landmarks on Santa Fe Trail. $$

HISTORIC DODGE CITY

Memorable for buffalo hunts, longhorn cattle and frontier marshals, Dodge City was laid out by construction crews of the Santa Fe Railroad and named for nearby Fort Dodge. Vast herds of buffalo—estimated at 24 million or more—which then covered the surrounding plains, had been hunted here for years. The railroad provided transportation to make the hides commercially profitable. A skilled hunter could earn $100 a day at the industry's height; by 1875 the herds were nearly exterminated. Cattle drives, also stimulated by the railroad, took the buffalo's place in the town's economy. In the 1870s, Dodge City became the cowboy capital of the region. Among its notable peace officers were Bat Masterson and Wyatt Earp. The prevalence of sudden and violent death resulted in the establishment of Boot Hill cemetery. In the mid-1880s the era of the cattle drives ended, and by 1890 much of the grazing land had been plowed for crops. Visitors to Doge City can get a peak into the Wild West's past by exploring the many preserved historic buildings, including those on restored historic Front Street.
Information: Convention & Visitors Bureau, 400 W. Wyatt Earp Blvd., 620-225-8186, 800-653-9378; www.visitdodgecity.org

EL DORADO

El Dorado, the seat of Butler County, is located on the western edge of the Flint Hills. The city's growth can be attributed to oil—two refineries are located here. Stapleton # 1, the area's first gusher, tapped in 1915, is commemorated by a marker at the northwestern edge of the town.
Information: Chamber of Commerce, 383 E. Central, 316-321-3150; www.eldoradochamber.com

WHAT TO SEE AND DO

El Dorado State Park
618 N.E. Bluestem Rd., El Dorado, 316-321-7180.
The largest of Kansas's state parks, El Dorado is made up of four areas totaling 4,000 acres. Rolling hills, wooded valleys and open prairie make up the natural environment of the park. El Dorado Lake is also within the park. Daily.

Kansas Oil Museum
383 E. Central Ave., El Dorado, 316-321-9333; www.kansasoilmuseum.org
Displays at this museum depict the area's oil, ranching and agricultural history, including a model rotary drilling rig. Outdoor historic oil field exhibits include a restored cable-tool drilling rig, shotgun lease house and antique engines. Monday-Saturday 9 a.m.-5 p.m., Sunday 1-5 p.m.

HOTELS

★★Best Western Red Coach Inn
2525 W. Central St., El Dorado, 316-321-6900, 800-780-7234; www.bestwestern.com
73 rooms. Pets accepted, some restrictions; fee. Restaurant. Fitness room. Indoor pool, whirlpool. Airport transportation available. $

39

KANSAS

★
★
★
★
★

EMPORIA

This was the home of one of America's most famous newspaper editors, William Allen White. His *Emporia Gazette* editorials, written from the 1890s to the 1940s, attracted nationwide attention and earned White a Pulitzer prize. Emporia is the seat of Lyon County and on the edge of the Flint Hills area.

Information Convention & Visitors Bureau, 719 Commercial St, 620-342-1803, 800-279-3730; www.emporiakschamber.org

WHAT TO SEE AND DO

Emporia Gazette Building
517 Merchant St., Emporia, 620-342-4800
This building houses William Allen White's widely-quoted newspaper. Located here is a small one-room museum that displays newspaper machinery used in White's time. Monday-Friday; weekends by appointment; closed holidays.

Flint Hills National Wildlife Refuge
310 W. Maple Ave., Hartford, 620-392-5553
Consisting of 18,500 acres located on the upstream portion of John Redmond River, this park offers hiking and camping. Wild food gathering is permitted. Bald eagles can be spotted in fall and winter. Fishing and hunting in legal seasons. Daily; some portions closed during fall migration of waterfowl.

National Teachers Hall of Fame
1200 Commercial, Emporia, 620-341-5660, 800-968-3224; www.nthf.org

This organization is committed to drawing the public's attention to exceptional teachers through a museum, teacher's resource center and an induction ceremony that recognizes five of the nation's most outstanding Pre-Kindergarten through Grade 12 educators each year. Monday-Saturday.

David Traylor Zoo of Emporia
75 Sodens Rd., Emporia, 620-342-6558; www.emporiazoo.org
This zoo has nearly 400 specimens of birds, mammals and reptiles representing more than 80 species housed in natural habitats. Drive or walk through. Daily.

HOTELS

★★Best Western Hospitality House
3021 W. Hwy. 50, Emporia,
620-342-7587, 800-362-2036;
www.bestwestern.com
143 rooms. Pets accepted, some restrictions. Complimentary continental breakfast. Restaurant. Bar. Fitness room. Indoor pool, whirlpool. Business center. $

HAYS

Fort Hays, a former military post on the old frontier, gave this railroad town its name. Oil, grain, cattle, educational and medical facilities, and tourism are important to the area.

Information: Convention and Visitors Bureau, 1301 Pine St., 785-628-8202, 800-569-4505; www.haysusa.com

WHAT TO SEE AND DO

Ellis County Historical Society and Museum
100 W. Seventh St., Hays, 785-628-2624
More than 26,000 items are on display in this museum including antique toys and games, musical instruments and rotating exhibits including quilts from the 1800s to present. Also here are a one-room schoolhouse and the oldest stone church in Ellis

County. June-August: Tuesday-Friday; also Saturday afternoons; rest of year: Tuesday-Friday.

Historic Fort Hays
1472 Hwy. 183, Hays, 785-625-6812;
www.kshs.org/places/forthays
This former U.S. Army post was in use from 1865 to 1889 as a base for defending the railroad that ran through the area. Wild

West legends Wild Bill Hickok and Buffalo Bill Cody are just some of the figures who passed through the fort. Daily.

Sternberg Museum of Natural History
3000 Sternberg Dr., Hays, 785-628-4286; www.fshu.edu/sterberg
This museum features natural history, paleontological and geological collections. Tuesday-Sunday.

SPECIAL EVENTS
Pioneer Days at Historic Fort Hays
1472 Hwy. 183 Alt., Hays, 785-625-6812
Two full days are filled with demonstrations of butter churning, tatting, rope making, rug weaving, whittling and stonepost cutting at this annual event. September.

Wild West Festival
Frontier Park, 1301 Pine St., Hays, 785-628-8202; www.wildwestfestival.com
This annual event features family-oriented activities, concerts, food booths and a fireworks display. Early July.

HOTELS
★Hampton Inn
4002 General Hays Rd., Hays, 785-621-4444, 800-426-7866; www.hamptoninn.com
117 rooms. Pets accepted, some restrictions. Complimentary continental breakfast. Airport transportation available. **$**

★★Holiday Inn
3603 Vine St., Hays, 785-625-7371, 888-465-4329; www.holiday-inn.com
191 rooms. Restaurant. Bar. Fitness room. Indoor pool, whirlpool. Airport transportation available. **$**

RESTAURANTS
★ Gutierrez
1106 E. 27 St., Hays, 785-625-4402; www.thelocalsfavorite.com
Mexican, American menu. Lunch, dinner. Bar. Children's menu. **$$**

HUTCHINSON
In 1887, drillers for natural gas discovered some of the world's richest rock salt deposits under the town of Hutchinson. Today, the town is a major salt-producing center.
Information: Greater Hutchinson Convention and Visitors Bureau, 117 N. Walnut, 620-662-3391, 800-691-4262; www.hutchchamber.com

KANSAS

WHAT TO SEE AND DO
Historic Fox Theatre
18 E. First Ave., Hutchinson, 620-663-5861
This theater exemplifies Art Deco architecture and is on the National Register of Historic Places. Professional entertainment, classic and independent film and arts education programs are offered.

HOTELS
★ Best Western Sundome
11 Des Moines Ave., South Hutchinson, 620-663-4444; 800-530-5426; www.bestwestern.com
Pets accepted, some restrictions. Complimentary breakfast. Restaurant. Business center. High-speed Internet. **$**

★★ Grand Prairie Hotel and Convention Center
1400 N. Lorraine St., Hutchinson, 620-669-9311; www.grandprairiehotel.com
220 rooms. Pets accepted; fee. Restaurant. Indoor pool. **$**

★

★

IOLA

Most of the expansion of this small eastern Kansas town happened after natural gas was discovered in the area in the 1900s. The town retains its historic feel with a preserved downtown with Victorian buildings.

Information Chamber of Commerce, 208 W. Madison, 620-365-5252; www.iola.com/guide.html

WHAT TO SEE AND DO

Old Jail Museum
203 N. Jefferson, Iola,
620-365-3051
A historic building, this jail has been restored and is now open for tours. Tuesday through Saturday, May through September.

Boyhood Home of Major General Frederick Funston
207 N. Jefferson, Iola, 620-365-3051
This house, built in 1860, was the home of Fred Funston, a decorated soldier noted for directing the recovery efforts following the San Francisco earthquake of 1906.

Originally located on a homestead about five miles north of Iola, the house has been restored according to the Victorian decor of the 1880s and 1890s. Many original family items are on display. May-September,: Wednesday-Saturday.

HOTELS

★★Best Western Inn
1315 N. State St., Iola,
620-365-5161, 800-769-0007;
www.bestwestern.com
59 rooms. Pets accepted, some restrictions; fee. Restaurant. Outdoor pool. $

LAWRENCE

42

KANSAS

★
★
★
★
★
★

Lawrence had a stormy history in the territorial years. It was founded by the New England Emigrant Aid Company, which aimed to populate the area with anti-slavery proponents transplanted from New England and other "free states" as a means of warding off slavery. The center of Free State activities, the town was close to a state of war from 1855 until the Free Staters triumphed in 1859. The Confederate guerrilla leader, William Quantrill, made one of his most spectacular raids on Lawrence in 1863, burning the town and killing 150 citizens. After the Civil War, the town experienced a gradual and peaceful growth. It is the site of the University of Kansas.

Information: Convention and Visitors Bureau, 734 Vermont, 785-865-4411, 800-529-5267; www.visitlawrence.com

WHAT TO SEE AND DO

Haskell Indian Nations University
155 Indian Ave., Lawrence, 785-749-8450;
www.haskell.edu
This school was founded in 1884 to provide education for Native Americans. More than 120 tribes are represented among the students. The campus is a registered historic landmark. The American Indian Athletic Hall of Fame is located here.

Lawrence Arts Center
940 New Hampshire St., Lawrence,
785-843-2787
Galleries featuring the work of local artists and craftspeople; performance hall for theater, dance, and music; art classes and workshops for all ages.

Old West Lawrence Historic District
402 N. Second St., Lawrence, 785-865-4499
Take a self-guided tour through this area of notable 19th-century homes.

University of Kansas
Corner of 15th and Iowa Streets,
Lawrence, 785-864-3131; www.ku.edu
With 26,000 students, this university stretches over a 1,000-acre campus. Kansas Jayhawks athletics (especially basketball) are a prime attraction in Lawrence. Some campus attractions include the Campanile Bell Tower, Museum of Natural History, Museum of Anthropology and Spencer Museum of Art. All buildings are closed holidays.

HOTELS

★Best Western Lawrence
2309 Iowa St., Lawrence, 785-843-9100;
www.bestwestern.com

100 rooms. Pets accepted; fee. Complimentary continental breakfast. High-speed Internet access. Fitness room. Indoor pool, whirlpool. Business center. **$**

★★Holiday Inn Lawrence
200 McDonald Dr., Lawrence,
785-841-7077, 888-465-4329;
www.holiday-inn.com/lawrenceks
196 rooms. Pets accepted; fee. High-speed Internet access, wireless Internet access. Restaurant. Bar. Indoor pool, whirlpool. Airport transportation available. Business center. **$**

★★★Eldridge Hotel
701 Massachusetts St., Lawrence,
785-749-5011, 800-527-0909;
www.eldridgehotel.com
This hotel, with a history dating to the Civil War, is located in the heart of quaint downtown Lawrence near the University of Kansas. The setting is charming, but the décor is crisp and contemporary. The original ceilings and woodwork have been nicely maintained.
48 rooms, all suites. High-speed Internet access, wireless Internet access. Restaurant. Bar. **$$**

SPECIALTY LODGINGS

Halcyon House Bed & Breakfast
1000 Ohio St., Lawrence, 785-841-0314,
888-441-0314; www.thehalcyonhouse.com
This Victorian inn was built in 1885 but has been updated with modern touches like high-speed Internet access.
9 rooms. Children over 12 years only. Complimentary full breakfast. High-speed Internet access. Victorian inn built in 1885. **$**

43

KANSAS

LEAVENWORTH

Leavenworth was the first incorporated town in Kansas Territory. At first strongly pro-slavery, Leavenworth had many border conflicts, but during the Civil War it was loyal to the Union. In the years just before the war, the town was the headquarters for a huge overland transportation and supply operation sending wagons and stagecoaches northwest on the Oregon Trail and southwest on the Santa Fe Trail. Fort Leavenworth, adjoining the

city, is the oldest military post west of the Mississippi River that has been in continuous operation (since 1827). A federal penitentiary is on the grounds adjacent to the fort.
Information: Leavenworth Convention and Visitors Bureau, 518 Shawnee St., 913-682-4113, 800-844-4114; www.lvarea.com

WHAT TO SEE AND DO

Fort Leavenworth
600 Thomas Ave., Fort Leavenworth, 913-684-5604

Features of interest at this base are the U.S. Army Command and General Staff College, U.S. Disciplinary Barracks, National Cemetery, Buffalo Soldier Monument and branches of the Oregon and Santa Fe trails. The Frontier Army Museum features artifacts of pioneer history and the Army of the West. Daily.

Frontier Army Museum
Fort Leavenworth,100 Reynolds Dr., Leavenworth, 913-684-3191

Discover the history of Fort Leavenworth and the United States Regular Army on the Frontier. See historic army uniforms, weapons and equipment, including a 1917 JN4D Jenny biplane and the carriage that Abraham Lincoln traveled in when he visited in 1859. Monday-Friday 9 a.m.-4 p.m., Saturday 10 a.m.-4 p.m.

Parker Carousel
320 S. Esplanade, Leavenworth, 913-682-1331; www.firstcitymuseums.org

This restored 1913 carousel features hand-carved, one-of-a-kind horses. Daily.

HOTELS

★Days Inn
3211 S. Fourth St., Leavenworth, 913-651-6000, 888-540-4020, www.daysinn.com

52 rooms. Complimentary continental breakfast. Outdoor pool. $

44

LEAWOOD

A Kansas City suburb was established after World War II and grew after the building of several housing developments. It's now one of the fastest growing cities in Kansas.
Information: www.leawood.org

RESTAURANTS

★ Gates Bar-B-Q
2001 W. 103 Rd., Leawood, 913-383-1752; www.gatesbbq.com

American menu. Lunch, dinner, late-night. Closed holidays. $$

★★★Hereford House
5001 Town Center Dr., Leawood, 913-327-0800; www.herefordhouse.com

Jack Webb founded the original branch of this steakhouse in Kansas City in 1957. Now, this Town Center Plaza location is one of three, with charcoal-grilled steaks and friendly, no-hassle service. Steak menu. Lunch, dinner. Bar. Children's menu. Outdoor seating. $$$

★★Yahooz
4701 Town Center Dr., Leawood, 913-451-8888; www.eatpbj.com

American, steak menu. Lunch, dinner, Sunday brunch. Bar. Children's menu. Reservations recommended. Outdoor seating. $$$

LIBERAL

Liberal's name comes from the generosity of one of its first settlers, S.S. Rogers. Although water was scarce in southwestern Kansas, Rogers never charged parched and weary travelers for the use of his well—a "liberal" fee.

Information: Tourist Information Center, 1 Yellow Brick Rd., 620-626-0170; www.liberal.net

WHAT TO SEE AND DO
Coronado Museum

567 E. Cedar St., Liberal, 620-624-7624; www.sewardcountymuseum.com
Displays at this museum depict early life of in Liberal. Some exhibits trace Francisco Coronado's route through Kansas. Also included are Dorothy's House from *The Wizard of Oz* and an animated display of the story. Daily; Winter: Tuesday-Sunday.

Mid-America Air Museum
2000 W. Second St., Liberal, 620-624-5263
See an aviation collection of 99 aircraft including civilian aircraft, military aircraft from World War II, and planes of the Korean and Vietnam era. Also here is the Liberal Army Airfield exhibit. Daily; closed holidays.

RESTAURANTS
★King's Pit Bar-B-Q
355 E. Pancake Blvd., Liberal, 620-624-2451
American menu. Lunch, dinner. Children's menu. $$

MANHATTAN

Several early settlements were combined to form Manhattan. Lying in a limestone bowl-shaped depression resulting from glacial action, the town developed as a trading center for farm products. Kansas State University is located in Manhattan.

Information: Convention and Visitors Bureau,
501 Poyntz Ave.,
785-776-8829,
800-759-0134;
www.manhattan.org

KANSAS

★
★
★
★
★

WHAT TO SEE AND DO

Kansas State University
17th and Anderson Streets, Manhattan, 785-532-6250; www.ksu.edu
With more than 20,000 students, this campus, established around 1863, has buildings constructed of native limestone.

Sunset Zoo
2333 Oak St., Manhattan, 785-587-2737; www.ci.manhattan.ks.us/sunsetzoo
A zoo with more than 300 animals, residents here include Brownie, thought to be the oldest living grizzly bear in the world. He's kept company by snow leopards, cheetahs, red pandas, bobcats, reptiles, birds and more. Daily.

Tuttle Creek State Park
5800 A River Pond Rd., Manhattan, 785-539-7941
This 1,156-acre park is located on a 13,350-acre lake. There is a special observation area with distant views of the Blue River Valley and Randolph Bridge, the largest in Kansas. Beach, bathhouse, fishing, boating, camping.

HOTELS

★★Clarion Hotel
530 Richards Dr., Manhattan, 785-539-5311; www.choicehotels.com

193 rooms. Pets accepted, some restrictions; fee. High-speed Internet access, wireless Internet access. Two restaurants, bar. Fitness room. Indoor pool, children's pool, whirlpool. Airport transportation available. Business center. **$**

★★Holiday Inn Manhattan at the Campus
1641 Anderson Ave., Manhattan, 785-539-7531, 888-465-4329; www.holiday-inn.com
113 rooms. Pets accepted. WiFi. Restaurant. Bar. Fitness room. Outdoor pool. Business center. **$**

RESTAURANTS

★★★Harry's
418 Poyntz Ave., Manhattan, 785-537-1300; www.harrysmanhattan.com
The historic Wareham hotel is the setting for this restaurant, named in honor of the hotel's first owner, Harry Wareham. Though the restaurant has been restored to look much as it did when it first opened in the 1920s, the menu is decidedly up-to-date, with dishes such as risotto and fried smoked portobellos, or grilled lobster salad with spicy roma tomato chutney. American menu. Lunch, dinner. Closed Sunday. Bar. Children's menu. Business casual attire. Reservations recommended. **$$$**

★ # MCPHERSON

Both the city and the county bear the name of Civil War hero General James Birdseye McPherson, who was killed in the Battle of Atlanta in 1864. This small town of 14,000 residents has a historic downtown and a restored opera house dating to the 1880s.
Information: Convention and Visitors Bureau, 306 N. Main, 316-241-3340, 800-324-8022; www.mcphersonks.org

WHAT TO SEE AND DO

Maxwell Wildlife Refuge
101 N. Main St., Canton
This 2,650-acre prairie provides a natural environment for elk, deer and buffalo. The refuge has an observation tower, a 46-acre fishing lake, boat ramp and nature trail. Daily.

HOTELS

★★Best Western Holiday Manor
2211 E. Kansas Ave., McPherson, 620-241-5343, 888-841-0038; www.bestwestern.com
110 rooms. Pets accepted, some restrictions; fee. Restaurant. Indoor pool, outdoor pool, whirlpool. **$**

46

KANSAS

OVERLAND PARK

The suburb Overland Park, which wasn't incorporated until 1960, is located directly south of Kansas City and has a historic downtown.

Information: Convention and Visitors Bureau, 9001 W. 110th St., 913-491-0123, 800-262-7275; www.opcvb.org

WHAT TO SEE AND DO

Deanna Rose Children's Farmstead

138th St. and Switzer Rd., Overland Park, 913-897-2360; www.opkansas.org
Feed and pet farm animals, hop on a horse-drawn wagon or walk through a replica of an early 1900s Kansas farmhouse at this farmstead. Memorial Day-Labor Day: daily 9 a.m.-8 p.m.; April-Memorial Day and Labor Day-October: daily 9 a.m.-5 p.m.

Overland Park Arboretum and Botanical Gardens

8909 W. 179th St., Overland Park, 913-685-3604; www.opkansas.org
This park features 300 acres of land, including three miles of hiking trails (some wheelchair accessible) through gardens. Naturalized areas feature a Meadow Garden, Butterfly Garden and Woodland Garden. Guided tours by appointment. Daily, weather permitting.

HOTELS

★★Courtyard Kansas City Overland Park Convention Center

11001 Woodson St., Overland Park, 913-317-8500, 800-321-2211; www.courtyard.com
168 rooms. High-speed Internet access. Restaurant. Fitness room. Indoor pool, whirlpool. Business center. $

★★Doubletree Hotel Overland Park-Corporate Woods

10100 College Blvd., Overland Park, 913-451-6100, 800-222-8733; www.doubletree.com
356 rooms. Restaurant. Bar. Fitness room. Indoor pool, whirlpool. Airport transportation available. $$

★★Embassy Suites Hotel Kansas City-Overland Park

10601 Metcalf Ave., Overland Park, 913-649-7060, 800-362-2779; www.embassysuites.com
199 rooms, all suites. Complimentary full breakfast. Wireless Internet access. Restaurant. Bar. Fitness room. Indoor pool, whirlpool. $

★★Hampton Inn Kansas City/Overland Park

10591 Metcalf Frontage Rd., Overland Park, 913-341-1551, 800-426-7866; www.hamptoninn.com
134 rooms. Complimentary continental breakfast. High-speed Internet access, wireless Internet access. Restaurant. Bar. Outdoor pool, whirlpool. Business center. $

★★Holiday Inn Overland Park-West

8787 Reeder Rd., Overland Park, 913-888-8440, 888-825-7538; www.holiday-inn.com
192 rooms. High-speed Internet access. Restaurant. Bar. Fitness room. Indoor pool, outdoor pool, whirlpool. Business center. $

★La Quinta Inn & Suites Overland Park

10610 Marty St., Overland Park, 913-648-5555; www.lq.com
143 rooms. Complimentary breakfast. Pets accepted. Outdoor pool. High-speed Internet access. $

★★★ Marriott Overland Park

10800 Metcalf Ave., Overland Park, 913-451-8000, 800-228-9290; www.overlandparkmarriott.com
Located in an industrial area of Overland Park, this well-landscaped suburban hotel can be easily seen from the Interstate (I-435). The Metcalf South Mall is approxi-

KANSAS

★
★
★
☆
☆

mately one mile away, and the convention center is within two miles of the hotel.

397 rooms. High-speed Internet access. Three restaurants, bar. Fitness room. Indoor pool, outdoor pool, whirlpool. Airport transportation available. Business center. **$$**

RESTAURANTS

★★★40 Sardines
11942 Roe Ave., Overland Park,
913-451-1040; www.40sardines.com
Open since June 2002, 40 Sardines continues to be one of the region's most popular restaurants. Chef and owner Debbie Gold's seasonal menu changes weekly and highlights several of the area's local farms and purveyors. The extensive menu has items ranging from wild boar and veal sweetbreads to tomato-braised beef short ribs and a wood-grilled rib eye. Of course, sardines (or rather, grilled Portuguese sardines) are available as well. The sleek bar has an intriguing cocktail menu. The wine list features 1,200 bottles that focus on both boutique wineries and many different wine-producing regions.
American menu. Lunch, dinner. Bar. Business casual attire. Reservations recommended. **$$$**

★★Fiorella's Jack Stack Barbecue
9520 Metcalf Ave., Overland Park,
913-385-7427; www.jackstackbbq.com
American, barbecue menu. Lunch, dinner. Closed holidays. Bar. Children's menu. Casual attire. **$$**

★★Il Trullo
9056 Metcalf Ave., Overland Park,
913-341-3773. www.iltrullo-kc.com
Italian menu. Lunch, dinner. Closed Sunday-Monday. Bar. Children's menu. Casual attire. Reservations recommended. **$$**

★★ India Palace
9918 W. 87th St., Overland Park,
913-381-1680
Indian menu. Lunch, dinner. **$$**

★★★ J. Gilbert's Wood Fired Steaks
8901 Metcalf Ave., Overland Park,
913-642-8070; www.jgilberts.com
The restaurants in this mini-chain (there are locations in Ohio, Virginia and Connecticut) all have a fireplace as their focal point, a visual reminder of this eatery's dedication to preparing simply delicious wood-fired steaks. The prime Kansas City strip is a favorite, while dishes like pan-seared halibut satisfy those who are less carnivorous.
Steak menu. Dinner. Closed holidays. Bar. Children's menu. Casual attire. Reservations recommended. Outdoor seating. **$$$**

★★Johnny Cascone's
6863 W. 91st St.,
Overland Park, 913-381-6837; www.cascones.com
Italian menu. Lunch, dinner. Bar. Children's menu. Casual attire. Reservations recommended. **$$**

★★K. C. Masterpiece Barbecue & Grill
10985 Metcalf Ave.,
Overland Park,
913-345-2255;
www.masterpiecebbq.com
American, barbecue menu. Lunch, dinner. Bar. Children's menu. Casual attire. **$$**

★★★Nikko
10800 Metcalf Rd, Overland Park,
913-451-8000 , 913-451-5914
A Japanese steakhouse complete with tableside teppanyaki chefs, this restaurant is located inside the Marriott hotel. Entrees, from steak to seafood and more, include soup, salad, shrimp, steamed rice and vegetables.
Japanese menu. Dinner. Children's menu. Valet parking. **$$**

★★Raoul's Velvet Room
7222 W. 119th St., Overland Park,
913-469-0466; www.raoulsvelvetroom.com
American menu. Dinner, late-night. Bar. Casual attire. Reservations recommended. Outdoor seating. **$$**

★Sushi Gin
9559 Nall Ave., Overland Park,

913-649-8488; www.sushigin.com
Japanese menu. Lunch, dinner. Children's menu. $$

★★Yia Yia's Eurobistro
4701 W. 119th St., Overland Park,

913-345-1111; www.eatpbj.com
Continental menu. Lunch, dinner, Sunday brunch. Bar. Children's menu. Casual attire. Reservations recommended. Outdoor seating. $$

PRAIRIE VILLAGE

This Kansas City suburb began in the 1940s as a planned community designed by J.C. Nichols, who also created nearby Country Club Plaza, the nation's first suburban shopping center.
www.pvkansas.com

RESTAURANTS
★Jun's Japanese Restaurant
7660 State Line Rd., Prairie Village, 913-341-4924
Japanese menu. Breakfast, lunch, dinner. Closed Sunday. $$

★★★Tatsu's
4603 W. 90th St., Prairie Village, 913-383-9801, www.tatsus.com

This quiet French restaurant grew from a small pastry and lunch shop opened by chef/owner Tatsu Arai in 1980. Since then, it has become a top Kansas City dining destination. The classic French cuisine includes dishes such as beef bourguignon, poached salmon with champagne sauce or lemon butter sauce and roasted boneless duck breast with peppercorn cream sauce. French menu. Lunch, dinner. Bar. $$

★
★
★
★
★

SALINA

Salina got its start as a trading post for gold hunters stopping through on their way to Pikes Peak. The arrival of the Union Pacific Railroad in 1867 brought new growth, and the wheat crops in the 1870s established a permanent economy. Alfalfa, now one of the state's major crops, was first introduced in Kansas by a Salina resident in 1874. The city was rebuilt in 1903 after the Smoky Hill flood destroyed most of the community. Aviator Steve Fossett made history in 2005 when he launched the first solo, non-stop, round-the-world, non-refueled flight in the Virgin Atlantic GlobalFlyer from the Salina airport.
Information: Chamber of Commerce, 120 W. Ash, Salina, 785-827-9301; www.salinakansas.org

WHAT TO SEE AND DO
Salina Art Center
242 S. Santa Fe, Salina, 785-827-1431; www.salinaartcenter.org
This center features art exhibits as well as a hands-on art laboratory for children. The cinema shows current art house releases. Tuesday-Sunday afternoons.

Smoky Hill Museum
211 W. Iron Ave., Salina, 785-309-5776; www.smokyhillmuseum.org

Area history is told through photos and artifacts at this museum. Changing exhibits are featured, as is a general store period room. Tuesday-Sunday; closed holidays.

HOTELS
★★Holiday Inn Salina
1616 W. Crawford St., Salina, 785-823-1739, 888-465-4329; www.holiday-inn.com/salinaks
192 rooms. Pets accepted; fee. Wireless Internet access. Two restaurants, bar. Fit-

ness room. Indoor pool, whirlpool. Airport transportation available. **$**

RESTAURANTS
★Gutierrez

640 Westport Blvd., Salina, 785-825-1649; www.gutzsalina.com

Mexican menu. Lunch, dinner. Bar. Children's menu. Casual attire. **$$**

SHAWNEE

This Kansas City suburb was founded in the 1850s and features many parks, an outdoor pioneer museum and a historic downtown.
Information: www.shawneekscvb.com

RESTAURANTS
★★Leona Yarbrough's.

10310 Shawnee Mission Pkwy., Shawnee, 913-248-0500; www.yarbroughrestaurant.com

American menu. Lunch, dinner. Children's menu. **$$**

★★Paulo & Bill

16501 Midland Dr., Shawnee, 913-962-9900

Italian, American menu. Lunch, dinner. Closed holidays. Bar. Children's menu. Outdoor seating. **$$**

TOPEKA

KANSAS

★
★
★
★
★
☆

The capital city of Kansas is located on the Kansas River (locally called the Kaw). World-famous psychiatric clinic and research center, the Menninger Foundation, is located here, and Herbert Hoover's vice president, Charles Curtis, who was part Kaw and a descendant of one of Topeka's earliest settlers, was born here.
Information: Convention and Visitors Bureau, 1275 S.W. Topeka Blvd., 785-234-1030, 800-235-1030; www.topeka.org

SPOT★ LIGHT

★TOPEKA COMES FROM A TRIBAL NAME MEANING "GOOD PLACE TO GROW POTATOES."

★ACTRESS ANNETTE BENING IS A TOPEKA NATIVE.

★DESEGREGATION CASE BROWN V. BOARD OF EDUCATION ORGINATED IN TOPEKA.

WHAT TO SEE AND DO

Brown v. Board of Education National Historic Site

1515 S.E. Monroe St., Topeka, 785-354-4273; www.nps.gov/brvb

This site commemorates the U.S. Supreme Court's groundbreaking 1954 decision declaring segregation in public schools unconstitutional. Here you'll find Monroe Elementary School, one of Topeka's four formerly segregated elementary schools for African-American children, along with interpretive exhibits and educational programs. Monday-Friday 8 a.m.-4 p.m.; closed federal holidays.

Combat Air Museum

Forbes Field, Hangars 602 and 604, J St., Topeka, 785-862-3303; www.combatairmuseum.org

Jets, cargo transports, fighters and trainers from 1917 to 1980 are displayed here, as well as military artifacts. Guided tours, by appointment. Daily; closed holidays.

Gage Park

9635 S.W. Gage Blvd., Topeka, 785-368-3700.

Tennis, swimming, softball and volleyball facilities are available here, along with playground equipment for different ages and abilities. The newly restored carousel was built in 1908 and operates from 10 a.m. to 8 p.m. during the summer and on weekends only in September and October. This park is to the Topeka Zoo.

Cedar Crest Governor's Mansion

1 S.W. Cedar Crest Rd., Topeka, 785-296-3636; www.ksgovenor.org/cedarcrest

This massive house features period architecture with Loire Valley overtones spread out on 244 acres. Built in 1928 and bequeathed to the state in 1955, it became the governor's residence in 1962. Guided tours, Monday afternoons.

Kansas State Historical Society

6425 S.W. Sixth Ave., Topeka, 785-272-8681; www.kshs.org

WILDLIFE ON THE PRAIRIE

East central Kansas boasts beautiful tall grass prairies, some of the few remaining in the United States. Take this drive in early spring, when the old grass is burned to make way for spring growth, or in early summer, when wildflowers are abundant. Head west from Topeka on Interstate 70 to Manhattan. Nearby, the Konza Prairie is a major site for prairie research, with hiking and wildlife-watching. Continue south on Highway 177 to the Tallgrass Prairie National Preserve near Strong Falls. Covered-wagon train trips are offered at El Dorado, northeast of Wichita on Highway 177. From Wichita, take Interstate 135 north to McPherson and visit the McPherson-Maxwell Game Preserve, with one of the states' largest bison herds, as well as elk, deer and buffalo. Return to Interstate 70 at Salina, then head back east to your starting point.

The Kansas Museum of History includes the Library of Kansas and information on Native American and Western history and genealogy. Tuesday-Saturday.

State Capitol

300 W. 10th St., Topeka, 785-296-3966; www.kshs.org/places/capitol

The design of this building was based on the U.S. Capitol. On the grounds are statues of Lincoln and Pioneer Woman, both by Topeka-born sculptor Merrell Gage. Murals on the second floor are by John Steuart Curry; those on the first floor are by David H. Overmeyer. Monday-Friday.

Topeka Zoo

635 S.W. Gage Blvd., Topeka, 785-368-9180; www.topeka.org/zoo

KANSAS

An orangutan and gorilla exhibit, black bear exhibit, lion display, tropical rain forest and more are featured at this museum. Daily 10 a.m.-5 p.m.

SPECIAL EVENTS
Huff 'n Puff Hot Air Balloon Rally
Lake Shawnee, Topeka, 785-234-1030;

www.huff-n-puff.org
Dozens of hot air balloons take to the skies in this annual event. September.

Washburn Sunflower Music Festival
1700 S.W. College Ave., Topeka, 785-231-1010;
www.sunflowermusicfestival.org

ACROSS THE PRAIRIE LANDSCAPE

This loop trail passes through prairie landscapes and across the Kansas of past, present and future. Begin in Wichita, the state's largest city. The city's historic role as a cow capital along the Chisholm Trail is preserved at the Old Cowtown Museum, a historic village with 40 buildings from the city's early boom years in the 1870s. Nearby is the Witchita Art Museum, with a fine collection of American Impressionists and a grand outdoor sculpture garden. Gardeners will enjoy Botanica, The Witchita Garden, which has a number of theme gardens.

Drive northeast on Interstate 35 to Cassoday, home to several good antique stores, and join Highway 177 northbound. Known as the Flint Hills Scenic Byway, this route passes through a rugged landscape of rolling hills, mesas and virgin prairie. Stop in Cottonwood Falls to visit the Chase County Courthouse, which is the oldest in Kansas. The building was constructed from local limestone in a striking French Renaissance style.

Just north is the Tallgrass Prairie National Preserve, which protects 11,000 acres of native prairie grassland that is home to 40 species of grasses, 200 species of birds, 30 species of mammals and up to 10 million insects per acre. A number of trails lead across the plains, which in spring are carpeted with wildflowers. The preserves headquarters are located at the Z Bar Ranch, an imposing stone ranch house cum mansion from the 1880s.

Council Grove is one of Kansas's most historic towns. In fact, the entire settlement has been designated a National Historic Landmark. Council Grove was the last provisioning stop on the old Sante Fe Trail between the Missouri River and Sante Fe, and the town is filled with landmarks of the frontier West.

Continue north on Highway 57 to Junction City, located at the confluence of the Republican and Smoky Hill rivers. The town owes its existence to Fort Riley, founded in 1853 to protect pioneers traveling along the Sante Fe and Oregon trails. The fort, just north of town along Highway 57, contains a number of historic sites, including the state's first territorial capital, an early home of General George Custer, and the U.S. Cavalry Museum, which chronicles the history of the mounted horse soldier from the Revolutionary War to 1950.

Continue east on Interstate 70 to Abilene, famous as an Old West cow town and as the boyhood home of President Dwight D. Eisenhower. In addition to the frontier and presidential museums you would expect, Abilene offers a couple of unusual attractions, including dinner excursions on an antique train and the American Indian Art Center, which represents 90 artists from 30 Native American nations.

This annual festival features international symphonic musicians performing nightly. First two weeks in June.

HOTELS

★★Clubhouse Inn & Suites Topeka
924 S.W. Henderson Rd., Topeka, 785-273-8888, 800-258-2466; www.clubhouseinn.com
121 rooms. Pets accepted, some restrictions; fee. Complimentary full breakfast. WiFi. Restaurant. Bar. Outdoor pool, whirlpool. Business center. **$**

★★Days Inn Topeka
1510 S.W. Wanamaker Rd., Topeka, 785-272-8538, 800-329-7466; www.daysinn.com
62 rooms. Pets accepted; fee. Complimentary continental breakfast. WiFi. Restaurant. Bar. Indoor pool, whirlpool. **$**

★★Ramada Downtown Topeka
420 S.E. Sixth Ave., Topeka, 785-234-5400, 800-272-6232; www.ramada.com
214 rooms. Pets accepted, some restrictions; fee. Complimentary full breakfast. High-speed Internet access. Restaurant. Bar. Fitness room. Indoor pool, outdoor pool, whirlpool. Business center. **$**

RESTAURANTS

★Carlos O'Kelly's
3425 S. Kansas Ave., Topeka, 785-266-3457; www.carlosokellys.com
Mexican menu. Lunch, dinner. Bar. Children's menu. Casual attire. **$$**

★★McFarland's
4133 S.W. Gage Center Dr., Topeka, 785-272-6909.
American menu. Lunch, dinner. Closed Monday. Bar. Children's menu. **$$**

WICHITA

The largest city in Kansas has a metropolitan flavor, with its tall buildings and wide streets. Still a major marketing point for agricultural products, the city is now best known as an aircraft production center. McConnell Air Force Base is here.

The town's first settlers were the Wichita, who built a village of grass lodges on the site. The following year James R. Mead set up a trading post and in 1865 sent his assistant, Jesse Chisholm, on a trading expedition to the Southwest. His route became famous as the Chisholm Trail, over which longhorn cattle were driven through Wichita to the Union Pacific at Abilene. As the railroad advanced to the southwest, Wichita had its turn as a "cow capital" in the early 1870s. By 1880, farmers drawn by the land boom had run fences across the trail and the cattle drives were shifted west to Dodge City. Wheat production and the discovery of oil after World War I revived the city.

Information: Convention and Visitors Bureau, 100 S. Main, 316-265-2800, 800-288-9424; www.visitwichita.com

★
★
★
★
★

WHAT TO SEE AND DO

Allen-Lambe House Museum and Study Center

255 N. Roosevelt St., Wichita, 316-687-1027; http://allenlambe.org

Designed in 1915 by Frank Lloyd Wright as a private residence, this structure is considered the last of Wright's prairie houses. The house features furniture designed by Wright in collaboration with interior designer George M. Niedecken. Guided tours by appointment only, minimum of five people.

Botanica, The Wichita Gardens

701 Amidon, Wichita, 316-264-9799; www.botanica.org

Displays of exotic flowers and plants native to Kansas fill this botanical garden. April-December: daily; rest of year: Monday-Friday.

Cheney State Park

16000 N.E. 50 St., Cheney, 316-542-3664

A 1,913-acre park on a 9,537-acre lake, this area is popular with sailboat and windsurfing enthusiasts. Large-scale regattas are a featured part of the many lake activities. Beach, bathhouse, fishing, boating, picnicking, concessions, camping.

Corbin Education Center

1845 Fairmount, Wichita

This Prairie-style structure, located on the campus of Wichita State University, was designed by Frank Lloyd Wright.

Mid-America All-Indian Center Museum

650 N. Seneca, Wichita, 316-262-5221; www.theindiancenter.org

This museum features changing exhibits of past and present Native American art. Tuesday-Sunday.

Lake Afton Public Observatory

25000 W. 39th St. S., Wichita, 316-978-7827; http://webs.wichita.edu/lapo

Public programs offer the opportunity to view a variety of celestial objects through a 16-inch reflecting telescope. Programs begin 30 minutes after sunset. September-May: Friday-Saturday; June-August: Friday-Sunday; closed December 23-January 1.

Old Cowtown Museum

1865 Museum Blvd., Wichita, 316-660-1871; www.oldcowtown.org

This 40-building historic village museum depicts Wichita life in the 1870s. The Diamond W Chuckwagon Supper features all-you-can-eat barbecue and a performance by the Prairie Wranglers, a country-western band.

Sedgwick County Zoo

5555 Zoo Blvd., Wichita, 316-660-9453; www.scz.org

See animals in their natural habitats at this Wichita zoo. A new Asian tiger exhibit is being constructed and is expected to open in 2009. Daily.

Wichita Art Museum

1400 W. Museum Blvd., Wichita, 316-268-4921; www.wichitaartmuseum.org

This museum features traveling exhibits, a collection of American art, paintings and sculpture by Charles M. Russell, pre-Columbian art and works by contemporary and historic Kansas artists. Tuesday-Sunday; closed holidays.

Wichita Center for the Arts

9112 E. Central Ave., Wichita, 316-634-2787; www.ctfa.com

With changing and permanent exhibits, this center features a gallery, theater and art school. Tuesday-Sunday.

Wichita-Sedgwick County Historical Museum

204 S. Main St., Wichita, 316-265-9314; www.wichitahistory.org

Local history, Native American artifacts, period rooms, a costume collection and more on are display at this museum. Tuesday-Sunday.

54

KANSAS

SPECIAL EVENTS

Wichita River Festival
1820 E. Douglas Ave., Wichita,
316-267-2817;
www.wichitariverfestival.com
This annual festival includes a twilight pop concert and fireworks, antique bathtub races, a hot air balloon launch, athletic events and entertainment. Mid-May.

HOTELS

★Clubhouse Inn & Suites Wichita
515 S. Webb Rd., Wichita,
316-684-1111, 800-258-2466;
www.clubhouseinn.com
119 rooms. Pets accepted; fee. Complimentary full breakfast. High-speed Internet access, wireless Internet access. Outdoor pool, whirlpool. **$**

★Days Inn Wichita West
550 S. Florence St., Wichita,
316-942-1717, 800-329-7466;
www.daysinn.com
42 rooms. Complimentary continental breakfast. WiFi. **$**

★★Holiday Inn Wichita
549 S. Rock Rd., Wichita,
316-686-7131, 888-465-4329,
www.holiday-inn.com
250 rooms. Pets accepted, some restrictions; fee. WiFi. Restaurant. Bar. Fitness room. Indoor pool, outdoor pool, whirlpool. Airport transportation available. Business center. **$**

★★★Hyatt Regency Wichita
400 W. Waterman, Wichita,
316-293-1234, 800-633-7313;
www.hyatt.com
Perched on the Arkansas River, this contemporary hotel has updated rooms with duvet-topped beds. The Southwinds Bar and Grill serves red meat of every kind (the grilled spicy cowboy ribeye steak is a standout) in an upscale setting.
303 rooms. Restaurant. Bar. Fitness room. Indoor pool. Business center. **$**

★★★ Marriott Wichita
9100 E. Corporate Hills Dr., Wichita,
316-651-0333, 800-610-0673;
www.marriott.com
After a complete renovation in 2007, this hotel is now a smoke-free environment with updated guest rooms that feature luxury beds, flat-screen TVs and wireless Internet access. The Black Angus Grille serves steakhouse classics, while Corrigan's Sports Bar is a prime place for catching up on the latest scores and noshing on pub fare.
294 rooms. Restaurant. Bar. Fitness room. Indoor pool, outdoor pool, whirlpool. Airport transportation available. Business center. **$$**

★Quality Suites Airport
658 Westdale Dr., Wichita,
316-945-2600, 800-318-2607;
www.choicehotels.com
50 rooms, all suites. Pets accepted, some restrictions; fee. Complimentary full breakfast. High-speed Internet access, wireless Internet access. Fitness room. Outdoor pool. Airport transportation available. **$**

RESTAURANTS

★★★ Olive Tree
2949 N. Rock Rd., Wichita, 316-636-1100;
www.olivetree-bistro.com
This family-owned, European-style bistro has an extensive wine list and a menu with both small and large plates of Mediterranean-inspired dishes. Entrees are eclectic and include everything from Thai green curry made with eggplant to fennel pollen roasted chicken.
American menu. Dinner, late-night, Sunday brunch. **$$**

55

KANSAS

MISSOURI

WHEN THE UNITED STATES PURCHASED ALL OF THE VAST FRENCH TERRITORY OF LOUISIANA in 1803, Missouri, with its strategic waterways and the already-thriving town of St. Louis, became a gateway to the West and remained one throughout the entire westward expansion. Its two largest cities, St. Louis and Kansas City, sit on its eastern and western edges like bookends. St. Louis was the Midwest's first great city, the center of commerce and transportation by thanks to its location on two major rivers. Kansas City was once the quintessential cow town and, the Gateway Arch notwithstanding, was the true way station to the West—to cattle trails and to the frontier.

Today, Missouri offers diverse array of sights. St. Louis and Kansas City have fine dining (and great barbecue), nightlife and music (especially blues and jazz). St. Louis has a world-famous zoo and one of the largest city parks in the nation. It has a significant art museum as well as the International Bowling Hall of Fame. St. Louis, home to the Cardinals and a legion of knowledgeable fans, is often hailed as the nation's best baseball town. Kansas City has the world's first planned shopping center (Country Club Plaza), a 60-acre waterpark and did we mention barbecue?

For outdoor recreation, Missouri could vie for the title of Land of Awesome Lakes. Its largest one, Lake of the Ozarks, is 92 miles end to end and has 1,150 miles of shoreline. There's also the 55,000-acre Truman Lake, part of the Harry S. Truman State Park, southeast of Kansas City, and Pomme de Terre Lake, 78 acres of water near Springfield.

Then there are the rivers, and we don't just mean the Mississippi and Missouri. Four state parks dot the Meramec River, which runs for nearly 100 miles. Nearly 90 percent is shallow, which makes it a perfect waterway for float trips. Another of Missouri's river gems is the Black, running through Poplar Bluff and north into the Arcadia Valley. It, too, promises great floating.

Wherever you are in the state, there's something to explore. Around Hannibal by the Mississippi, you can recapture Mark Twain's riverboat days. Along the Missouri River in St. Joseph, the flavor is more Lewis and Clark and pioneers. Southwest is Springfield, a gateway to both the Ozarks and to Branson, that one-of-a-kind capital of corn-pone, country and crooning. In the middle is Jefferson City, a prototypical sleepy capital town with a beautiful capitol standing astride the Missouri River.

★ SPOTLIGHT

★ Famous Missourians include Mark Twain, Walter Cronkite and Harry S. Truman.

★ No one is sure how the state's nickname, "The Show Me State" originated. Most think it has something to do with Missourians stubborn need for proof.

★ The state takes its name for a branch of the Sioux tribe who lived in the area.

★ The rivalry between the University of Missouri and the University of Kansas is the second oldest in the nation.

MISSOURI'S EL CAMINO REAL

Originally an Indian trail, this route became the El Camino Real, laid out during the late 18th century when Spain ruled the North American territory west of the Mississippi. Leave St. Louis on Interstate 55 south to exit 186, then drive east to Highway 61. Head south on Highway 61 to Kimmswick, a little town on the Mississippi that thrived from the 1860s to the end of the 19th century, when it was a busy center for riverboat traffic.

Lucianna Gladney Ross, daughter of the founder of the 7-Up soft-drink company, discovered the handsome but dilapidated town and spearheaded a movement to restore it to its original condition. Today, Kimmswick is part open-air museum, part shopping boutique. Many of the older buildings contain restaurants, antique stores and other specialty retail shops. The Old House Restaurant (Second and Elm Streets) was once a stagecoach stop and tavern frequented by Ulysses S. Grant. It features old-fashioned home-cooked meals and desserts.

Just west of Kimmswick, the 425-acre Mastodon Historic Site preserves an important archaeological area that contains the bones of American mastodons. The fossil remains of these and other now-extinct animals were first found in the early 1800s in what is now called the Kimmswick Bone Bed. The area became known as one of the most extensive Pleistocene bone beds in the country, attracting archaeological and paleontological interest from around the world. A museum tells the natural and cultural story of the area.

Follow Highway 61 south along the Mississippi to Ste. Genevieve, founded in the 1750s as a French village. Ste. Genevieve is one of the oldest European settlements west of the Mississippi and contains an important collection of French Colonial architecture. Now a National Historic District, the entire town gives testament to the lasting quality of French craftsmanship.

South of Perryville to the east of Highway 66 is a cluster of villages settled by Germans: Altenburg, Frohna and Wittenberg. Altenburg has a collection of original structures from the 1830s and a museum of that commemorates the early Lutheran farming history of the area. Continue south on Highway 66, and follow Highway 177 east to Trail of Tears State Park. This 3,415-acre park is a memorial to the Cherokee Indians who died during a forced relocation to Oklahoma. The park's many trails are good for hiking, and the bluffs and cliffs along the river are roosting sites for bald eagles.

Follow Highway 177 to Cape Girardeau, which began as a fur-trading fort. The town sweeps up from the Mississippi to a high promontory, with a number of 19th-century buildings along the waterfront, and has the distinction of being the hometown of Rush Limbaugh.

From Cape Girardeau, follow Highway 61 south to New Madrid. In 1789, this site was selected to be the capital of the colony that Spain hoped to establish in the Louisiana Territory. Not much became of Spain's plans for this colony, and now New Madrid is most famous for the devastating 1811 earthquake that centered on the New Madrid Fault. With an estimated magnitude reaching more than 8 on the Richter scale, this earthquake was one of the largest in recent geologic history. Approximately 190 miles.

MISSOURI

BONNE TERRE

French settlers named this town bonne terre, meaning "good earth," when they discovered the abundance of lead ore in the area.

Information: Chamber of Commerce, 11 S.W. Main St., 573-358-4000; www.bonterre.net

WHAT TO SEE AND DO

Bonne Terre Mine Tours

39 N. Allen St., Bonne Terre, 573-358-2148

A one-hour walking tour takes visitors through lead and silver mines that operated from 1864 to 1962. See historic mining tools, ore cars, ore samples, an underground lake, flower garden and museum exhibits. May-September: daily; rest of year: Friday-Monday.

Mark Twain National Forest

Hwy. 8, Bonne Terre, 573-438-5427

This park has a wimming beach, boat launch, nature trails and camping. Daily.

Washington State Park

Hwy. 21, DeSoto, 636-586-2995

A more than 1,400-acre park containing petroglyphs (interpretations available). Swimming pool, fishing, canoeing on Big River; hiking trails, playground, cabins, camping. Daily.

BRANSON

The resort town of Branson has become a mecca for fans of country music and old-fashioned acts. Variety shows, comedy acts and performers of all ages hit the stages of the many theaters in town nightly.

Information: Branson/Lakes Area Chamber of Commerce, 269 Hwy. 248, 417-334-4084, 800-214-3661; www.branson.com

WHAT TO SEE AND DO

Andy Williams Moon River Theater

2500 W. Hwy. 76, Branson, 417-334-4500; www.andywilliams.com

This theater is the domain of 1960s singer Andy Williams, who is sometimes joined on stage by guest performers, which in the past have included Charo and Glen Campbell. April-December.

Baldknobbers Jamboree

2845 W. Hwy. 76, Branson, 417-334-4528; www.baldknobbers.com

This country music variety show features comedy, music and skits. March-mid-April:

Friday-Saturday; mid-April-mid-December: Monday-Saturday.

Branson Scenic Railway

206 E. Main St., Branson, 417-334-6110; 800-287-2462

Forty-mile roundtrip through Ozark Foothills. Mid-March-mid-December, schedule varies; closed holidays.

College of the Ozarks

100 Opportunity Ave.,

★
★
★
★
★
★

Point Lookout, 417-334-6411
(1906) (1,500 students). This is a small liberal arts college of 1,500 where students work, rather than pay, for their education.

Dutton Family Theater
3454 W. Hwy. 76, Branson, 417-332-2772;
www.theduttons.com
A musical variety show featuring all seven member of the Dutton family and their spouses playing a variety of instruments. April-December.

Elvis and the Superstars Show
205 S. Commercial, Branson,
417-336-2112, 800-358-4795;
www.elvisinbranson.com
A musical tribute to Elvis Presley, this show features an impersonator belting out tunes by the King from his early days to Vegas years. Year-round.

Grand Country Music Hall
1945 W. Hwy. 76, Branson, 417-335-2484;
www.grandcountry.com
Shows at this performance space include everything from *Amazing Pets* to the *Ozarks Mountain Jamboree.*

Hughes Brothers Celebrity Theatre
3425 W. Hwy. 76, Branson, 417-334-0076
The five Utah-born Hughes brothers, along with their wives and children entertain six days a week in this musical variety show.

Jim Stafford Theatre
3440 W. Hwy. 76, Branson, 417-335-8080;
www.jimstafford.com
Novelty singer Jim Stafford, who had several hits in the '70s, performs at this theater.

Jimmy Osmond's American Jukebox Show
3600 W. Hwy. 76, Branson, 417-336-6100;
www.osmondfamilytheater.com
The youngest Osmond performs hit songs from the '40s to the present at this theater. April-December.

Presley's Country Jubilee
2920 W. Hwy. 76, Branson, 417-334-4874
Four generations of a family perform country music and more. March-mid-December.

Ripley's Believe It Or Not! Museum
3326 W. Hwy. 76, Branson,
417-337-5300; www.ripleys.com
This outpost of the curiousities museum has hundreds of exhibits in eight galleries.

Shepherd of the Hills
5586 W. Hwy. 76, Branson, 417-334-4191
Jeep-drawn conveyance tours include authentically furnished Old Matt's Cabin, home of the prominent characters in Harold Bell Wright's Ozark novel *The Shepherd of the Hills.* Late April-late October, daily.

WIDE OPEN COUNTRY
The beautiful Ozark hills drew people to southwest Missouri long before Branson became famous for its country music theaters. From Springfield, drive 41 miles south on Highway 65 to Branson. Touring options here include a railroad that travels through the Ozarks to Arkansas, and the Ducks, amphibious vehicles that roll around town and onto Table Rock Lake. Other area attractions beyond the music theaters packing Highway 76 (Country Boulevard) include the Shepherd of the Hills homestead and outdoor theater and Silver Dollar City theme park. Once you've had your fill of Branson, head east out of town on Highway 76, a scenic stretch through part of the Mark Twain National Forest, then take Highway 5 north. Stop at Mansfield to see the Laura Ingalls Wilder farm, where the author wrote the Little House books. Return to Springfield via Highway 60 west. Approximately 150 miles.

59

MISSOURI

Showboat Branson Belle
Branson, 417-336-7171
Lunch and dinner cruises depart from Highway 165 near Table Rock Dam. April-December, daily.

Stone Hill Winery
601 Hwy. 165, Branson, 417-334-1897; www.stonehillwinery.com
Guided tours and bottling demonstrations. Daily; closed holidays.

Table Rock Dam and Lake
4600 Hwy. 165, Branson, 417-334-4101
This 43,100-acre reservoir, formed by impounding waters of White River, offers swimming, water skiing, scuba diving, fishing for bass, crappie, and walleye, boating, hunting for deer, turkey, rabbit and waterfowl, picnicking, playgrounds and camping. Daily.

SPECIAL EVENTS
Festival of American Music and Craftsmanship
399 Indian Point Rd., Branson, 800-475-9370
Celebrating arts, crafts and cooking from across America, with demonstrations, exhibits, and entertainment. Early September-late October.

HOTELS
★★Best Western Mountain Oak Lodge
8514 Hwy. 76, Branson, 417-338-2141, 800-868-6625; www.bestwestern.com
145 rooms. Complimentary continental breakfast. Restaurant, bar. Indoor pool. $

★★Clarion Hotel at the Palace
2820 W. Hwy. 76, Branson, 417-334-7666, 800-725-2236; www.choicehotels.com
166 rooms. Complimentary continental breakfast. Restaurant, bar. Indoor pool, whirlpool. $

★★Days Inn
3524 Keeter St., Branson, 417-334-5544, 800-329-7466; www.daysinnbranson.com
424 room. Pets accepted; fee. Complimentary continental breakfast. Restaurant. Outdoor pool, children's pool, whirlpool. $

★Hampton Inn
3695 W. Hwy. 76, Branson, 417-337-5762, 800-426-7866; www.hamptoninn.com
110 rooms. Complimentary continental breakfast. Indoor pool, whirlpool. $

★★Radisson Hotel Branson
120 S. Wildwood Dr., Branson, 417-335-5767, 800-333-3333; www.radisson.com/bransonmo
472 rooms. Restaurant, bar. Fitness room. Indoor pool, outdoor pool, whirlpool. $

★Ramada Inn
1700 W. Hwy. 76, Branson, 417-334-1000, 800-641-4106; www.ramadabranson.com
296 rooms. Pets accepted; fee. Outdoor pool. $

★★★Big Cedar Lodge
612 Devils Pool Rd., Ridgedale, 417-335-2777; www.bigcedarlodge.com
Guests can stay in one of three lodges, a cabin or a cottage. The resort offers boating and swimming on the lake, tennis, golf, horseback riding, a 10,000-acre nature park with hiking trails and more.
224 rooms. Restaurant, bar. Children's activity center. Fitness room. Two outdoor pools. Tennis. $

★★★Chateau on the Lake
415 N. Hwy. 265, Branson, 417-334-1161, 888-333-5253; www.chateauonthelake.com
Chateau on the Lake has a mountaintop location overlooking Table Rock Lake. The resort is located close to town, with a spa and salon, as well as an old-fashioned soda fountain.
300 rooms. Pets accepted, some restrictions; fee. Restaurant, bar. Fitness room. Indoor pool, outdoor pool, whirlpool. Tennis. Business center. $$

60

MISSOURI

★
★
★
★
★

★★★Lodge Of The Ozarks Entertainment Complex
3431 W. Hwy. 76, Branson,
417-334-7535, 877-866-2219;
www.lodgeoftheozarks.com
This hotel offers large rooms and is walking distance from theaters, shopping, and other attractions.
190 rooms. Complimentary continental breakfast. Restaurant, bar. Indoor pool, whirlpool. **$**

★★★Thousand Hills Golf and Conference Resort
245 S. Wildwood Dr., Branson,
417-336-5873, 877-262-0430;
www.thousandhills.com
This sprawling resort has both cabins and condominiums available for rent along-side the Thousand Hills Golf Course. Most have jacuzzi tubs, fireplaces and fully stocked kitchens. The resort also has a fitness center, indoor and outdoor pools and tennis courts.
Pets not accepted. Golf. Fitness Center. **$$$**

RESTAURANTS
★★Candlestick Inn
127 Taney St., Branson,
417-334-3633; www.candlestickinn.com
Seafood, steak menu. Lunch, dinner. Bar. Children's menu. **$$$**

★Uncle Joe's Bar-B-Q
2819 Hwy. 76 W., Branson, 417-334-4548
American menu. Lunch, dinner. Closed December-January. Children's menu. **$$**

★Mr G's Chicago-Style Pizza
201 N. Commercial, Marvel Cave Park,
417-335-8156
Italian menu. Lunch, dinner. Bar. **$**

CAPE GIRARDEAU
On early maps, a rocky promontory on the Mississippi River, 125 miles below St. Louis, was labeled Cape Girardot (or Girardeau), named for a French ensign believed to have settled there about 1720. In 1792, an agent for the Spanish government, Louis Lorimier, set up a trading post at the site of the present city and encouraged settlement.

Cape Girardeau's location assured flourishing river traffic before the Civil War. The war, however, ended river trade and the earliest railroads bypassed the town, triggering further decline. In the late 1880s, the arrival of new railroads and the 1928 completion of a bridge across the Mississippi contributed to industrial growth and the widening of Cape Girardeau's economic base. Southeast Missouri State University (1873), which has a mural in its library depicting the history of the area, is located in the town.

Information: Convention and Visitors Bureau, 100 Broadway, 573-335-1631, 800-777-0068; www.capegirardeaucvb.org

WHAT TO SEE AND DO
Bollinger Mill State Historic Site
113 Bollinger Mill Rd.,
Cape Girardeau, 573-243-4591
This day-use park features a historic 19th-century gristmill and the oldest covered bridge in the state (1868). Guided tours are available. Daily.

Cape River Heritage Museum
538 Independence, Cape Girardeau,
573-334-0405
Exhibits on Cape Girardeau's early heritage, 19th-century industry, education, and culture. March-December: Friday-Saturday; also by appointment.

Court of Common Pleas Building

Spanish and Themis Streets,
Cape Girardeau

Central portion built about 1854 to replace previous log structure. During the Civil War, cells in the basement housed prisoners. Outstanding view of the Mississippi River from the park.

Glenn House

325 S. Spanish St., Cape Girardeau,
573-334-1177

A Victorian house with period furnishings, memorabilia of the Mississippi River and steamboat era is displayed here. April-December: Friday-Sunday.

Old St. Vincent's Church

Spanish and Main Streets, Cape Girardeau
English Gothic Revival church showing Roman influences. More than 100 medieval-design plaster masks. Hand-carved doors. Tours by appointment.

St. Louis Iron Mountain and Southern Railway

Jackson, 573-243-1688, 800-455-7245
A 1946 steam locomotive pulls vintage 1920s cars through scenic woodlands. Trips range from 80 minutes to five hours. April-October: Saturday-Sunday.

Trail of Tears State Park

429 Moccasin Spring, Cape Girardeau,
573-334-1711

A more than 3,000-acre park on limestone bluffs overlooking the Mississippi River. Commemorates the forced migration of the Cherokee Nation over the Trail of Tears to Oklahoma. Daily.

HOTELS

★★Drury Inn

104 S. Vantage Dr., Cape Girardeau,
573-334-7151, 800-378-7946;
www.druryhotels.com
139 rooms. Pets accepted, some restrictions. Complimentary full breakfast. Restaurant, bar. Fitness room. Outdoor pool, children's pool. $

★★Holiday Inn

3253 William St., Cape Girardeau,
573-334-4491, 888-465-4329;
www.holidayinn.com
102 rooms. Restaurant, bar. Fitness room. Indoor pool, outdoor pool, children's pool. $

★Pear Tree Inn

3248 William St., Cape Girardeau,
573-334-3000, 800-378-7946;
www.druryhotels.com
78 rooms. Pets accepted, some restrictions. Complimentary continental breakfast. Outdoor pool, children's pool. $

RESTAURANTS

★BG's Olde Tyme Deli & Saloon

205 S. Plaza Way, Cape Girardeau,
573-335-8860
American menu. Lunch, dinner. Bar. Children's menu. $

★Broussard's Cajun Cuisine

120 N. Main St., Cape Girardeau,
573-334-7235
Cajun/Creole menu. Lunch, dinner. Bar. $$

CARTHAGE

Carthage was founded as the seat of Jasper County in 1842. The first major Civil War battle west of the Mississippi River was fought here July 5, 1861. Belle Starr, a Confederate spy and outlaw, lived here as a girl. Annie Baxter, the first woman in the United States to hold elective office, was elected County Clerk in Carthage in 1890, and James Scott, a ragtime musician and composer, began his career here in 1906. Many interesting Victorian houses can still be found in Carthage.
Information: Chamber of Commerce, 107 E. Third St., 417-358-2373; www.carthagenow.com

WHAT TO SEE AND DO
Battle of Carthage Civil War Museum
205 E. Grant, Carthage
Features artifacts, a wall-sized mural and a diorama depicting the progress of the battle. Daily.

Jasper County Courthouse
302 S. Main, Carthage, 417-358-0421
Built in 1894 of Carthage marble, with a mural by Lowell Davis depicting local history. Monday-Friday.

HOTELS
★Carthage Inn
2244 Grand Ave., Carthage,
417-358-2499, 888-454-2499
40 rooms. Pets accepted, some restrictions;

fee. Complimentary continental breakfast. $

SPECIALTY LODGINGS
Grand Avenue Bed and Breakfast
1615 Grand Ave., Carthage, 417-358-7265;
www.grand-avenue.com
This bed and breakfast is housed in a Queen Anne-style house built in 1890. 4 rooms. Complimentary full breakfast. High-speed Internet access. Outdoor pool. $

RESTAURANTS
★★Bamboo Garden
104 N. Garrison Ave., Carthage,
417-358-1611
Chinese menu. Lunch, dinner. $

CHESTERFIELD
This is suburb was under water during the Great Flood of 1993 due to parts being located in the Chesterfield Valley. It is the largest city west of St. Louis.
www.chesterfieldmochamber.com

RESTAURANTS
★★Annie Gunn's
16806 Chesterfield Airport Rd.,
Chesterfield, 636-532-7684
American menu. Lunch, dinner, late-night. Bar. Outdoor seating. $$$

★★Paul Manno's
75 Forum Center, Chesterfield,
314-878-1274
Italian menu. Dinner. Closed Sunday; also late June-early July. Bar. Business casual attire. Reservations recommended. $$

CHILLICOTHE
Chillicothe, seat of Livingston County, is a Shawnee word meaning "our big town." It was named for Chillicothe, Ohio. Sloan's Liniment was developed here about 1870 by Earl Sloan. An Amish community located approximately 25 miles northwest of town, near Jamesport, has many interesting shops.
Information: Chamber of Commerce, 715 Washington St., 660-646-4050, 877-224-4554; www.chillicothemo.com

WHAT TO SEE AND DO
General John J. Pershing Boyhood Home State Historic Site
1000 Pershing Dr., Laclede, 660-963-2525;
www.mostateparks.com/pershingsite.htm
This 11-room house, built in 1858, was the childhood home of the World War I hero. Also here is a statue of "Black Jack" Pershing, a Wall of Honor and the relo-

cated Prairie Mound School, the one-room schoolhouse where Pershing taught before entering West Point. Daily.

Pershing State Park
29277 Hwy. 130, Chillicothe, 660-963-2299
This 3,500-acre memorial to General John J. Pershing offers fishing, canoeing, hiking trails, picnicking, camping. North of the

park is the Locust Creek covered bridge, the longest of four remaining covered bridges in the state. Daily.

HOTELS

★Best Western Chillicothe Inn & Suites
1020 S. Washington St., Chillicothe, 660-646-0572, 800-990-9150; www.bestwestern.com

58 rooms. Pets accepted; fee. Complimentary continental breakfast. Outdoor pool. **$**

★★Grand River Inn
606 W. Business 36, Chillicothe, 660-646-6590, 888-317-8290; www.grandriverinn.com
60 rooms. Pets accepted; fee. Complimentary continental breakfast. Restaurant, bar. Outdoor pool, whirlpool. **$**

COLUMBIA

An educational center from its earliest years, Columbia is the home of Columbia College, Stephens College and the University of Missouri, the oldest state university west of the Mississippi. Established as Smithton, the town was moved a short distance to ensure a better water supply and renamed Columbia. In 1822, the Boone's Lick Trail was rerouted to pass through the town. Classes began at the University of Missouri in 1841, and the town has revolved around the institution ever since. The School of Journalism, founded in 1908,

was the first degree-granting journalism school in the world.

Information: Convention and Visitors Bureau, 300 S. Providence Rd., 573-875-1231, 800-652-0987; www.visitcolumbiamo.com

WHAT TO SEE AND DO

Nifong Park
3801 Ponderosa Dr., Columbia, 573-443-8936
The park includes a visitor center, restored 1877 Maplewood house (April-October, Sunday, limited hours), Maplewood Barn Theater (summer), Boone County Historical Society Museum, petting zoo, lake and picnicking. Park daily.

Shelter Gardens
1817 W. Broadway, Columbia, 573-445-8441

Miniature mid-American environment with a pool and stream, domestic and wild flowers, more than 300 varieties of trees and shrubs, rose garden. Concerts in summer. Daily, weather permitting.

Stephens College
1200 E. Broadway, Columbia, 573-442-2211
On this 240-acre campus is the Firestone Baars Chapel on Walnut Street designed in 1956 by Eero Saarinen. Open Monday through Friday.

64

MISSOURI

★
★
★
★
★
★

University of Missouri-Columbia
311 Jesse Hall, Columbia, 573-882-6333;
www.missouri.edu
This 1,334-acre campus with more than 22,000 students contains numerous collections, exhibits, galleries and attractions.

Edison Electric Dynamo
Lobby of U. of Missouri Engineering
Building, E. Sixth St. and Stewart Rd.,
Columbia
The recently restored dynamo, given to the university in 1882 by its inventor, Thomas Alva Edison, was used on campus in 1883 for the first demonstration of incandescent lighting west of the Mississippi. Monday-Friday.

Ellis Library
Lowry Mall between Memorial Union
and Jesse Hall, Ninth St. and Conley Ave.,
Columbia, 573-882-4391
One of the largest libraries in the Midwest. A rare book room contains a page from a Gutenberg Bible. The State Historical Society of Missouri, located on the east ground wing, has early newspapers and works by Missouri artists.

Museum of Anthropology
Tucker Hall, Columbia, 573-882-3764
Artifacts from 9000 B.C. to the present. Monday-Friday.

Museum of Art and Archaeology
1 Pickard Hall, Columbia, 573-882-3591

Comprehensive collection including more than 13,000 objects from around the world, from the paleolithic period to the present. Cast gallery has items made from original Greek and Roman sculptures. Tuesday-Sunday.

HOTELS
★★Holiday Inn
2200 I-70 Dr. S.W., Columbia,
573-445-8531, 800-465-4329;
www.holiday-inn.com
311 rooms. Pets accepted. Restaurant, bar. Fitness room. Indoor pool, outdoor pool, whirlpool. Adjacent to Exposition Center. $

★★Quality Inn
1612 N. Providence Rd., Columbia,
573-449-2491, 800-228-5751;
www.qualityinn.com
142 rooms. Pets accepted, some restrictions; fee. Restaurant, bar. Fitness room. Indoor pool, whirlpool. $

RESTAURANTS
★★Boone Tavern
811 E. Walnut St., Columbia,
573-442-5123; www.boonetavern.com
American menu. Lunch, dinner. Closed holidays. Bar. Children's menu. Outdoor seating. $$

★Flat Branch Pub & Brewing
115 S. Fifth St., Columbia,
573-499-0400; www.flatbranch.com
American menu. Lunch, dinner. Bar. Children's menu. Outdoor seating. $$

MISSOURI

ELLISVILLE
This town is located 13 miles west of St. Louis. Though it was settled in the 1830s, it was not incorporated until 1932.
www.ellisville.mo.us

RESTAURANT
★★★GP Agostino's
15846 Manchester Rd., Ellisville,
636-391-5480; www.agostinosstlouis.com
The owners, Agostino and Rosa, were born and raised in Palermo, Sicily, and their upbringings are reflected in the cuisine and service of this fine Italian restaurant.
Italian menu. Lunch, dinner, late-night. Bar. Jacket required (dinner). $$

EXCELSIOR SPRINGS

Excelsior Springs was established in 1880 when two settlers, Anthony W. Wyman and J. V. D. Flack, discovered various natural springs on Wyman's property. Today the city is a health resort offering visitors bottled water from the springs and medicinal baths in the city-operated bathhouse.
Information: Chamber of Commerce, 101 E. Broadway, 816-630-6161; www.exsmo.com

WHAT TO SEE AND DO
Excelsior Springs Historical Museum
101 E. Broadway, Excelsior Springs, 816-630-0101
Includes murals, a bank, antiques, antique bedroom, doctor's office, dental equipment. Tuesday-Saturday.

Jesse James's Farm
Jesse James Farm Rd., Excelsior Springs, 816-628-6065
This house is where outlaw James was born and raised with his brother Frank. Daily.

Watkins Woolen Mill State Park and State Historic Site
26600 Park Rd. N., Lawson, 816-296-3357

Woolen factory and gristmill built and equipped in 1860; contains original machinery. Original owner's house, summer kitchen, ice house, smokehouse and school. Guided tours daily.

HOTEL
★★★The Inn On Crescent Lake
1261 St. Louis Ave., Excelsior Springs, 816-630-6745, 866-630-5253; www.crescentinn.com
This inn was built in 1915 on 22 acres of landscaped yard, surrounded by two crescent-shaped ponds. The rooms are individually decorated and have private baths. 10 rooms. Children over 12 years only. Complimentary full breakfast. Restaurant. Fitness room. Outdoor pool. **$**

FULTON

Named in honor of Robert Fulton, inventor of the steamboat, this town was home to both architect General M. F. Bell, who designed many of Fulton's historic buildings, and Henry Bellaman, author of the best-selling novel *King's Row,* which depicted life in Fulton at the turn of the century. The town is home to Westminster College (1851), William Woods University (1870) and the Missouri School for the Deaf.
Information: Kingdom of Callaway Chamber of Commerce, 409 Court St., 573-642-3055, 800-257-3554; www.fultonmissouri.org

WHAT TO SEE AND DO
Westminster College
501 Westminster Ave., Fulton, 573-642-3361
Winston Churchill delivered his "Iron Curtain" address here on March 5, 1946.

Winston Churchill Memorial and Library
Seventh St. and Westminster Ave., Fulton, 573-592-5369
To memorialize Churchill's "Iron Curtain" speech, the bombed ruins of Sir Christopher

Wren's 17th-century Church of St. Mary, Aldermanbury, were dismantled, shipped from London to Westminster College, reassembled and finally restored. The church was rehallowed in 1969 with Lord Mountbatten of Burma and Churchill's daughter, Lady Mary Soames, in attendance. The undercroft of the church houses a museum, gallery and research library with letters, manuscripts, published works, photos, memorabilia. Daily.

GEORGE WASHINGTON CARVER NATIONAL MONUMENT

Born a slave on the farm of Moses Carver, George Washington Carver (1864-1943) rose to become an eminent teacher, humanitarian, botanist, agronomist and pioneer conservationist. Carver was the first African American to graduate from Iowa State University. He received both a bachelor's and a master's degree in science. He then headed the Department of Agriculture at Booker T. Washington's Tuskegee Institute in Alabama.

Authorized as a national monument in 1943, this memorial to Carver honors a vital part of the American historical heritage. The visitor center contains a museum and audiovisual presentation depicting Carver's life and work. A self-guided trail passes the birthplace site, the statue of Carver by Robert Amendola, the restored 1881 Moses Carver house, the family cemetery and the woods and streams where Carver spent his boyhood. Daily.

Information: 5646 Carver Rd., Diamond, 417-425-4151; www.nps.gov/gwca

HANNIBAL

Hannibal is world-famous as the home town of the great novelist Samuel Clemens (Mark Twain) as well as the setting of *The Adventures of Tom Sawyer,* which records many actual events of Clemens's boyhood. He served his printer's apprenticeship here and gained a fascination with steamboats in the days when the river was the source of the town's prosperity.

Information: Visitors and Convention Bureau, 505 N. Third St., 573-221-2477; www.visithannibal.com

MISSOURI

★
★
★
★
☆

WHAT TO SEE AND DO

Mark Twain Riverboat Excursions
Center St., Hannibal, 573-221-3222, 800-621-2322
One-hour cruises on the Mississippi River; also two-hour dinner cruises. Early May-October: daily.

Becky Thatcher House
209-211 Hill St., Hannibal
House where Laura Hawkins (Becky Thatcher) lived during Samuel Clemens's boyhood; upstairs rooms have authentic furnishings. Daily.

Mark Twain Cave
7097 Country Rd. 453, Hannibal, 573-221-1656
This is the cave in *The Adventures of Tom Sawyer* in which Tom and Becky Thatcher were lost and where Injun Joe died. Tours daily; closed holidays.

Mark Twain Museum and Boyhood Home
208 Hill St., Hannibal, 573-221-9010
Museum houses Mark Twain memorabilia, including books, letters, photographs, and family items. Daily.

John M. Clemens Justice of the Peace Office
Hill St., Hannibal, 63401
Restored courtroom where Twain's father presided as justice of the peace.

Pilaster House and Grant's Drugstore
Hill and Main Streets, Hannibal
The Clemens family lived in this Greek Revival house, which contains a restored old-time drugstore, pioneer kitchen, doctor's office and quarters where John Clemens, Twain's father, died.

Molly Brown Birthplace and Museum
600 Butler St., Hannibal, 573-221-2100

Antique-filled home has memorabilia of the "unsinkable" Molly Brown, who survived the *Titanic* disaster. April-May, September-October: weekends; June-August: daily.

Optical Science Center and Museum
216 Main St., Hannibal, 573-221-2020
Hands-on learning stations provide first-hand optical demonstrations. Computerized light show, wrap around theater. April-October: daily.

Rockcliffe Mansion
Hill St., Hannibal, 573-221-4140
Restored Beaux Arts mansion overlooking the river; 30 rooms, many original furnishings. Samuel Clemens addressed a gathering here in 1902. Guided tours. Daily.

SPECIAL EVENTS
Tom Sawyer Days
505 N. Third St., Hannibal, 573-221-2477
National fence painting contest, frog jumping, entertainment. Four days early in July.

HOTELS
★Hotel Clemens
401 N. Third St., Hannibal, 573-248-1150; www.hotelclemens.us
78 rooms. Complimentary continental breakfast. Indoor pool, whirlpool. Airport transportation available. **$**

MARK TWAIN'S HANNIBAL

Start a tour of Hannibal, an old Mississippi riverboat town and hometown to Samuel Longhorn Clemens—better known as Mark Twain—at the Hannibal Convention and Visitors Bureau (505 N. Third St). Towering above the visitor center is the Mark Twain Lighthouse, located at the crest of Cardiff Hill. This is the largest inland lighthouse in the United States, offering great views of Hannibal and the Mississippi from the top.

A block south of the Visitors Bureau is the Mark Twain Boyhood Home and Museum (208 Hill St.), which features the original 1843 Clemens home, restored to look as it did when Twain lived here in the 1840s. Next door (211 Hill St.) is the period home of Laura Hawkins, Mark Twain's youthful sweetheart and the inspiration for the character Becky Thatcher in Twain's novels. On the corner of Hill and Main Streets is the Clemens Law office, where Twain's father, J. M. Clemens, presided as Hannibal's justice of the peace. Attached to the building is a historic courtroom, which served as the model for scenes from *The Adventures of Tom Sawyer*. At the base of Cardiff Hill at Main Street is the Tom and Huck Statue, which commemorates Twains most famous characters, Huck Finn and Tom Sawyer. Frederick Hibbard sculpted this bronze statue in 1926.

Stretching along Main Street are a number of historic buildings and shops. Follow Main Street south, passing boutiques in historic storefronts. A worthy stop is Mrs. Clemens' Antique Mall (305 N. Main), which features two floors of antiques and an ice-cream parlor. At Bird and Main Streets stands the handsome Pilaster House/Grant's Drug Store, dating from the 1830s. The Clemens family lived here briefly in the 1940s, and Judge Clemens died here in 1847. Today, the building is preserved as an 1890s apothecary.

At Main and Center Streets is the Mark Twain Museum, a restored structure that contains a collection of original Norman Rockwell paintings used for illustrated editions of *Adventures of Huckleberry Finn*. The museum also serves as a memento of Hannibal's riverboat past.

★Super 8
120 Huckleberry Heights Dr., Hannibal,
573-221-5863, 800-800-8000;
www.super8.com
59 rooms. Pets accepted, some restrictions; fee. Complimentary continental breakfast. Outdoor pool. **$**

★★★Garth Woodside Mansion B&B
11069 New London Rd., Hannibal,
573-221-2789, 888-427-8409;
www.hannibal-missouri.com
With eight guest rooms, each with its

own private bath, this Second Empire/ Victorian mansion where Mark Twain was often a guest is located on 33 acres of grass, woodland, gardens and ponds. 8 rooms. Complimentary full breakfast. High-speed Internet access. **$**

RESTAURANTS
★Logue's
121 Huckleberry Heights Dr., Hannibal,
573-248-1854
American menu. Breakfast, lunch, dinner. Children's menu. **$**

HERMANN

German immigrants, unhappy with the English atmosphere of Philadelphia, bought this land and founded the town with the purpose of maintaining their German culture. Grape cultivation and wine making started early and thrived until Prohibition. Today the town has several working wineries and plenty of German-influenced buildings, restaurants and shops.
Information: 573-486-2744, 800-932-8687; www.hermanmo.com

WHAT TO SEE AND DO
Deutsche Schule Arts and Crafts
German School Building, 312 Schiller St., Hermann, 573-486-2744
Exhibits from more than 100 craftspeople, including handmade quilts, baskets and woodcutting. Daily.

Deutschheim State Historic Site
109 W. Second St., Hermann,
573-486-2200
This site includes the authentically furnished Pommer-Gentner House (1840) on Market Street and Strehly House and Winery (circa 1840-1867) on West Second Street. Kitchen, herb, and flower gardens; special events. Tours. Daily.

Graham Cave State Park
217 Hwy. TT, Montgomery, 573-564-3476
Native Americans occupied this cave approximately 10,000 years ago. About 350 acres with fishing, nature trails, playground, camping. Daily.

Hermannhof Winery
330 E. First St., Hermann, 573-486-5959

This 150-year-old winery includes 10 wine cellars. Sausage making; cheeses. Sampling. Daily.

Historic Hermann Museum
312 Schiller St., Hermann, 573-486-2017
Heritage Museum in 1871 building, with artifacts of early settlers; River Room depicts the history of early river men; children's museum has toys, furniture of 1890s; handmade German bedroom set; 1886 pump organ. Mechanism of town clock may be seen. April-October; Tuesday-Sunday.

SPECIAL EVENTS
Great Stone Hill Grape Stomp
Stone Hill Winery and Restaurant, 1110 Stone Hill Hwy., Hermann, 800-909-9463; www.stonehillwinery.com
Jump into in a barrel full of juicy grapes to celebrate the beginning of grape harvest. Second Saturday in August.

HOTEL
★Hermann Motel
112 E. 10th St., Hermann, 573-486-3131; www.hermannmotel.com
24 rooms. **$**

★
★
★
★
★

RESTAURANT
★★Vintage
1110 Stone Hill Hwy., Hermann,
573-486-3479, 800-909-9463;
www.stonehillwinery.com

American, German menu. Lunch, dinner. Closed mid-December-mid-February. Children's menu. Reservations recommended. $$

INDEPENDENCE
Independence was an outfitting point for westbound wagon trains from 1830 to 1850. The scene of much of the Mormon Wars in the early 1830s, it was ravaged by raiders and occupied by Union and Confederate troops during the Civil War. Today it's best known as the hometown of President Harry S. Truman.
Information: Tourism Division, 111 E. Maple, 816-325-7111, 800-748-7323

WHAT TO SEE AND DO
1859 Marshal's Home and Jail Museum
217 N. Main St., Independence,
816-252-1892
Restored building contains dungeonlike cells, marshal's living quarters, regional history museum. One-room schoolhouse (1870). April-October: daily; November-December and March: Tuesday-Sunday.

Bingham-Waggoner Estate
313 W. Pacific, Independence,
816-461-3491
Famous Missouri artist George Caleb Bingham lived here from 1864 to 1870; also the homestead of the Waggoner family, millers of "Queen of the Pantry" flour. April-October: daily.

Fort Osage
105 Osage, Sibley, 816-795-8200
Restoration of one of the first U.S. outposts in the Louisiana Territory following the purchase from France. Built in 1808 by William Clark of the Lewis and Clark expedition, the fort includes officers' quarters, soldiers' barracks, trading post, factor's house, museum; costumed guides. Mid-April-mid-November: Wednesday-Sunday; rest of year: Saturday-Sunday.

Harry S. Truman Courtroom and Office Museum
Jackson County Courthouse,
112 W. Lexington, Independence,
816-795-8200

Restored office and courtroom where Truman began his political career as presiding county judge. Tours. Sunday-Thursday, by appointment.

Harry S. Truman National Historic Site (Truman House)
Main and Truman Streets,
Independence, 816-254-9929;
www.nps.gov/hstr
This was Truman's residence from the time of his marriage to Bess Wallace in 1919 until his death in 1972. An excellent example of late 19th-century Victorian architecture. The house, built by Bess Truman's grandfather, was the birthplace of Margaret Truman and served as the summer White House from 1945 to 1953. Memorial Day-Labor Day: daily; rest of year: Tuesday-Sunday.

National Frontier Trails Center
318 W. Pacific, Independence,
816-325-7575
Partially restored flour mill at the site of the Santa Fe, California and Oregon trails serves as a museum, interpretive center, library and archive of westward pioneer expansion; Daily.

Truman Farm Home
12301 Blue Ridge Blvd., Grandview,
816-254-2720
Harry Truman lived in this two-story, white frame house in the decade preceding World War I. During these years—"the best years," according to Truman—he farmed the sur-

MISSOURI

★
★
★
★
★

rounding 600 acres, worked as a mason and postmaster, served as a soldier and courted Bess Wallace. Interior features period furnishings, including original family pieces. Mid-May-late August: Friday-Sunday.

Truman Presidential Museum and Library
500 W. Hwy. 24, Independence,
www.trumanlibrary.org
Includes presidential papers, mementos of public life and a reproduction of President Truman's White House office. Graves of President and Mrs. Truman in courtyard. Museum daily; closed holidays. Library, Monday-Friday.

SPECIAL EVENTS
Santa-Cali-Gon
210 W. Truman Rd., Independence,
816-252-4745
Celebration commemorating the Santa Fe, California and Oregon trails. Contests, arts and crafts, square dancing. Labor Day weekend.

HOTELS
★Comfort Inn East
4200 S. Noland Rd., Independence,
816-373-8856; www.choicehotels.com
171 rooms. Pets accepted; fee. Complimentary continental breakfast. Indoor pool, outdoor pool, whirlpool. $

SPECIALTY LODGINGS
Woodstock Inn Bed & Breakfast
1212 W. Lexington Ave., Independence,
816-833-2233, 800-276-5202;
www.independence-missouri.com
11 rooms. Complimentary full breakfast. High-speed Internet access. In a historic area of town near the Truman house and library. $

RESTAURANTS
★★Rheinland
208 N. Main St., Independence,
816-461-5383
German menu. Breakfast, lunch, dinner, brunch. Children's menu. $$

★★Salvatore's
12801 Hwy. 40 E., Independence,
816-737-2400; www.salvatores.us
Italian menu. Lunch, dinner. Bar. Children's menu. Outdoor seating. $$

★★★V's Italiano
10819 Hwy. 40 E. Independence,
816-353-1241; www.vsrestaurant.com
This family style Italian restaurant serves up heaping portions of classic dishes like veal parmigian and osso buco. Entrees come with fresh slices of Italian rum cake. American, Italian menu. Lunch, dinner, Sunday brunch. Bar. Children's menu. Casual attire. $$

JEFFERSON CITY
Jefferson City was chosen for the state capital in 1826. Near a river landing, it consisted of a foundry, a shop and a mission. Goverment business drives this small historic town. Named for Thomas Jefferson, it is known locally as "Jeff City."
Information: Jefferson City Convention and Visitors Bureau, 213 Adams St., 573-634-3616, 800-769-4183; www.visitjeffersoncity.com

WHAT TO SEE AND DO
Cole County Historical Society Museum
109 Madison St., Jefferson City,
573-635-1850
One of three four-story row houses built in the Federal style, the museum features Victorian furnishings and household items, plus inaugural gowns from

Missouri's first ladies dating from 1877. Tuesday-Saturday.

Governor's Mansion
100 Madison St., Jefferson City,
573-751-4141
This Renaissance Revival house (1871) was designed by George Ingham Barnett and features period furnishings, stenciled ceilings,

period wall coverings and late 19th-century chandeliers. Tours Tuesday and Thursday; closed August and December.

State Capitol
High St. and Broadway, Jefferson City, 573-751-4127
On a bluff overlooking the Missouri River, this building of Carthage stone is the third state capitol in Jefferson City; both predecessors burned. A Thomas Hart Benton mural is in the House Lounge, on the third floor west wing. Also here are paintings by N. C. Wyeth and Frank Brangwyn. Daily.

Jefferson Landing State Historic Site
Jefferson and Water Streets, Jefferson City, 573-751-3475
Restored mid-1800s riverboat landing. Lohman Building (1839) features exhibits and audiovisual presentation on the history of Jefferson City and the Missouri Capitol. Union Hotel (1855) contains a gallery of exhibits by local artisans Tuesday-Saturday.

HOTELS

★★Best Western Capital Inn
1937 Christy Dr., Jefferson City, 573-635-4175, 800-780-7234; www.bestwestern.com
79 rooms. Pets accepted, some restrictions. Complimentary continental breakfast. Restaurant, bar. Indoor pool. **$**

★★Hotel Deville
319 W. Miller St., Jefferson City, 573-636-5231, 800-392-3366; www.devillehotel.com

98 rooms. Restaurant, bar. Outdoor pool. **$**

★★★Capitol Plaza Hotel
451 W. McCarty St., Jefferson City, 573-635-1234, 800-338-8088; www.jqhhotels.com
This full-service hotel offers renovated guest rooms, a pool, whirlpool and cascading waterfall in the atrium, a restaurant, cafe and lounge and more. It is located across from the Truman building and near attractions.
255 rooms. Pets accepted, some restrictions; fee. Restaurant, bar. Fitness room. Indoor pool. **$**

RESTAURANT

★★Madison's Café
216 Madison St., Jefferson City, 573-634-2988; www.madisonscafe.com
Italian menu. Lunch, dinner. Children's menu. Casual attire. **$$**

JOPLIN

The discovery of lead here convinced an early settler to establish a town. As the mining boom continued, another community, Murphysburg, grew up on the west side of Joplin Creek. The two towns were rivals until 1873 when both agreed to merge. Today Joplin, one of Missouri's larger cities, is home to many manufacturing industries.

Information: Convention and Visitors Bureau, 222 W. Third St., 417-625-4789, 800-657-2534; www.joplincvb.com

WHAT TO SEE AND DO

Dorothea B. Hoover Historical Museum
W. Seventh St. and Schifferdecker Ave., Joplin, 417-623-1180; www.joplinmuseum.org
Period rooms with late 19th-century furnishing; miniatures, including a circus, photographs, musical instruments, Victorian doll house and playhouse; antique toys; dolls; Native American artifacts; cut glass.

Thomas Hart Benton Exhibit
303 E. Third St., Joplin
Includes mural, "Joplin at the Turn of the Century, 1896-1906," as well as photographs, clay models, personal letters, and other paintings by Benton. Monday-Friday.

HOTELS

★Drury Inn
3601 S. Range Line Rd., Joplin, 417-781-8000, 800-378-7946; www.druryhotels.com
109 rooms. Pets accepted. Complimentary continental breakfast. Fitness room. Indoor pool, whirlpool. **$**

★★Holiday Inn
3615 Range Line Rd., Joplin, 417-782-1000, 800-465-4329; www.holiday-inn.com
262 rooms. Pets accepted, some restrictions. Restaurant, bar. Fitness room. Indoor pool, outdoor pool, whirlpool. **$**

RESTAURANTS

★Kitchen Pass
1212 S. Main St., Joplin, 417-624-9095; www.kitchenpass.net
Seafood, steak menu. Lunch, dinner. Closed Sunday; holidays. Bar. Children's menu. **$$**

★Wilder's
1216 Main St., Joplin, 417-623-7230
Seafood, steak menu. Dinner. Bar. **$$$**

73

MISSOURI

★
★
★
★
★

KANSAS CITY

Kansas City was developed as a steamboat landing for the town of Westport, four miles south on the Santa Fe Trail, and a competitor with Independence as the trail's eastern terminus and outfitting point. The buildings that sprang up along this landing eclipsed Westport, which was eventually incorporated into the new city. Kansas City's roaring overland trade was disturbed by the border warfare of the 1850s and the Civil War, but peace and the railroads brought new prosperity. A network of railway lines following the natural water-level routes that converge at the mouth of the Kansas River made Kansas City a great terminus.

Famous for their "booster" spirit, its citizens were aroused to the need for civic improvement in the 1890s by the crusade of William Rockhill Nelson, the *Kansas City Star* publisher. As a result, today's Kansas City boasts 52 boulevards totaling 155 miles and more fountains than any city except Rome. It's also known around the world for its superb barbecue and its rhythm and blues scene.

Information: Kansas City Convention & Visitors Bureau, 1100 Main St., 816-221-5242, 800-767-7700; www.visitkc.com

MISSOURI

SPOT★LIGHT

★COUNT BASIE AND CHARLIE PARKER LED THE KANSAS CITY JAZZ MOVEMENT.

★THE KANSAS CITY STRIP STEAK, FROM THE STRIP LOIN, IS A PRIME CUT.

★ERNEST HEMINGWAY WROTE FOR THE KANSAS CITY STAR DURING WORLD WAR I.

WHAT TO SEE AND DO

Arabia Steamboat Museum
400 Grand Blvd., Kansas City,
816-471-4030; www.1856.com
Excavated pioneer artifacts from the steamboat *Arabia,* which went down in 1856. The boat, discovered in 1988, carried 200 tons of cargo. Replica of main deck; hands-on displays. Daily.

Art and Design Center
4510 State Line Rd., Kansas City
More than 20 shops and galleries located in an historic area.

City Market
Kansas City, Main to Grand Streets,
Third to Fifth Streets
Outdoor farmers' market since early 1800s. April-September: daily. Indoor farmers' market, year-round, daily.

Country Club Plaza
4745 Central St., Kansas City,
816-753-0100
The nation's first planned shopping center (1922) consists of 55 acres encompassing more than 180 shops and 25 restaurants in and around Spanish/Moorish-style

arcaded buildings. The plaza features tree-lined walks, statues, fountains and murals; re-creations of Spain's Seville light and Giralda tower; horse-drawn carriage rides; free entertainment. Daily.

Crown Center
**2450 Grand, Kansas City,
816-274-8444**
This entertainment complex offers shopping, theaters, restaurants and hotels around a landscaped central square; exhibits and ice skating (mid-November-March). Shops daily.

Kaleidoscope
**2450 Grand Blvd., Kansas City,
816-274-8300;
www.hallmarkkaleidoscope.com**
Participatory creative art exhibit for children ages 5-12. Discovery Room features hands-on creative area. Mid-June-August: Monday-Saturday; rest of year: Saturday or by appointment. Adults may view activity through one-way mirrors. Three 90-minute sessions per day; tickets available half-hour before each session.

Jesse James Bank Museum
103 N. Water St., Liberty, 816-781-4458
Restored site of the first daylight bank robbery by the James gang in 1866. Jesse James memorabilia; hand-scribed bank ledger books and other relics of early banking. Monday-Saturday.

John Wornall House Museum
**6115 Wornall Rd., Kansas City,
816-444-1858**
Restored farmhouse interprets the lives of prosperous Missouri farm families from 1830 to 1865; herb garden. Tuesday-Sunday; closed January.

Kansas City Chiefs (NFL)
**Arrowhead Stadium, One Arrowhead Dr.,
Kansas City,
816-920-9300, 800-676-5488;
www.kcchiefs.com**
Professional football team.

Kansas City Museum
**Union Station, 3218 Gladstone Blvd.,
Kansas City, 816-483-8300;
www.kcmuseum.com**
Science, history and technology exhibits housed in former estate of lumber millionaire Robert A. Long; re-creation of 1821 trading post, 1860 storefront and functioning 1910 drugstore; planetarium; gift shop. Tuesday-Sunday.

Kansas City Royals (MLB)
**Kauffman Stadium, One Royal Way,
Kansas City, 816-921-8000;
www.kcroyals.com**
Professional baseball team.

Kansas City Wizards (MLS)
**Arrowhead Stadium, One Arrowhead Dr.,
Kansas City, 816-920-9300;
www.kcwizards.com**
Professional soccer team.

Kansas City Zoo
**Swope Park, 6800 Zoo Dr.,
Kansas City, 816-513-5700;
www.kansascityzoo.org**
Explore 200 acres landscaped to resemble natural animal habitats. Sea lion and wild bird shows; IMAX theater; miniature train, pony, and camel rides. Daily.

Nelson-Atkins Museum of Art
**4525 Oak St., Kansas City, 816-751-1278;
www.nelson-atkins.org**
Collections range from Sumerian art of 3000 BC to contemporary paintings and sculpture; period rooms; decorative arts; Kansas City Sculpture Park featuring Henry Moore sculpture garden. Tuesday-Sunday.

Union Cemetery
227 E. 28th St., Kansas City
Some notables buried here include artist George Caleb Bingham and Alexander Majors, founder of the Pony Express; graves of more than 1,000 Civil War soldiers.

Westport
**Broadway and Westport Rd.,
Kansas City**

★
★
★
★
☆

Renovated 1830s historic district includes specialty shops, galleries and restaurants; Pioneer Park traces Westport's role in the founding of Kansas City. Daily.

Worlds of Fun
4545 N.E. Worlds of Fun Ave.,
Kansas City, 816-454-4545;
www.worldsoffun.com
A 170-acre entertainment complex with amusement rides, live entertainment, children's area, special events, restaurants; includes looping steel and wooden roller coasters. Late May-August: daily; April and September-October: weekends.

SPECIAL EVENTS
Kansas City Pro Rodeo
Benjamin Ranch, 6401 E. 87th St.,
Kansas City, 816-761-1234
Saddle bronco riding, steer wrestling, bareback riding, barrel racing, calf roping and bull riding are some of the events held at the Benjamin Ranch. Week of July 4.

Kansas City Symphony
1020 Central St., Kansas City,
816-471-0400
Concert series of symphonic and pop music. Friday-Sunday, some Wednesdays.

Lyric Opera
1029 Central St., Kansas City,
816-471-7344
Opera productions in English. Performances on Monday, Wednesday, Friday-Saturday. April-May and mid-September-mid-October; holiday production in December.

Missouri Repertory Theatre
Center for the Performing Arts,
4949 Cherry St., Kansas City,
816-235-2700
Professional equity theater company; classic and contemporary productions. Annual performance of *A Christmas Carol.* September-May: Tuesday-Sunday.

St. Patrick's Day Parade
Pershing and Grand Streets,

Kansas City, 816-931-7373;
www.kcirishparade.com
One of the nation's largest, this St. Patrick's Day parade is approximately one mile long and features a variety of themed floats, bands, and performers. March.

Starlight Theater
Swope Park, 4600 Starlight Rd.,
Kansas City, 816-363-7827
Outdoor amphitheater featuring Broadway musicals and contemporary concerts. Performances nightly. Early June-August.

HOTELS
★Baymont Inn
2214 Taney St., North Kansas City,
816-221-1200, 800-301-0200;
www.baymontinn.com
93 rooms. Complimentary continental breakfast. $

★★Doubletree Hotel
1301 Wyandotte St., Kansas City,
816-474-6664, 800-222-8733;
www.doubletree.com
388 rooms. Pets accepted, some restrictions; fee. Restaurant, bar. Fitness room. Outdoor pool. Business center. $$

★★★Hotel Savoy
219 W. Ninth St., Kansas City,
816-842-3575, 800-728-6922;
www.bandbonline.com
This restored 1888 landmark building features original architectural details such as stained and leaded glass, tile floors and tin ceilings. The Savoy Grille is located on the property and many attractions are nearby.
22 rooms. Complimentary full breakfast. Restaurant, bar. $

★★★Hotel Phillips
106 W. 12th St., Kansas City,
816-221-7000, 800-433-1426;
www.hotelphillips.com
Located downtown, this boutique hotel is a convenient base. While the historic Art Deco integrity of this 1931 landmark has been preserved, modern amenities have been added to the rooms and suites. Phillips

Chophouse has a 1930s feel. Live music can be heard at 12 Baltimore Cafe and Bar. 217 rooms. High-speed Internet access. Two restaurants, two bars. Fitness room. Airport transportation available. Business center. **$$**

★★★Hyatt Regency Crown Center
2345 McGee St., Kansas City,
816-421-1234, 888-591-1234;
www.hyatt.com
Connected to the Crown Center by an elevated walkway and located near the Truman Sports Complex, an amusement park and the international airport, this hotel is convenient and comfortable.
731 rooms. High-speed Internet access, wireless Internet access. Five restaurants, bars. Fitness room. Outdoor pool, whirlpool. Tennis. Airport transportation available. Business center. **$$**

★★★The Raphael Hotel
325 Ward Pkwy., Kansas City,
816-756-3800, 800-695-8284;
www.raphaelkc.com
This hotel is located in the midtown area near shops, restaurants and other attractions.
123 rooms. High-speed Internet access. Restaurant, bar. Airport transportation available. Business center. **$$**

★★★The Raphael Hotel
325 Ward Pkwy., Kansas City,
816-756-3800, 800-695-8284;
www.raphaelkc.com
This hotel is located in the midtown area near shops, restaurants and other attractions.
123 rooms. High-speed Internet access. Restaurant, bar. Airport transportation available. Business center. **$$**

★★★InterContinental Kansas City at the Plaza
401 Ward Pkwy., Kansas City,
816-756-1500, 888-424-6835;
This elegant and contemporary hotel is located within the Plaza shopping and dining area. It has a 24-hour business center and a fitness center with outdoor pool and spa treatments. The Oak Room restaurant serves steaks and chops.
366 rooms. Pets accepted; fee. High-speed Internet access. Restaurant, bar. Fitness room. Outdoor pool, children's pool. Airport transportation available. Business center. **$$**

★★★Marriott Kansas City Airport
775 Brasilia Ave., Kansas City,
816-464-2200, 800-228-9290;
www.marriott.com
Located on the Kansas City International Airport's grounds, this hotel has been updated with luxury bedding and high-speed Internet access.
378 rooms. Restaurant, bar. Fitness room. Indoor pool, whirlpool. Airport transportation available. Business center. **$**

★★★Marriott Kansas City Country Club Plaza
4445 Main St., Kansas City,
816-531-3000, 800-228-9290;
www.marriott.com/mcipl
Situated 10 minutes from downtown, this hotel is within walking distance of the city's top shopping and restaurants. A non-smoking hotel, this location has updated rooms with luxury bedding.
295 rooms. Wireless Internet access. Restaurant, bar. Fitness room. Indoor pool, whirlpool. Airport transportation available. Business center. **$**

★★★Marriott Kansas City Downtown
200 W. 12th St., Kansas City,
816-421-6800, 800-228-9290;
www.marriott.com
This large hotel is located downtown near the city market, casinos and family attractions.
983 rooms. Pets accepted; fee. Wireless Internet access. Two restaurants, two bars. Fitness room (fee). Indoor pool. Airport transportation available. Business center. **$$**

★★Quarterage Hotel
560 Westport Rd., Kansas City,
816-931-0001, 800-942-4233;

www.quarteragehotel.com
123 rooms. Complimentary full breakfast. High-speed Internet access. Airport transportation available. Business center. **$**

★★★The Raphael Hotel
325 Ward Pkwy., Kansas City, 816-756-3800, 800-695-8284; www.raphaelkc.com
This hotel is located in the midtown area near shops, restaurants and other attractions. 123 rooms. High-speed Internet access. Restaurant, bar. Airport transportation available. Business center. **$$**

★★★Sheraton Suites Country Club Plaza
770 W. 47th St., Kansas City, 816-931-4400, 800-325-3535; www.sheraton.com
This is an all-suite hotel offering many facilities, including a restaurant, lounge, indoor and outdoor heated pools, whirlpool and weight room. The hotel is located near sports, cultural and family attractions. 257 rooms, all suites. Pets accepted. High-speed Internet access. Restaurant, bar. Fitness room. Indoor pool, outdoor pool, whirlpool. Airport transportation available. Business center. **$**

★★★The Westin Crown Center
1 Pershing Rd., Kansas City, 816-474-4400, 800-228-3000; www.westin.com/crowncenter
Located in the downtown area within Hallmark's Crown Center, where visitors will find shops, restaurants and theaters, this hotel is also near the Liberty Memorial and the Bartle Convention Center. 729 rooms. Pets accepted, some restrictions. High-speed Internet access. Two restaurants, two bars. Children's activity center. Fitness room (fee). Outdoor pool, whirlpool. Tennis. Airport transportation available. Business center. **$$**

SPECIALTY LODGINGS
Southmoreland On The Plaza
116 E. 46th St., Kansas City, 816-531-7979; www.southmoreland.com

Each room in this quiet bed-and-breakfast is uniquely furnished and decorated. Rooms feature either a fireplace, Jacuzzi tub, or a private deck. The property is located near the Country Club Plaza shopping district and other attractions. 13 rooms. Children over 13 years only. Complimentary full breakfast. Wireless Internet access. **$**

RESTAURANTS
★★★★The American Restaurant
200 E. 25th St., Kansas City, 816-545-8000; www.theamericankc.com
The flagship restaurant of the Crown Center, the American has attracted Kansas City diners for 40 years. With a concept designed by the legendary James Beard, the father of American cooking, and Joe Baum, the restauranteur of the former Windows on the World in New York City, the restaurant is as elegant as ever, with downtown views, polished service, and one of the city's best wine lists. The kitchen staff, led by executive chef Celina Tio, prepares American fare using local seasonal produce. American menu. Lunch, dinner. Closed Sunday. Bar. Children's menu. Business casual attire. Reservations recommended. Valet parking. **$$$**

★★★Andre's Tearoom
5018 Main St., Kansas City, 816-561-3440, 800-892-1234; www.andreschocolates.com
An offshoot of legendary Swiss chocolate maker Andres Bollier's candy shop, this tearoom serves continental favorites such as leek and gruyere pie or vol au vent in a quaint setting. After lunch, stock up on truffles or a linzer torte to take home. Continental menu. Lunch. Closed Sunday-Monday. Business casual attire. **$**

★Arthur Bryant's Barbeque
1727 Brooklyn Ave., Kansas City, 816-231-1123; www.arthurbryantsbbq.com
American menu. Lunch, dinner. Closed holidays. Casual attire. **$**

78

MISSOURI

★Berliner Bear

7815 Wornall Rd., Kansas City,
816-444-2828
German menu. Lunch, dinner. Closed Monday. Bar. Children's menu. Casual attire. **$$**

★★★Bluestem

900 Westport Rd., Kansas City,
816-561-1101; www.bluestemkc.com
Bluestem is the product of two acclaimed chefs, Colby and Megan Garrelts, who worked at such restaurants as Aureole in Las Vegas and Tru in Chicago. The space is divided into a 40-seat restaurant, clad in cobalt blue walls and warm candlelight, and an adjacent wine bar that offers more casual fare. A three-, five- or seven-course prix menu is available, as well as a twelve-course tasting menu. Entrees might include a torchon of foie gras, wild Tasmanian salmon with oxtail or LaBelle duck with sweet potato gnocchi and apple emulsion. Desserts are outstanding, simplistic in their approach but full of intense flavors.
American menu. Dinner, brunch. Bar. Business casual attire. Reservations recommended. **$$$**

★★Bugatti's Little Italy

3200 N. Ameristar Dr., Kansas City,
816-414-7000; www.ameristarcasinos.com
Italian menu. Breakfast, lunch, dinner, brunch. Bar. **$$**

★★Californos

4124 Pennsylvania, Kansas City,
816-531-7878; www.californos.com
American menu. Lunch, dinner. Closed Sunday; holidays. Bar. Casual attire. Reservations recommended. Valet parking. Outdoor seating. **$$**

★★Cascone's Italian Restaurant

3733 N. Oak, Kansas City, 816-454-7977; www.cascones.com
Italian menu. Lunch, dinner. Bar. Children's menu. Casual attire. Reservations recommended. Outdoor seating. **$$**

★★Chappell's

323 Armour Rd., North Kansas City,
816-421-0002;
www.chappellsrestaurant.com
Steak menu. Lunch, dinner. Closed Sunday. Bar. Children's menu. Casual attire. **$$**

★★Classic Cup Café

301 W. 47th St., Kansas City,
816-753-1840; www.classiccup.com
American menu. Breakfast, lunch, dinner, Sunday brunch. Bar. Casual attire. Outdoor seating. **$$**

★★★EBT

1310 Carondelet Dr., Kansas City,
816-942-8870; www.ebtrestaurant.com
Mid-1900s sandstone columns and two ornate brass elevators provide the setting for this restaurant, with dishes such as pistachio-encrusted salmon and pepper steak. Tableside presentations are offered, and there is an extensive wine list.
American menu. Lunch, dinner. Closed Sunday-Monday. Bar. Children's menu. Business casual attire. Reservations recommended. **$$$**

★★Figlio

209 W. 46th Terrace, Kansas City,
816-561-0505; www.dineoutinkc.com
Italian menu. Lunch, dinner, brunch. Bar. Children's menu. Casual attire. Reservations recommended. Valet parking. Outdoor seating. **$$**

★★Fiorella's Jack Stack Barbecue

13441 Holmes St., Kansas City,
816-942-9141, 877-419-7427;
www.jackstackbbq.com
American menu. Lunch, dinner. Bar. Children's menu. Casual attire. Reservations recommended. Outdoor seating. **$$**

★★Garozzo's Ristorante

526 Harrison, Kansas City,
816-221-2455; www.garozzos.com
Italian menu. Lunch, dinner. Bar. Children's menu. Casual attire. Reservations recommended. **$$**

79

MISSOURI

★
★
★
★
★

★★Golden Ox
1600 Genessee St., Kansas City,
816-842-2866; www.goldenox.com
Steak menu. Lunch, dinner. Bar. Children's
menu. Casual attire. $$$

★★★Grand Street Café
4740 Grand St., Kansas City,
816-561-8000; www.eatpbj.com
A stylish and modern botanical theme is found
throughout this dining room. Double cut pork
chops with cinnamon apples and brown sugar
jus, caramelized sea scallops with Maine lob-
ster butter and a crispy potato pancake, and
grilled filet mignon with a veal demi-cabernet
sauce and French green beans are among the
menu items. Brunch is popular. A small, cozy
patio with eight tables offers al fresco dining.
American menu. Lunch, dinner, brunch.
Bar. Children's menu. Business casual
attire. Reservations recommended. Outdoor
seating. $$$

★★Hardware Cafe
5 E. Kansas Ave., Liberty,
816-792-3500
American menu. Breakfast, lunch, dinner.
Closed Sunday. Children's menu. Old-fashioned soda fountain, historical building. No
credit cards accepted. $$

★★Jess & Jim's Steak House
517 E. 135th St., Kansas City,
816-941-9499;
www.jessandjims.com
Steak menu. Lunch, dinner. Bar. Children's
menu. Casual attire. $$$

★★★JJ's
910 W. 48th St., Kansas City,
816-561-7136; www.jjs-restaurant.com
Upscale European fare is served at this
friendly bistro. Entrées spotlight fresh,
local ingredients and might include Kansas
City strip steak with smoked gouda mashed
potoates.
American menu. Lunch, dinner. Bar. Business casual attire. Reservations recom-
mended. Valet parking. $$$

★L.C.'s Bar-B-Q
5800 Blue Park Way, Kansas City,
816-923-4484
American menu. Lunch, dinner. Closed
Sunday. $$

★★★Le Fou Frog
400 E. Fifth St., Kansas City,
816-474-6060; www.lefoufrog.com
This French bistro is a good place to dine
when seeing a show at the convention center. Sauces are light and presentation is
excellent. Portions are big, from the escar-
got to the steak au poivre.
French menu. Lunch, dinner. Closed Monday. Bar. Casual attire. Reservations recommended. Valet parking. Outdoor seat-
ing. $$$

★★★Lidia's Kansas City
101 W. 22nd St., Kansas City,
816-221-3722; www.lidiasitaly.com
Created by the acclaimed New York res-
taurateur Lidia Bastianich, this trendy
restaurant offers a rustic atmosphere, with
rough brick walls and exposed wooden
beams. The menu is classic, with dishes
such as salmon alla griglia.
Italian menu. Lunch, dinner. Bar. Children's
menu. Business casual attire. Reservations
recommended. Outdoor seating. $$

★★★Marina Grog & Galley
22 A St., Lees Summit, 816-578-5511;
www.marinagrogandgalley.com
Take in beautiful lake views from the
elegant dining room.
Seafood menu. Dinner. Bar. Children's
menu. Outdoor seating. $$$

★★Macaluso's on 39th
1403 W. 39th St., Kansas City,
816-561-0100; www.macalusoson39th.com
Italian menu. Dinner. Closed Sunday. Bar.
Casual attire. Reservations recommended.
$$$

★★★O'Dowd's Little Dublin
4742 Pennsylvania Ave., Kansas City,
816-561-2700;
www.odowdslittledublin.com

This authentic Irish pub, with much of its interior built in Ireland then shipped here, serves the best fish and chips in town. Irish menu. Lunch, dinner, late-night. Closed Memorial Day. Bar. Children's menu. Casual attire. Reservations recommended. Outdoor seating. $

★Phoenix Piano Bar & Grill
302 W. Eighth St., Kansas City, 816-472-0001; www.phoenixjazz.net
American menu. Lunch, dinner, late-night. Closed Sunday. Piano bar; pictures of famous jazz musicians. Casual attire. Outdoor seating. $$

★★★Plaza III Steakhouse
4749 Pennsylvania Ave., Kansas City, 816-753-0000; www.plazaiiisteakhouse.com
The epitome of the Kansas City steakhouse, this restaurant serves USDA prime aged cuts of Midwestern beef, chops, fresh fish, and lobster. Lunch includes the famous steak soup.
Steak menu. Lunch, dinner. Bar. Children's menu. Business casual attire. Reservations recommended. Valet parking. $$$

★★★Raphael Dining Room
325 Ward Pkwy., Kansas City, 816-756-3800, 800-821-5343; www.raphaelkc.com
Housed in the Raphael Hotel, this restaurant has an elegant dining room and refined service. The Kansas City strip steak with port wine sauce and melted gorgonzola is a menu standout.

International menu. Breakfast, lunch, dinner. Bar. Business casual attire. Reservations recommended. Valet parking. $$$

★★Shiraz
320 Southwest Blvd., Kansas City, 816-472-0015; www.shirazkc.com
Mediterranean menu. Lunch, dinner. Closed Sunday. Bar. Casual attire. Reservations recommended. Valet parking. Outdoor seating. $$

★Smuggler's Inn
1650 Universal Plaza Dr., Kansas City, 816-483-0400
American menu. Lunch, dinner. Bar. $$

★★Stephenson's Apple Farm
16401 E. Hwy. 40, Kansas City, 816-373-5405; www.stephensons.bigstep.com
American menu. Lunch, dinner. Bar. Children's menu. Casual attire. Reservations recommended. Outdoor seating. $$

★★★The Majestic Steakhouse
931 Broadway, Kansas City, 816-471-8484; www.majesticgroup.com
The historic Fitzpatrick Saloon building in downtown Kansas City is home to one of the best, most entertaining steakhouses in town. It's also a great place to indulge in a cigar. The restaurant features turn-of-the-century decor with stained-glass windows, ceiling fans and an ornate tin ceiling.
Steak menu. Lunch, dinner. Bar. Business casual attire. Reservations recommended. $$$

★
★
★
★
★

LAKE OZARK
This resort community rests on the huge, man-made reservoir Lake of the Ozarks. In summer the area is packed with tourists who come to boat and float on the lake or stay in its many resorts.
www.funlake.comi

WHAT TO SEE AND DO
Jacob's Cave
23114 Hwy. TT, Versailles, 573-378-4374; www.jacobscave.com

Famous for its depth illusion, reflective pools, prehistoric bones and the world's largest geode. Daily; closed holidays.

Lake of the Ozarks
Hwy. 54, Lake Ozark, www.funlake.com
Completed in 1931, the 2,543-foot-long Bagnell Dam impounds the Osage River to form this 54,000-acre recreational lake, which has an irregular 1,150-mile shoreline. Fishing, boating and swimming are excellent here.

Lake of the Ozarks State Park
403 Hwy. 134, Kaiser, 573-348-2694
This more than 17,000-acre park, the largest in the state, has 89 miles of shoreline with two public swimming and boat launching areas. On the grounds is a large cave with streams of water that continuously pour from stalactites.

HOTELS
★★★The Lodge of Four Seasons
Horseshoe Bend Pkwy., Lake Ozark, 573-365-3000, 800-843-5253; www.4seasonsresort.com
Located in the Ozark Hills, the property overlooks the winding shoreline. Many of the rooms and two- and three-bedroom condominiums have views of the lake or Japanese garden and pool. A golf course and health spa are on the premises.
350 rooms. Restaurant, bar. Children's activity center. Fitness room, spa. Outdoor pool, children's pool, whirlpool. Golf. Airport transportation available. $$

RESTAURANTS
★★Bentley's
Hwy. 54 Business, Lake Ozark, 573-365-5301
Seafood, steak menu. Dinner. Closed Sunday; holidays. Bar. Children's menu. $$

★★J.B. Hook's Great Ocean Fish & Steaks
2260 Bagnell Dam Blvd., Lake Ozark, 573-365-3255; www.jbhooks.com
Seafood, Steak menu. Lunch, dinner. Bar. Outdoor seating (lunch only). $$

LEBANON
Lebanon was founded in the mid-1800s beside an Indian trail that today is Interstate 44. As the seat of the newly-created Laclede County, the town was originally called Wyota. The name was changed when a respected minister asked that it be renamed after his hometown of Lebanon, Tennessee.
Information: Lebanon Area Chamber of Commerce, 500 E. Elm St., 417-588-3256; www.lebanonmissouri.com

WHAT TO SEE AND DO
Bennett Spring State Park
26250 Hwy. 64A, Lebanon, 417-532-4338
Nearly 3,100 acres. Swimming pool, trout fishing (March-October); picnicking, store, dining lodge, camping, cabins. Nature center. Daily.

SPECIAL EVENTS
Hillbilly Days
Bennett Springs State Park, Lebanon, 417-588-3256
Arts and crafts, contests, country music, antique cars. Father's Day weekend.

HOTELS
★★Best Western Wyota Inn
1225 Millcreek Rd., Lebanon, 417-532-6171, 800-780-7234; www.bestwestern.com
52 rooms. Pets accepted, some restrictions; fee. Complimentary continental breakfast. Restaurant. Outdoor pool. $

LEXINGTON

This historic city with more than 110 antebellum houses was founded by settlers from Lexington, Kentucky. The site of a three-day battle during the Civil War, many of the Union Army's entrenchments are still visible today. Situated on bluffs overlooking the Missouri River, Lexington was an important river port during the 19th century. Today the area is one of the state's largest producers of apples.

Information: Tourism Bureau, 817 Main St., 660-259-4711; www.historiclexington.com

WHAT TO SEE AND DO

Battle of Lexington State Historic Site
Extension Hwy. N., Lexington,
660-259-4654
The site of one of the Civil War's largest western campaign battles (September 18-20, 1861). Anderson House, which stood in the center of the battle and changed hands from North to South three times, has been restored. Daily.

Lafayette County Courthouse
1001 Main St., Lexington, 660-259-4315
Built in 1847, this is the oldest courthouse in constant use west of the Mississippi. It has a Civil War cannonball embedded in the east column. Monday-Friday.

Lexington Historical Museum
112 S. 13th St., Lexington, 660-259-6313
Built as a Presbyterian church in 1846, this structure contains Pony Express and Battle of Lexington relics, photographs and other historical Lexington items. Mid-April-mid-October: daily.

Log House Museum
817 Main St., Lexington, 660-259-4711
Exhibits include candle making, quilting, hearth cooking. Wednesday-Sunday; also by appointment.

RESTAURANT

★Long Branch
28855 Sunset Dr., Macon,
660-385-4600
Lunch, dinner. Bar. Children's menu. $$

NEVADA

Settled by families from Kentucky and Tennessee, Nevada became known as the "bushwhackers capital" due to the Confederate guerrillas headquartered here during the Civil War. The town was burned to the ground in 1863 by Union troops and was not rebuilt until after the war. Today Nevada is a shopping and trading center for the surrounding area.

Information: Nevada-Vernon Chamber of Commerce, 201 E. Cherry, 417-667-5300, 800-910-4276; www.nevada-mo.com

WHAT TO SEE AND DO

Bushwhacker Museum
231 N. Main St., Nevada, 417-667-5841
The museum, operated by the Vernon County Historical Society, includes a restored 19th-century jail as well as Civil War relics, period clothing and tools. May-September: daily; October: weekends.

SPECIAL EVENTS

Bushwhacker Days
231 N. Main St., Nevada, 417-667-5300

Parade; arts and crafts, antique machine and car shows; street square dance, midway. Mid-June.

HOTELS

★Days Inn
2345 E. Marvel Rd., Nevada,
417-667-6777, 800-329-7466;
www.daysinn.com
46 rooms. Pets accepted; fee. Complimentary continental breakfast. Outdoor pool, whirlpool. $

MISSOURI

MISSOUREE OR MISSOURAH?

As in many states, you might need to check with a local to learn how to pronounce the name of the town in which you're standing. New Madrid is "New MAD-drid," Versailles is "Ver-SAILS." But while town names usually have an undisputed, if vexing (Iowa's Des Moines is "duh-MOYN") right way to say them, it won't do you much good to ask someone how to say "Missouri." On TV, East Coast anchorman and pundits seem to grapple with a foreign language as they strain to utter the state's name in the "authentic" way: "Miz-zur-uh" (as opposed to Miz-zur-ee). But is it? Even though in any Missouri political race, there are always candidates who try to establish their native's credentials and just-folks image with the "-uh" ending, if you ask someone who lives in the state the right way to say it, the answer is far from clear. Some say the "-uh" locution reigns in the south of the state, but you will find plenty of natives there who go with "-ee." Others say it's a western thing, but there are lots of self-declared "Missouree" natives in Kansas City. The consensus seems to be, especially around St. Louis, that while the "-uh" has a lot of adherents among older generations in rural areas, you won't stand out like a lost tourist if you go with "Missouree," the most common pronunciation. Just don't push it by saying, "Show me."

84

MISSOURI

★
★
★
★
★

OSAGE BEACH

A major resort community on the Lake of the Ozarks, the town came into existence with the 1931 completion of the lake.
Information: Lake Area Chamber of Commerce, 1 Willmore Lane, Lake Ozark, 573-964-1008, 800-451-4117; www.lakeareachamber.com

SPECIAL EVENTS

Lee Mace's Ozark Opry
Hwy. 54, Osage Beach, 573-348-3383
This musical variety show is performed Monday-Saturday evenings. Late April-mid-October.

HOTELS

★★Best Western Dogwood Hills Resort Inn
1252 Hwy. KK, Osage Beach,
573-348-1735, 800-780-7234;
www.dogwoodhillsresort.com
47 rooms. Pets accepted; fee. Restaurant (March-October), bar. Outdoor pool, whirlpool. Golf. **$**

★★Inn At Grand Glaize
5142 Hwy. 54, Osage Beach,
573-348-4731, 800-348-4731
www.innatgrandglaize.com
151 rooms. Restaurant, bar. Fitness room. Outdoor pool, children's pool, whirlpool. **$**

★★★Tan-Tar-A Resort
Hwy. KK, Osage Beach, 573-348-3131;
www.tan-tar-a.com
This property is on the scenic Lake of the Ozarks and offers more than 30 recreational activities, including indoor and outdoor pools, water skiing, a full spa, jogging, golf and more. The hotel is near many area restaurants and attractions.

365 rooms. Restaurant, bar. Children's activity center. Fitness room. One indoor pool, four outdoor pools, two children's pools, whirlpool. Golf. Tennis. **$**

RESTAURANTS

★★Domenico's Carry-Out Pizza
4737 Hwy. 54, Osage Beach,
573-348-2844
Italian, American menu. Dinner. Closed holidays. Bar. Children's menu. **$$**

★★Happy Fisherman
4676 Hwy. 54, Osage Beach,
573-348-3311
American menu. Dinner. Closed mid-December-January. Bar. Children's menu. **$$**

★★Potted Steer
5085 Hwy. 54, Osage Beach,
573-348-5053
Dinner. Closed Sunday-Monday. Bar. **$$**

★★The Brass Door
5167 Hwy. 54, Osage Beach,
573-348-9229; www.the-brass-door.com
Steak menu. Dinner. Children's menu. **$$$**

★★Vista Grande
4579 Hwy. 54, Osage Beach,
573-348-1231
American, Mexican menu. Lunch, dinner. Bar. Children's menu. **$$**

PILOT KNOB

This village of less than 700 people was the site of the Civil War Battle of Pilot Knob. Union and Confederate forces clashed over control of nearby Fort Davidson in 1864.

WHAT TO SEE AND DO

Johnson's Shut-Ins State Park
Hwy. N., Middle Brook, 573-546-2450
This nearly 8,500-acre area, left in its wilderness state, has a spectacular canyonlike defile along the river. The park is at the southern end of the 20-mile-long Ozark backpacking trail, which traverses Missouri's highest mountain, Taum Sauk. Swimming, fishing, hiking, picnicking, playground, improved camping. Daily.

HOTELS

★★Wilderness Lodge
Peola Rd., Lesterville,
573-637-2295, 888-969-9129;
www.wildernesslodgeresort.com
27 rooms. Restaurant (public by reservation), bar. Outdoor pool. Business center.**$**

85

MISSOURI

ROLLA

According to legend, this town was named by a homesick settler from Raleigh, North Carolina, who spelled the name as he pronounced it. Called "the child of the railroad" because it began with the building of the St. Louis-San Francisco Railroad, the town is located in a scenic area with several streams nearby. Mark Twain National Forest maintains its headquarters in Rolla.
Information: Rolla Area Chamber of Commerce, 1301 Kings Hwy., 573-364-3577, 888-809-3817; www.rollachamber.org

WHAT TO SEE AND DO

Maramec Spring Park and Remains of Old Ironworks
21880 Maramec Spring Dr., Rolla,
573-265-7387
The spring discharges an average of 96 million gallons per day. The ironworks was first established in 1826; the present furnace was built in 1857. Nature center; observation tower; two museums. Daily.

Mark Twain National Forests
401 Fairgrounds Rd., Rolla, 573-364-4621
More than 192,000 acres; cradles the head-waters of the Gasconade, Little Piney and Big Piney rivers. Paddy Creek Wilderness Area covers about 6,800 acres with 30 miles of hiking and riding trails.

St. James Winery
540 Sidney St., 573-265-7912
Dry and semi-dry wines, sparkling wines, concord, catawba and berry wines are all produced here. Daily.

HOTELS
★Best Western Coachlight
1403 Martin Springs Rd., Rolla, 573-341-2511, 800-780-7234; www.bestwestern.com
88 rooms. Pets accepted, some restrictions. Complimentary continental breakfast. $

★Drury Inn
2006 N. Bishop Ave., Rolla, 573-364-4000, 800-378-7964; www.druryhotels.com
86 rooms. Pets accepted, some restrictions. Complimentary continental breakfast. Outdoor pool. $

★★Zeno's Motel and Steak House
1621 Martin Springs Dr., Rolla, 573-364-1301; www.zenos, biz.
51 rooms. Restaurant, bar. Indoor pool, outdoor pool, whirlpool. $

RESTAURANTS
★Johnny's Smoke Stak
201 Hwy. 72, Rolla, 573-364-4838
American menu. Lunch, dinner. Children's menu. $

SEDALIA

Known as the "queen city of the prairies," Sedalia was a prosperous railhead town in the 1800s with great cattle herds arriving for shipment to eastern markets. During the Civil War, the settlement functioned as a military post. A monument at Lamine and Main Streets marks the site of the Maple Leaf Club, one of the city's many saloons that catered to railroad men. The monument is dedicated to Scott Joplin, who composed and performed the "Maple Leaf Rag" here, triggering the ragtime craze at the turn of the 20th century. Whiteman Air Force Base is 21 miles west of Sedalia.
Information: Chamber of Commerce, 600 E. Third St., 660-826-2222, 800-827-5295; www.sedaliachamber.com

WHAT TO SEE AND DO
Bothwell Lodge State Historic Site
19350 Bothwell State Park, Sedalia, 660-827-0510
An Arts and Crafts house built between 1897 and 1928 for a local businessman, the lodge is open for tours. The park includes approximately 180 acres, with hiking trails and picnic areas. Daily.

Pettis County Courthouse
415 S. Ohio, Sedalia, 660-826-4892
Historic courthouse contains local artifacts and exhibits. Monday-Friday.

Sedalia Ragtime Archives
State Fair Community College Library, Maple Leaf Room, 3201 W. 16th St., Sedalia, 660-530-5800
Includes original sheet music, piano rolls, tapes of interviews with Eubie Blake. Monday-Friday; closed school holidays.

SPECIAL EVENTS
Missouri State Fair
2503 W. 16th St., Sedalia, 660-530-5600
One of the country's leading state fairs, this event has been held here since 1901. Stage shows, rodeo, competitive exhibits, livestock, auto races. August.

MISSOURI

Scott Joplin Ragtime Festival
Sedalia, 660-826-2271
Entertainment by ragtime greats. Early June.

HOTEL
★★Best Western State Fair Motor Inn
3120 S. Limit Ave., Sedalia,
660-826-6100, 800-780-7234;
www.bestwestern.com
117 rooms. Pets accepted, some restrictions. Restaurant, bar. Fitness room. Indoor pool, children's pool, whirlpool. Airport transportation available. **$**

SIKESTON
Although settlers were in this region before the Louisiana Purchase, John Sikes established the town of Sikeston in 1860 on El Camino Real, the overland route from St. Louis to New Orleans, at the terminus of the Cairo and Fulton Railway (now the Union Pacific).
Information: Sikeston-Miner Convention and Visitors Bureau, 1 Industrial Dr., 888-309-6591; www.sikeston.net

SPECIAL EVENTS
Bootheel Rodeo
Rodeo Grounds, Sikeston, 800-455-2855
Country music and rodeo events; parade. First full week in August.

HOTELS
★★Best Western Coach House Inn
220 S. Interstate Dr., Sikeston,
573-471-9700, 877-471-9700;
www.bestwestern.com
63 rooms. Pets accepted, some restrictions; fee. Restaurant, bar. Outdoor pool. **$**

★Drury Inn
2602 E. Malone Ave., Sikeston,
573-471-4100, 800-378-7946;
www.druryhotels.com

80 rooms. Pets accepted, some restrictions. Complimentary continental breakfast. Indoor pool, outdoor pool, whirlpool. **$**

RESTAURANTS
★Fisherman's Net
915 S. Kings Hwy., Sikeston,
573-471-8102; www.fishermansnet.net
Seafood menu. Lunch, dinner. Closed Sunday-Monday. Children's menu. **$**

★Lambert's
2305 E. Malone, Sikeston,
573-471-4261; www.throwedrolls.com
American menu. Lunch, dinner. Children's menu. No credit cards accepted. **$$**

SPRINGFIELD
In the southwest corner of the state and at the northern edge of the Ozark highlands, Springfield, known as Ozark Mountain Country's Big City, is near some of Missouri's most picturesque areas. A few settlers came here as early as 1821, but settlement was temporarily discouraged when the government made southwestern Missouri a reservation. Later, the tribes were moved west and the town developed. Its strategic location made it a military objective in the Civil War. Confederates took the town in the Battle of Wilson's Creek, August 10, 1861; Union forces recaptured it in 1862. "Wild Bill" Hickok, later one of the famous frontier marshals, was a scout and spy for Union forces headquartered in Springfield. Perhpas the city's most famous native son is actor Brad Pitt, who grew up here and later attended the University of Missouri in Columbia.
Information: Convention and Visitors Bureau, 3315 E. Battlefield Rd., 417-881-5300, 800-678-8767; www.springfieldmo.org

WHAT TO SEE AND DO

Bass Pro Shops Outdoor World Showroom and Fish and Wildlife Museum

1935 S. Campbell Ave., Springfield, 417-887-7334; www.outdoor-world.com

This 300,000-square-foot sporting goods store features a four-story waterfall, indoor boat and RV showroom, art gallery and indoor firing range. The restaurant has a 30,000-gallon saltwater aquarium. Daily.

Springfield

Dickerson Park Zoo

3043 N. Fort, Springfield, 417-864-1800; www.dickersonparkzoo.org

Animals are housed at this zoo in naturalistic settings. Features an elephant herd; train rides. Daily.

Discovery Center

438 St. Louis St., Springfield, 417-862-9910; www.discoverycenter.org

This interactive hands-on museum includes its "Discovery Town Theatre" where kids can be a star on stage, create a newspaper, run a make-believe TV station, or dig for dinosaur bones. Tuesday-Sunday.

★ Laura Ingalls Wilder-Rose Wilder Lane Museum and Home

3068 Highway A, Mansfield, 417-924-3626

The house where Laura Ingalls Wilder wrote the Little House books houses artifacts and memorabilia of the author, her husband Almanzo and daughter Rose Wilder Lane. Included are four handwritten manuscripts and many items mentioned in Wilder's books, including Pa's fiddle. March-mid-November: daily.

HOTELS

★ Best Western Deerfield Inn

3343 E. Battlefield St., Springfield, 417-887-2323, 877-822-6560; www.bestwestern.com

103 rooms. Complimentary continental breakfast. Indoor pool. **$**

★ Best Western Route 66 Rail Haven

203 S. Glenstone Ave., Springfield, 417-866-1963, 800-780-7234; www.bestwestern.com

93 rooms. Pets accepted, some restrictions. Complimentary continental breakfast. Outdoor pool, whirlpool. **$**

★★ Clarion Hotel

3333 S. Glenstone Ave., Springfield, 417-883-6550, 800-756-7318; www.clarionhotel.com

199 rooms. Pets accepted; fee. Restaurant, bar. Outdoor pool. **$**

★ Hampton Inn

222 N. Ingram Mill Rd., Springfield, 417-863-1440, 800-426-7866; www.hamptoninn.com

99 rooms. Complimentary continental breakfast. Fitness room. Outdoor pool, whirlpool. **$**

★★★ Sheraton Hawthorn Park Hotel

2431 N. Glenstone Ave., Springfield, 417-831-3131, 800-223-0092; www.sheraton.com

201 rooms. Restaurant, bar. Fitness room. Indoor pool, outdoor pool, whirlpool. Airport transportation available. **$**

SPECIALTY LODGINGS
The Mansion At Elfindale
1701 S. Fort, Springfield,
417-831-5400, 800-443-0237;
www.mansionatelfindale.com
This inn is housed in a mansion constructed in 1890.
13 rooms. Children over 11 years only. Complimentary full breakfast. **$**

Walnut Street Inn
900 E. Walnut St., Springfield,
417-864-6346, 800-593-6346;
www.walnutstreetinn.com
This bed and breakfast is located in a Queen Anne-style Victorian house built in 1894.
14 rooms. Complimentary full breakfast. **$**

RESTAURANTS
★★Gee's East Wind
2951 E. Sunshine, Springfield,
417-883-4567;
www.blueheronpottedsteer.com
Chinese, American menu. Lunch, dinner. Closed Sunday; last week in June, first week in July. Bar. Children's menu. **$$**

★J. Parriono's Pasta House
1550 E. Battlefield, Springfield,
417-882-1808
Italian menu. Lunch, dinner. Bar. Children's menu. **$$**

★★★Le Mirabelle
2620 S. Glenstone Ave., Springfield,
417-883-2550
Tucked away at the end of a shopping center, the candlelit, flower-filled dining room of this classic French restaurant is a pleasant surprise. Open since 1976, its extensive menu has featured nearly 30 entrees including roast duckling and Dover sole.
French menu. Dinner. Closed Sunday. Bar. **$$**

ST. CHARLES
St. Charles, one of the early settlements on the Missouri River, was the first capital of the state from 1821 to 1826. Between 1832 and 1870, a wave of German immigrants settled here and developed the town, but St. Louis, by virtue of its location on the Mississippi, became the state's most important city. Frenchtown, a northern ward of old St. Charles, is home to many antiques shops.
Information: Convention and Visitors Bureau, 230 S. Main, 636-946-7776, 800-366-2427; www.historicstcharles.com

WHAT TO SEE AND DO
Katy Trail State Park
St. Charles, 660-882-8196, 800-334-6946;
www.mostateparks.com/katytrail
A 236-mile bicycling and hiking trail across Missouri, this is among the longest of its kind in the United States.

First Missouri State Capitol State Historic Site
200-216 S. Main St., St. Charles,
636-940-3322
Eleven rooms of the capitol have been restored to their original state; nine rooms have 1820 period furnishings; also restoration of the Peck Brothers General Store and house. Daily.

Lewis and Clark Center
701 Riverside, St. Charles, 636-947-3199
Museum depicts the 1804-1806 expedition from St. Charles to the Pacific Ocean. Hands-on exhibits, life-size models of Sacagawea and the men of the expedition; Mandan and Sioux villages. Daily.

SPECIAL EVENTS
Lewis and Clark Heritage Days
Frontier Park, Riverside Dr., St. Charles,
800-366-2427

Reenactment of the explorers' encampment in 1804 prior to embarking on their exploration of the Louisiana Purchase; parade, fife and drum corps. Mid-May.

HOTELS

★★Holiday Inn
4341 Veteran's Memorial Pkwy., St. Peters, 636-928-1500, 800-767-3837; www.holiday-inn.com

195 rooms. Pets accepted; fee. Restaurant, bar. Fitness room. Indoor pool, outdoor pool, whirlpool. Business center. **$**

RESTAURANTS

★★St. Charles Vintage House
1219 S. Main St., St. Charles, 636-946-7155
American, German, seafood menu. Dinner. Closed Monday. Bar. Children's menu. Outdoor seating. Former winery (1860). **$$**

ST. JOSEPH

A historic city with beautiful parks, St. Joseph retains traces of the frontier settlement of the 1840s in its "original town" near the Missouri River. It was founded and named by Joseph Robidoux III, a French fur trader from St. Louis, who established his post in 1826. St. Joseph, the western terminus of the first railroad to cross the state, became the eastern terminus of the Pony Express, whose riders carried mail to and from Sacramento, California, from 1860 to 1861 using relays of fast ponies. The record trip, which carried copies of President Lincoln's inaugural address, was made in seven days and 17 hours. The telegraph ended the need for the Pony Express.

Information: Convention and Visitors Bureau, 109 S. Fourth St., 816-233-6688, 800-785-0360; www.stjomo.com

WHAT TO SEE AND DO

Albrecht-Kemper Museum of Art
2818 Frederick Blvd., St. Joseph, 816-233-7003
Exhibits of 18th-, 19th- and 20th-century American paintings, sculpture, graphic art. Formal gardens. Tuesday-Sunday.

Glore Psychiatric Museum
3406 Frederick Ave., St. Joseph
Housed in a ward of the original 1874 administration building, the museum displays the evolution of treatment philoso-

phy and techniques over a 400-year period. Daily.

Jesse James Home
1202 Penn St., St. Joseph, 816-232-8206
This is the one-story frame cottage where the outlaw had been living quietly as "Mr. Howard" until he was killed here on, April 3, 1882, by an associate, Robert Ford. Some original furnishings. Daily.

Patee House Museum
1202 Penn St., St. Joseph, 816-232-8206

★
★
★
★
★

Built in 1858 as a hotel, this building once served as headquarters of the Pony Express. Contains pioneer exhibits related to transportation and communication and includes restored 1860 Buffalo Saloon, wood-burning engine and the original last mail car from the Hannibal and St. Joseph railroad. April-October: daily; January-March and November: weekends.

Pony Express Museum
914 Penn St., St. Joseph,
816-279-5059, 800-530-5930
This museum is located in the old Pikes Peak (Pony Express) Stables, the starting point of the service's first westward ride. Original stables; displays illustrate the creation, operation, management and termination of the famed mail service. Daily.

Pony Express Region Tourist Information Centers
502 N. Woodvine Rd., St. Joseph,
816-232-1839
Housed in historic railroad cabooses, centers provide brochures and information on St. Joseph, northwest Missouri and northeast Kansas; free maps. Daily.

Robidoux Row Museum
3rd and Poulin streets, St. Joseph,
816-232-5861
Built by the city's founder, French fur trader Joseph Robidoux, as temporary housing for newly arrived settlers who had purchased land from him. Authentically restored; some original furnishings. Tours. Tuesday-Sunday.

HOTELS

★Days Inn
4312 Frederick Blvd., St. Joseph,
816-279-1671, 800-329-7466;
www.daysinn.com
100 rooms. Complimentary continental breakfast. Bar. Outdoor pool. $

★Drury Inn
4213 Frederick Blvd., St. Joseph,
816-364-4700; www.druryhotels.com
133 rooms. Pets accepted. Complimentary continental breakfast. Fitness room. Indoor pool. $

★★Holiday Inn
102 S. Third St., St. Joseph,
816-279-8000, 800-824-7402;
www.holiday-inn.com
170 rooms. Pets accepted. Restaurant, bar. Fitness room. Indoor pool, whirlpool. $

RESTAURANTS

★★36th Street Food & Drink Company
501 N. Belt Hwy., St. Joseph,
816-364-1564
American, Italian menu. Lunch, dinner. Closed Sunday. Bar. $$

★Barbosa's Castillo
906 Sylvanie St., St. Joseph,
816-233-4970
Mexican menu. Lunch, dinner. Closed Sunday. Bar. Children's menu. Valet parking. $$

91

MISSOURI

ST. LOUIS

One of the oldest settlements in the Mississippi Valley, St. Louis was founded by Pierre Laclede as a fur trading post and was named for Louis IX of France. Early French settlers, a large German immigration in the mid-1800s and a happy mix of other national strains contribute to the city's cosmopolitan flavor. In 1804, it was the scene of the transfer of Louisiana to the United States, which opened the way to westward expansion. During the Civil War, though divided in sympathy, the city was a base of Union operations. In 1904, the Louisiana Purchase

Exposition, known as the St. Louis World's Fair, brought international fame to the city.

For more than 200 years, St. Louis has been the dominant city in the state. It's the home of St. Louis University, the University of Missouri-St. Louis and Washington University. After the steamboat era, St. Louis grew westward away from the riverfront, which deteriorated into slums. This original center of the city has now been developed as the Jefferson National Expansion Memorial. Recent redevelopment of downtown and the riverfront is revitalizing the city. Busch Stadium brings St. Louis Cardinals fans into the downtown area and the rehabilitated Union Station offers visitors a vast shopping experience within a restored turn-of-the-century railroad station that was one of the nation's most magnificent. Information: Convention and Visitors Commission, 1 Metropolitan Square, 314-421-1023, 800-325-7962; www.explorestlouis.com

92

MISSOURI

SPOT★LIGHT

★AT 630 FEET, THE GATEWAY ARCH IS THE WORLD'S TALLEST MONUMENT.

★MUSICIANS CHUCK BERRY AND SHERYL CROW ARE FROM ST. LOUIS.

★ST. LOUIS WAS THE FIRST AMERICAN CITY TO HOST THE OLYMPICS IN 1904.

WHAT TO SEE AND DO

Anheuser-Busch Brewery
12th and Lynch Streets, St. Louis, 314-577-2333; www.budweisertours.com
Trace the making of Budweiser beer from farm fields to finished product in a tour of the nation's largest brewery. Inside the 150-year-old plant, you'll also experience a historic brewhouse, beechwood aging cellars, a packing facility and Clydesdale stables. Adults can sample Bud products. Daily.

Butterfly House and Education Center
Faust Park, 15193 Olive Blvd., Chesterfield, 636-530-0076; www.butterflyhouse.org
Three-story crystal palace conservatory with more than 2,000 butterflies in free flight. Educational programs, films, miracle of metamorphosis display. Memorial Day-Labor Day: daily; rest of year: Tuesday-Sunday.

Campbell House Museum
1508 Locust St., St. Louis, 314-421-0325

Mansion with original 1840-1880 furnishings. March-December: Wednesday-Sunday.

Cathedral of St. Louis
4431 Lindell Blvd., St. Louis,
314-373-8243
The city's cathedral, built in 1907, is a fine example of Romanesque architecture with Byzantine details. The interior mosaic work is among the most extensive in the world.

Christ Church Cathedral
1210 Locust St., St. Louis, 314-231-3454
This was the first Episcopal parish west of the Mississippi River, founded in 1819. English Gothic sandstone building; altar carved in England from stone taken from a quarry in Caen, France; Tiffany windows on north wall. Occasional concerts. Sunday-Friday. Tours by appointment.

Climatron
4344 Shaw Blvd., St. Louis, 314-577-5141
Seventy-foot high, prize-winning geodesic dome—first of its kind to be used as a conservatory—houses a two-level, half-acre tropical rain forest with canopies, rocky outcrops, waterfalls and mature tree collection; exhibits explain the many facets of a rain forest. Entrance to Climatron through series of sacred lotus and lily pools.

Delta Queen and Mississippi Queen
St. Louis, 800-543-1949;
www.deltaqueen.com
Paddlewheelers offer three- to eight-night cruises on the Ohio, Cumberland, Mississippi and Tennessee rivers.

Eads Bridge
St. Louis Riverfront area
Designed in 1874 by engineer James B. Eads, the Eads was the first bridge to span the wide southern section of the Mississippi and the first bridge in which steel and the cantilever were used extensively. The approach ramps are carried on enormous Romanesque stone arches.

Eugene Field House and Toy Museum
634 S. Broadway, St. Louis,

314-421-4689
This was the birthplace of the famous children's poet. The museum includes mementos, manuscripts and many original furnishings plus antique toys and dolls. Wednesday-Saturday, Sunday afternoons.

Gateway Arch
The Gateway Arch Riverfront, St. Louis,
877-982-1410; www.gatewayarch.com
Eero Saarinen's Gateway Arch is a 630-foot stainless steel arch that symbolizes the starting point of the westward expansion of the United States. Visitor center includes capsule transporter to observation deck. There is often a wait for observation deck capsules. Memorial Day-Labor Day: daily 8 a.m-10 p.m.; rest of year: daily 9 a.m-6 p.m.

Grant's Farm
10501 Gravois Rd., St. Louis,
314-843-1700; www.grantsfarm.com
This 281-acre wooded tract contains a log cabin (1856) and land once owned by Ulysses S. Grant. Anheuser-Busch Clydesdale barn; carriage house with horse-drawn vehicles, trophy room; deer park where deer, buffalo, longhorn steer and other animals roam freely in their atural habitat. May-September: Tuesday-Sunday; mid-April-May and September-mid-October: Wednesday-Sunday.

International Bowling Museum and Hall of Fame
111 Stadium Plaza, St. Louis,
314-231-6340; www.bowlingmuseum.com
View wacky bowling shirts and the sublime Hall of Fame, or bowl a few frames. The museum shares the building with the St. Louis Cardinals Museum, which boasts an outstanding collection of Redbirds memorabilia. April-September: daily 11 a.m-5 p.m.; October-March: Tuesday-Saturday 11 a.m-4 p.m..

Japanese Garden
4344 Shaw Blvd., St. Louis; 800-642-8842
Largest traditional Japanese garden in North America, with lake landscaped with many

MISSOURI

varieties of water irises, waterfalls, bridges and a teahouse.

Jefferson Barracks Historical Park
533 Grant Rd., St. Louis, 314-544-5714
This army post was established in 1826, and used through 1946. St. Louis County now maintains 424 acres of the original tract. Restored buildings include a stable (1851), a laborer's house (1851), two powder magazines (1851 and 1857), ordnance room, and visitor center. Picnicking. Buildings Wednesday-Sunday.

Jefferson National Expansion Memorial
11 N. Fourth St., St. Louis, 314-655-1700; www.nps.gov/jeff
The Jefferson National Expansion Memorial, located along the Mississippi River, pays tribute to Thomas Jefferson and his influence on freedom and democracy.

Old Courthouse
11 N. Fourth St., St. Louis, 314-655-1600
Begun in 1837 and completed in 1862, this building houses five museum galleries on St. Louis history, including various displays, dioramas and films. The first two trials of the Dred Scott case were held in this building. Guided tour. Daily.

Laclede's Landing
720 N. Second St., St. Louis, 314-241-1155
Early St. Louis commercial district (mid-1800s) includes a nine-block area of renovated pre-Civil War and Victorian buildings that house specialty shops, restaurants and nightclubs.

Missouri Botanical Garden
4344 Shaw Blvd., St. Louis, 314-577-5141, 800-642-8842; www.mobot.org
This 79-acre park includes rose, woodland, and herb gardens; scented garden for the blind; electric tram rides. Sections of the botanical garden are more than a century old. Daily.

Missouri History Museum-Missouri Historical Society
5700 Lindel Blvd., St. Louis, 314-746-4599; www.mohistory.org
Exhibits on St. Louis and the American West; artwork, costumes and decorative arts; toys, firearms; 19th-century fire-fighting equipment; St. Louis history slide show; ragtime-rock 'n' roll music exhibit; 1904 World's Fair and Charles A. Lindbergh collections. Daily.

Museum of Transportation
3015 Barrett Station Rd., Kirkwood, 314-965-7998; www.museumoftransport.org
One of the more interesting collections anywhere in the country, the Museum of Transportation houses an extensive collection of passenger and freight train equipment (ranging from elevated cars from Chicago to the last steam locomotive to operate in Missouri), as well as the riverboats and airplanes that local history has helped support. Daily.

Museum of Westward Expansion
11 N. Fourth St., St. Louis, 314-655-1700
The Museum of Westward Expansion offers exhibits on the people and events of 19th-century western America, special exhibits and films on St. Louis, construction of the arch and the westward movement. Daily.

NASCAR Speedpark
5555 St. Louis Mills Blvd., Hazelwood, 314-227-5600; www.nascarspeedpark.com
This mini-amusement park northwest of downtown, and one of five now open across North America, contains everything from an arcade to a rock-climbing wall to a NASCAR merchandise store. But its main draw is its multitude of racetracks. You can climb into a mock stock car and experience centrifugal forces, turns and crash impacts as you "drive" a full-motion NASCAR Silicon Motor Speedway simulator. Monday-Friday 10 a.m-9:30 p.m., Saturday 10 a.m-10 p.m., Sunday 11 a.m-7 p.m.

94

MISSOURI

Old Cathedral

209 Walnut St., St. Louis, 314-231-3250
The 1831 basilica of St. Louis, King of France, is located on the site of the first church built in St. Louis in 1770. Museum on the west side contains the original church bell and other religious artifacts. Daily.

Powell Symphony Hall

718 N. Grand Blvd., St. Louis,
314-534-1700
Decorated in ivory and 24-karat gold leaf, the hall, built in 1925 as a movie and vaudeville house, is now home of the St. Louis Symphony Orchestra (mid-September-mid-May). After-concert tours available by appointment.

Six Flags St. Louis

Six Flags Rd., Eureka,
636-938-4800; www.sixflags.com
This edition of the theme park franchise has rides and attractions for kids and grownups, plus live shows throughout summer. Among the two dozen or so rides here are several roller coasters. Mid-May-late August: daily from 10 a.m; early-April-mid-May and late August-Halloween: weekends from 10 a.m; closing times vary.

St. Louis Art Museum

1 Fine Arts Dr., St. Louis, 314-721-0072;
www.stlouis.art.museum
Built for the 1904 World's Fair as the Palace of Fine Arts, this museum has collections of American and European paintings, prints, drawings and decorative arts. Tuesday-Sunday.

St. Louis Blues (NHL)

Scotttrade Center, 1401 Clark Ave.,
St. Louis, 314-241-1888;
www.blues.nhl.com
Professional hockey team.

St. Louis Cardinals (MLB)

Busch Stadium, 250 Stadium Plaza,
St. Louis, 314-421-3060;
www.cardinals.mlb.com
Professional baseball team.

St. Louis Rams (NFL)

Edward Jones Dome, 901 N. Broadway,
St. Louis, 314-425-8830;
www.stlouisrams.com
Professional football team.

St. Louis Science Center

5050 Oakland Ave., St. Louis,
314-289-4444, 800-456-7572;
www.slsc.org
Features three buildings with more than 700 exhibits. Also Omnimax theater, planetarium, children's discovery room. Daily.

St. Louis Union Station

1820 Market St., St. Louis, 314-421-6655
This block-long stone chateauesque railroad station (1894) was the world's busiest passenger terminal from 1905 to the late 1940s. After the last train pulled out on October 31, 1978, the station and train shed were restored and redeveloped as a marketplace with more than 100 specialty shops and restaurants, nightclubs and a hotel.

St. Louis University

221 N. Grand, St. Louis,
314-977-8886, 800-758-3678;
www.slu.edu
The oldest university west of the Mississippi River, the campus was opened in 1818 and includes the Pius XII Memorial Library with its Vatican Microfilm Library (the only depository for copies of Vatican documents in the Western Hemisphere). Daily; closed holidays.

St. Louis Zoo

Forest Park, 1 Government Dr.,
St. Louis, 314-781-0900, 800-966-8877;
www.stlzoo.org
The St. Louis Zoo is considered one of the best in the country. Lions, cheetahs and giraffes roam in natural African settings, while other areas showcase exotic species from the poles to the tropics. Memorial Day-Labor Day: daily 8 a.m-7 p.m.; rest of year: daily 9 a.m-5 p.m.

95

MISSOURI

Ulysses S. Grant National Historic Site
7400 Grant Rd., St. Louis, 314-842-3298
The White Haven property was a focal point in Ulysses's and his wife Julia's lives for four decades. Grounds feature more than 50 species of trees and are a haven for a variety of wildlife. Visitors center includes exhibits and information on the Grants and White Haven. Guided tours. Daily.

Washington University
1 Brookings Dr., St. Louis, 314-935-5000
(1853) (11,000 students) A prestigious liberal arts institution with 11,000 students, the campus of this university includes the Graham Chapel, Edison Theatre and Francis Field (1904), site of the first Olympic Games in the United States.

SPECIAL EVENTS
Fair St. Louis
Jefferson National Expansion Memorial Park, St. Louis, 314-434-3434
Three-day festival with parade, food, air and water shows, entertainment. July 4 weekend.

Muny Opera
Forest Park, St. Louis, 314-361-1900
12,000-seat outdoor theater. Light opera and musical comedy. Mid-June-August.

St. Louis Symphony Orchestra
Powell Symphony Hall, 718 N. Grand Blvd., St. Louis, 314-534-1700
Classical music performances from September-May.

HOTELS
★★Cheshire Lodge
6300 Clayton Rd., St. Louis, 314-647-7300, 800-325-7378; www.cheshirelodge.com
Restaurant, two bars. Fitness room. Indoor pool, outdoor pool. $

★★★Chase Park Plaza
212 N. Kingshighway Blvd., St. Louis, 314-633-3000; www.chaseparkplaza.com

This historic hotel in St. Louis's Central West End has guest rooms decorated with period furnishings. A resort-like feel pervades the hotel, which has a five-screen movie theater, spa and salon, courtyard with outdoor pool and 24-hour concierge. 250 rooms. High-speed Internet access. Four restaurants, five bars. Fitness room, fitness classes available, spa. Outdoor pool. Business center. $$

★★★Clayton On The Park
8025 Bonhomme Ave., Clayton, 314-721-6543, 800-323-7500; www.claytononthepark.com
The suites at this tower are contemporary in design and offer the ameneties of an apartment, from fully stocked kitchens to separate living areas with work desks and high speed Internet. The onsite Finale restaurant offers creative American cuisines and live music inside, or on the rooftop veranda in good weather.
109 rooms, all suites. Pets accepted. Complimentary continental breakfast. High-speed Internet access. Restaurant, bar. Fitness room. $$

★★Courtyard St. Louis Downtown
2340 Market St., St. Louis, 314-241-9111, 800-321-2211; www.courtyard.com
151 rooms. Wireless Internet access. Fitness room. Indoor pool, whirlpool. $

★★Drury Inn
201 S. 20th St., St. Louis, 314-231-3900, www.druryinn.com
176 rooms. Pets accepted, some restrictions. Complimentary continental breakfast. Restaurant, bar. Fitness room. Indoor pool, whirlpool. Restored 1907 railroad hotel. $

★Drury Inn-Natural Bridge Road
10490 Natural Bridge Rd., St. Louis, 314-423-7700, 800-378-7946; www.druryhotels.com
172 rooms. Pets accepted. Complimentary continental breakfast. High-speed Internet access. Fitness room. Indoor pool, whirlpool. Airport transportation available. $

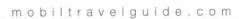

★Hampton Inn
2211 Market St., St. Louis,
314-241-3200, 800-426-7866;
www.hamptoninn.com
239 rooms. Pets accepted, some restrictions. Complimentary continental breakfast. Bar. Fitness room. Indoor pool, whirlpool. **$**

★★★Hilton St. Louis at the Ballpark
1 S. Broadway, St. Louis,
314-421-1776, 800-228-9290;
www.hilton.com
As its name suggests, this hotel is located across the street from the home of the Cardinals, Busch Stadium. The entire space has been recently renovated in a contemporary style, with rooms outfitted with granite bathrooms and duvet-topped beds.
684 rooms. High-speed Internet access. Two restaurants, bar. Fitness room. Indoor pool, whirlpool. Business center. **$$**

★★★Hilton St. Louis Downtown
400 Olive St., St. Louis,
314-436-0002, 800-445-8667;
www.hilton.com
A historic landmark, the Hilton St. Louis occupies the original Merchant Laclede building. All of St. Louis' attractions are within walking distance of this hotel, including the Gateway Arch, Busch Stadium and the America's Center.
195 rooms. High-speed, wireless Internet access. Restaurant, bar. Fitness room. Whirlpool. Business center. **$**

★★★Hilton St. Louis Frontenac
1335 S. Lindbergh Blvd., St. Louis,
314-993-1100, 800-325-7800;
www.hilton.com
Located between downtown St. Louis and Lambert International Airport, this hotel is near the St. Louis Zoo, the Science Center, Six Flags Amusement Park and adjacent to the upscale Plaza Frontenac shopping mall.
263 rooms. Wireless Internet access. Restaurant, bar. Fitness room. Outdoor pool. Airport transportation available. **$$**

★★Holiday Inn
811 N. Ninth St., St. Louis,

314-421-4000, 800-289-8338;
www.holiday-inn.com
295 rooms. Pets accepted. Wireless Internet access. Two restaurants, bar. Fitness room. Indoor pool, whirlpool. **$**

★★★Hyatt Regency St. Louis
1 St. Louis Union Station, St. Louis,
314-231-1234, 800-633-7313;
www.stlouis.hyatt.com
Located in the renovated Union Station railroad terminal, the main lobby and lounge of this hotel occupy the Grand Hall. The mall in the station has many stores and restaurants. Decor here is traditional, but contemporary details include an updated fitness center and luxury linens on the beds.
538 rooms. High-speed Internet access. Two restaurants, bar. Fitness room. Outdoor pool. Business center. **$$**

★★★Marriott St. Louis Airport
10700 Pear Tree Lane, St. Louis,
314-423-9700, 877-264-8771;
www.marriott.com
This airport hotel provides complimentary shuttle service and updated business and fitness centers. The Rock River Grill and Rock River Tavern serve a variety of classic American fare.
601 rooms. High-speed Internet access. Restaurant, bar. Fitness room. Indoor pool, outdoor pool, whirlpool. Airport transportation available. Business center. **$$**

★★★Omni Majestic Hotel
1019 Pine St., St. Louis,
314-436-2355, 800-843-6664;
www.omnihotels.com
This European-style hotel (1913) is located in downtown St. Louis and is listed in the National Register of Historic Buildings.
91 rooms. Pets accepted, some restrictions; fee. Wireless Internet access. Restaurant, bar. Fitness room. Business center. **$$**

★★Parkway Hotel
4550 Forest Park Blvd., St. Louis,
314-256-7777, 866-314-7700;
www.theparkwayhotel.com

MISSOURI

220 rooms. High-speed Internet access. Restaurant, bar. Fitness room. Business center. $

★★Radisson Hotel and Suites
200 N. Fourth St., St. Louis,
314-621-8200, 800-333-3333;
www.radisson.com/stlouismo
440 rooms. High-speed Internet access. Restaurant, bar. Fitness room. Outdoor pool. $$

★★★Renaissance St. Louis Grand Suites and Hotel
800 Washington Ave., St. Louis,
314-621-9600, 800-468-3571;
www.renaissancehotels.com
This historic downtown hotel is close to St. Louis' top attractions. There are five on-site restaurants and a full fitness center as well as an indoor pool.
918 rooms. Pets accepted. High-speed Internet access. Four restaurants, bar. Fitness room. Indoor pool, whirlpool. Airport transportation available. Business center. $

★★★Renaissance St. Louis Hotel Airport
9801 Natural Bridge Rd., St. Louis,
314-429-1100, 800-340-2594;
www.renaissancehotels.com
This hotel is adjacent to the Lambert International Airport and has been recently updated with pillowtop mattresses and an on-site Starbucks.
394 rooms. High-speed Internet access. Restaurant, bar. Fitness room. Indoor pool, outdoor pool, whirlpool. Business center. $$

★★★★The Ritz-Carlton, St. Louis
100 Carondelet Plaza, Clayton,
314-863-6300, 800-241-3333;
www.ritzcarlton.com
This sophisticated hotel features spacious and plush guest rooms, all with private balconies with views of the city skyline. A comprehensive fitness center includes lap and hydrotherapy pools. The Wine Room is a unique spot for sampling one of the hotel's more than 7,000 bottles of wine, while the Restaurant offers a fine dining experience.

301 rooms. Pets accepted; fee. High-speed, wireless Internet access. Two restaurants, bar. Fitness room. Indoor pool, whirlpool. Airport transportation available. Business center. $$$$

★★★Seven Gables Inn
26 N. Meramec Ave., Clayton,
314-863-8400, 800-433-6590;
www.sevengablesinn.com
Surrounded by upscale shops, galleries, and restaurants, this inn offers a blend of old-world charm and modern conveniences. The inn was inspired by sketches in Nathaniel Hawthorne's novel *The House of Seven Gables*.
32 rooms. Complimentary continental breakfast. Restaurant, bar. Airport transportation available. $

★★★Sheraton Clayton Plaza
7730 Bonhomme Ave., Clayton,
314-863-0400, 800-325-3535;
www.sheraton.com/clayton
This hotel, located in Clayton just outside St. Louis, is loaded with amenities from an indoor pool to an onsite Enterprise car rental desk, sundeck and fitness center.
257 rooms. Pets accepted, some restrictions. High-speed Internet access. Two restaurants, bar. Fitness room. Indoor pool, whirlpool. Airport transportation available. Business center. $$

★★★Sheraton St. Louis City Center Hotel and Suites
400 S. 14th St., St. Louis, 314-231-5007,
800-325-3535; www.sheraton.com
This downtown hotel has oversized rooms with queen-size sleeper sofas for extra guests. Other amenities include a fitness center, indoor pool and onsite sports bar.
288 rooms. Pets accepted, some restrictions. Restaurant. Fitness room. Indoor pool. Business center. $$

★Staybridge Suites
1855 Craigshire Rd., St. Louis,
314-878-1555, 800-238-8000;
www.staybridgesuites.com
106 rooms, all suites. Pets accepted; fee. Complimentary continental breakfast.

MISSOURI

★
★
★
★
★

High-speed Internet access. Outdoor pool, whirlpool. Airport transportation available. **$**

★★★The Westin St. Louis
811 Spruce St., St. Louis,
314-621-2000, 800-228-3000;
www.westin.com/stlouis
Adjacent to Busch Stadium and convenient to shopping and restaurants, this contemporary hotel has a spa, health club and an acclaimed restaurant and bar.
221 rooms. Pets accepted, some restrictions; fee. High-speed Internet access. Restaurant, bar. Fitness room, spa. Business center. **$$**

RESTAURANTS
★★Big Sky Café
47 S. Old Orchard, Webster Groves,
314-962-5757;
www.bigskycafe.net
American menu. Dinner. Bar. Outdoor seating. **$$**

★Blueberry Hill
6504 Delmar Blvd., St. Louis,
314-727-4444; www.blueberryhill.com
American menu. Lunch, dinner, late-night. Bar. Casual attire. Outdoor seating. Live music. **$**

*Bristol Seafood Grill
11801 Olive Blvd., Creve Coeur,
314-567-0272; www.bristolseafoodgrill.com
Seafood menu. Lunch, dinner, Sunday brunch. Bar. Children's menu. **$$$**

*Broadway Oyster Bar
736 S. Broadway, St. Louis, 314-621-8811;
www.broadwayoysterbar.com
Cajun/Creole menu. Lunch, dinner, late-night. Bar. Casual attire. Outdoor seating. **$$**

★Cafe Napoli
7754 Forsyth, Clayton, 314-863-5731;
www.cafenapoli.com
Italian menu. Lunch, dinner. Bar. Valet parking. **$$$**

★★★Cardwell's in Clayton
8100 Maryland, Clayton, 314-726-5055;
www.cardwellsinclayton.com
This restaurant's celebrity chefs dish up an innovative American-style menu in a modern dining room.
Seafood menu. Lunch, dinner. Closed Sunday. Bar. Children's menu. Outdoor seating. **$$**

★★Cardwell's at the Plaza
94 Plaza Frontenac, St. Louis,
314-997-8885;
 www.cardwellsattheplaza.com
International menu. Lunch, dinner. Bar. Children's menu. Business casual attire. Reservations recommended. Outdoor seating. **$$**

★Charlie Gitto's
207 N. Sixth St., St. Louis,
314-436-2828; www.charliegittos.com
American, Italian menu. Lunch, dinner. Closed Sunday. Bar. Children's menu. Casual attire. **$$**

★Chuy Arzola's
6405 Clayton Ave., St. Louis,
314-644-4430
Southwestern menu. Lunch, dinner. Bar. Children's menu. Casual attire. Outdoor seating. **$**

★Cicero's
6691 Delmar Blvd., University City,
314-862-0009; www.ciseros.com
American, Italian menu. Lunch, dinner, late-night. Bar. Children's menu. Outdoor seating. **$$**

★Cravings
8149 Big Bend Blvd.,
Webster Groves, 314-961-3534;
www.cravingsonline.com
American menu. Lunch, dinner. Closed Sunday-Monday. Valet parking. **$$**

★Crown Candy Kitchen
1401 St. Louis Ave., St. Louis,
314-621-9650;
www.crowncandykitchen.com

MISSOURI

American menu. Lunch, dinner. **$**

★★Cunetto House of Pasta
5453 Magnolia Ave., St. Louis,
314-781-1135; www.cunetto.com
Italian menu. Lunch, dinner. Closed Sunday. Bar. Casual attire. Outdoor seating. **$$**

★★Dierdorf & Hart's Steak House
701 E. Market St., St. Louis, 314-878-1801;
www.dierdorfharts.com
Steak menu. Dinner. Bar. Business casual attire. Reservations recommended. **$$$**

★★★Dominic's Restaurant
5101 Wilson Ave., St. Louis, 314-771-1632;
www.dominicsrestaurant.com
Friendly service and a menu of well-crafted, traditional Italian cuisine have earned this restaurant a loyal following since it opened in 1971. Entrees include breast of chicken alla Romano, lobster picante and veal T-bone chop with truffle sauce. Pasta dishes range from pappardele with mushrooms to risotto with lobster. The wine list is Italian-focused with many exceptional vintages.
Italian menu. Dinner. Closed Sunday. Bar. Children's menu. Business casual attire. Reservations recommended. Valet parking. **$$$**

★★Frank Papa's Ristorante
2241 S. Brentwood Blvd.,
Brentwood, 314-961-3344;
www.frankpapas.com
Italian menu. Dinner. Closed Sunday. Bar. **$$$**

★Frazer's Restaurant and Lounge
1811 Pestalozzi, St. Louis, 314-773-8646;
www.frazergoodeats.com
International menu. Dinner. Closed Sunday. Bar. Outdoor seating. **$$**

★★★The Gardens at Malmaison
3519 St. Albans Rd., St. Albans,
636-458-0131
A rustic replica of a French inn tucked away in the countryside outside of St. Louis, this restaurant offers a small, fresh seasonal menu.
French menu. Dinner. Closed Tuesday-Wednesday. Bar. Jacket required. Outdoor seating. **$$$**

★Gino's Restaurant
4502 Hampton Ave., St. Louis,
314-351-4187; www.ginosbarroma.com
Italian menu. Dinner. Closed Monday. Bar. Children's menu. Casual attire. Reservations recommended. Outdoor seating. **$$**

★★★Giovanni's
5201 Shaw Ave., St. Louis, 314-772-5958;
www.giovannisonthehill.com
This restaurant is best described as timeless Italian. The highlight is its focus on fresh seafood, which is flown in daily. The veal and beef dishes are also superlative.
Italian menu. Dinner. Closed Sunday. Bar. Business casual attire. Reservations recommended. Valet parking. **$$$**

★★Giuseppe's
4141 S. Grand Blvd., St. Louis,
314-832-3779;
www.giuseppesongrand.com
Italian menu. Lunch, dinner. Closed Monday. Bar. **$$**

★★★The Grill
100 Carondelet Plaza, Clayton,
314-863-6300, 800-241-3333;
www.ritzcarlton.com
Located in the Ritz-Carlton St. Louis hotel, this upscale dining room serves up contemporary interpretations of American classics. The decor includes extensive mahogany paneling and woodwork, overstuffed leather banquettes, dramatic lighting and a marble fireplace. Nightly entertainment is featured (piano or acoustic guitar), and on weekends, there's live music (jazz, blues, or swing) in the hotel lounge.
American menu. Dinner. Bar. Business casual attire. Reservations recommended. Valet parking. **$$$**

★★★Hacienda
9748 Manchester Rd., Rock Hill,

100

MISSOURI

314-962-7100; www.hacienda-stl.com
Built as a residence for a steamboat captain (1861), this rambling, casual restaurant consistently delivers in its preparation of the Mexican favorites.
Mexican menu. Lunch, dinner. Bar. Outdoor seating. **$$**

★**Hammerstone's**
2028 S. Ninth, St. Louis, 314-773-5565; www.hammerstones.net
American menu. Breakfast, lunch, dinner. Bar. Children's menu. Casual attire. Outdoor seating. **$$**

★**Hannegan's**
719 N. Second St., St. Louis, 314-241-8877; www.hannegans.admitonevip.com
American menu. Lunch, dinner. Bar. Children's menu. Casual attire. Outdoor seating. **$$**

★★**Harry's**
2144 Market St., St. Louis, 314-421-6969; www.harrysrestaurantandbar.com
American menu. Lunch, dinner, late-night. Bar. Casual attire. Reservations recommended. Valet parking. Outdoor seating. **$$$**

★★**Harvest**
1059 S. Big Bend Rd., St. Louis, 314-645-3522; www.harveststlouis.com
International menu. Dinner. Closed Monday. Bar. Business casual attire. Reservations recommended. **$$$**

★**House of India**
8501 Delmar Blvd., St. Louis, 314-567-6850; www.hoistl.com
Indian menu. Lunch, dinner. Casual attire. Reservations recommended. **$$**

★★**J. F. Sanfilippo's**
705 N. Broadway, St. Louis, 314-621-7213; www.sanfilippos.com
Italian menu. Lunch, dinner. Closed Sunday (except during football season). Bar. Children's menu. Casual attire. **$$**

★**John D. McGurk's**
1200 Russell Blvd., St. Louis, 314-776-8309; www.mcgurks.com
American, Irish menu. Lunch, dinner. Bar. Casual attire. **$$**

★★**Joseph's Italian Café**
107 N. Sixth St., St. Louis, 314-421-6366; www.josephsofstlouis.com
Italian menu. Lunch, dinner. Closed Sunday. Bar. Children's menu. Casual attire. Outdoor seating. **$$**

★★★**Kemoll's**
1 Metropolitan Square, St. Louis, 314-421-0555; www.kemolls.com
Since 1927, this downtown landmark restaurant has served classic specialties in an elegant atmosphere. The name was originally shortened from the Sicilian name Camuglia, and the restaurant is run by fourth-generation family members.
Italian menu. Dinner. Closed Sunday. Business casual attire. Reservations recommended. **$$$**

★**King & I**
3157 S. Grand Blvd., St. Louis, 314-771-1777; www.thaispicy.com
Thai menu. Lunch, dinner. Closed Monday. Bar. **$$**

★★**Lombardo's**
10488 Natural Bridge Rd., St. Louis, 314-429-5151; www.lombardosrestaurants.com
Italian menu. Lunch, dinner. Closed Sunday. Bar. Casual attire. Reservations recommended. **$$**

★★★**Kreis's**
535 S. Lindbergh Blvd., St. Louis, 314-993-0735; www.kreisrestaurant.com
This German-influenced steakhouse (think meat and potatoes) has been at the same location more than 50 years. It's housed in a renovated 1930s brick house with beamed ceilings.
Steak menu. Dinner. Bar. **$$**

★
★
★
★

★★★Lombardo's Trattoria
201 S. 20th St., St. Louis, 314-621-0666;
www.lombardosrestaurants.com
Family-owned and operated for three generations, this restaurant is located in a converted hotel. The menu lists family classics as well as creative seasonal entrees. Italian menu. Lunch, dinner. Closed Sunday. Bar. Business casual attire. Reservations recommended. Valet parking. **$$**

★★LoRusso's Cucina
3121 Watson Rd., St. Louis, 314-647-6222;
www.lorussos.com
Italian menu. Lunch, dinner. Closed Monday. Bar. Children's menu. Business casual attire. Reservations recommended. **$$**

★Maggie O'Brien's
2000 Market St., St. Louis,314-421-1388;
www.maggieobriens.com
American, Irish menu. Lunch, dinner. Bar. Children's menu. Casual attire. Valet parking. Outdoor seating. **$$**

★Marciano's
333 Westport Plaza, St. Louis,
314-878-8180
Italian menu. Lunch, dinner. Closed holidays. Bar. Children's menu. Business casual attire. Outdoor seating. **$$**

★★Mike Shannon's
100 N. Seventh St., St. Louis,
314-421-1540; www.shannonsteak.com
Steak menu. Lunch, dinner. Bar. Children's menu. Business casual attire. Reservations recommended. Outdoor seating. **$$**

★★Portabella
15 N. Cental Ave., Clayton,
314-725-6588; www.portabellarestaurant.com
Mediterranean menu. Lunch, dinner. Bar. **$$$**

★★Remy's
222 S. Bemiston, Clayton,
314-726-5757; www.grihome.com
Mediterranean menu. Lunch, dinner, late-night. Bar. Outdoor seating. **$$**

★Saleem's Lebanese Cuisine
6501 Delmar Blvd.,
St. Louis, 314-721-7947
Middle Eastern menu. Lunch, dinner. Closed Sunday. Bar. Casual attire. Outdoor seating. **$$**

★Riddle Penultimate
6307 Delmar Blvd., University City,
314-725-6985; www.riddlescafe.com
International menu. Dinner, late-night. Closed Monday. Bar. Outdoor seating. **$$**

WARM AND TOASTY
Ravioli: Classic Italian dish consisting of pasta squared around a filling of meat or cheese, boiled and topped with a sauce. In most places, yes, but in St. Louis the near-mandatory appetizer in classic Italian joints takes a twist on the recipe. In the Hill District that is home to many old-time Italian dining spots—as well in just about any of the many excellent strip-mall Italian restaurants in the suburbs—the ravioli takes a detour into some breading and then to the deep-frier before it reaches the plate.

Many establishments claim to have invented the dish. Among the more legitimate contenders is Charlie Gitto's (originally called Angelo's). The story goes that a chef accidentally dropped some raviolis into bread crumbs and decided to deep-fry them for the heck of it. A tradition was born.

Whatever the truth is, toasted ravioli—which is generally a concoction encasing savory beef or veal, topped with marina sauce and sprinkled with Parmesan cheese—is a St. Louis original and a comforting opener to any dinner.

102

MISSOURI

★
★
★
★
★

★★Sidney Street Café
2000 Sidney St., St. Louis, 314-771-5777;
www.sidneystreetcafe.com
American menu. Dinner. Closed Sunday-
Monday. Bar. Children's menu. Casual
attire. Reservations recommended. **$$**

★Spiro's.
3122 Watson Rd., St. Louis, 314-645-8383
American menu. Lunch, dinner. Closed
Monday. Children's menu. Reservations
recommended. **$$**

★★Schlafly Tap Room
2100 Locust St., St. Louis,
314-241-2337; www.schlafly.com
American menu. Lunch, dinner. Bar. Casual
attire. Outdoor seating. **$$**

★★★Schneithorst's Hofamberg Inn
1600 S. Lindbergh Blvd., Ladue,
314-993-4100; www.schneithorst.com
Unusual ethnic influences give traditional
German cuisine an unexpected new face on
this menu. Atlantic salmon with rain for-
est fruit relish and seafood strudel Johann
Strauss are a few examples. In true German
fashion, 33 specialty beers are available
on tap.
German, American menu. Breakfast, lunch,
dinner. Bar. Children's menu. Outdoor
seating. **$$**

★Thai Café
6170 Delmar Blvd.,
St. Louis, 314-862-6868
Thai menu. Lunch, dinner. Casual attire. **$$**

★★★★Tony's
410 Market St., St.Louis, 314-231-7007;
www.tonysstlouis.com
Italian food may bring to mind images
of pasta with red sauce, but at Tony's
you'll find a menu of authentic Italian
fare prepared with a measured and
sophisticated hand. Expect appetizers like
smoked salmon with mascarpone cheese
and asparagus and Belgian endive and
entrees like tenderloin of beef with foie
gras in a port wine demi-glaze. The room
has an urban, postmodern style, with

sleek low lighting, linen-topped tables,
and glossy, wood-paneled walls. The
chef's tasting menu is a nice choice for
gourmands with healthy appetites.

Italian menu. Dinner. Closed Sunday; also
first week of January and first week of
July. Bar. Jacket required. Reservations
recommended. Valet parking. **$$$**

★★★John Mineo's
13490 Clayton Rd.,
Town and Country, 314-434-5244
For decades, this Italian-continental
restaurant has lured diners with dishes such
as Dover sole and veal chop, as well as daily
fresh fish specials and house-made pasta.
Italian menu. Dinner. Bar. Jacket required.
$$$

★★Trattoria Marcella
3600 Watson Rd., St. Louis, 314-352-7706;
www.trattoriamarcella.com
Italian menu. Dinner. Closed Sunday-Mon-
day. Bar. Casual attire. Reservations rec-
ommended. **$$**

★Yacovelli's
407 Dunn Rd., Florissant,
314-839-1000; www.yacovellis.com
Italian menu. Dinner, brunch. Closed Mon-
day-Tuesday. Bar. Children's menu. **$$**

★★Yemanja Brasil
2900 Missouri Ave., St. Louis,
314-771-7457; www.brazildining.com
Brazilian menu. Dinner. Bar. Outdoor
seating. **$$**

★Zia's
5256 Wilson Ave., St. Louis, 314-776-0020;
www.zias.com
Italian menu. Lunch, dinner. Closed Sun-
day. Bar. Casual attire. Outdoor seating. **$$**

★Zinnia
7491 Big Bend Blvd.,
Webster Groves, 314-962-0572
American menu. Lunch, dinner. Closed
Monday. Bar. Outdoor seating. **$$$**

103

MISSOURI

★
★
★
★
★

SAINTE GENEVIEVE

Sainte Genevieve, the first permanent settlement in Missouri, developed on the banks of the Mississippi River early in the 18th century when Frenchmen began mining lead in the region. After a flood in 1785, the village was moved to higher ground. Once St. Louis's chief rival, Sainte Genevieve preserves its French heritage in its festivals, old houses and massive red brick church.

Information: Great River Road Interpretive Center, 66 S. Main., 573-883-7097, 800-373-7007; www.ste-genevieve.com

WHAT TO SEE AND DO

Bolduc House Museum
125 S. Main St., Ste. Genevieve, 573-883-3105

This restored French house (1770) with walls of upright heavy oak logs features period furnishings, orchard and an herb garden. April-November, daily.

Felix Valle Home State Historic Site
198 Merchant St., Ste. Genevieve, 573-883-7102

A restored and furnished Federal-style stone house (1818) of an early fur trader. Guided tours are available. Daily.

Guibourd-Valle House
1 N. Fourth St., Ste. Genevieve, 573-883-7544

Late 18th-century restored vertical log house on a stone foundation; French heirlooms. Attic with Norman truss and hand-hewn oak beams secured by wooden pegs. Courtyard; rose garden; stone well; costumed guides. April-October: daily; March and November: weekends.

Sainte Genevieve Museum
Merchant St. and DuBourg Place, Ste. Genevieve, 573-883-3461

Display of salt manufacturing, the state's first industry. Scale model of rail car transfer boat, *Ste. Genevieve*, which carried trains across the Mississippi. Native American artifacts; local mementos. Daily; closed holidays.

SPECIALTY LODGINGS

Southern Hotel Bed & Breakfast
146 S. Third St., Ste. Genevieve, 573-883-3493, 800-275-1412; www.southernhotelbb.com

8 rooms. Children over 12 years only. Complimentary full breakfast. Built in 1791. $

RESTAURANTS

★Anvil Saloon
46 S. Third St., Ste. Genevieve, 573-883-7323

German, American menu. Lunch, dinner. Closed holidays. Bar. Oldest commercially operated building in the city (circa 1850); early Western saloon décor. $$

★Old Brick House
90 S. Market St., Ste. Genevieve, 573-883-2724

American menu. Breakfast, lunch, dinner. Bar. Children's menu. One of the first brick buildings (1785) west of the Mississippi. $$

WENTZVILLE

Daniel Boone and his family were the first to settle in the area around Wentzville, which was named after Erasmus L. Wentz, principal engineer of the North Missouri Railroad. Between 1850 to 1880 the area was devoted to growing tobacco. The original Liggett and Myers Tobacco Company factory still stands in Wentzville.

Information: Chamber of Commerce, 5 W. Pearce, 636-327-6914; www.wentzvillemo.org

MISSOURI

★
★
★
★
★
☆

WHAT TO SEE AND DO

Cuivre River State Park
678 St. Rte 147, Troy, 636-528-7247
One of the state's largest and most natural parks, this 6,251-acre area contains rugged, wooded terrain, native prairie and an 88-acre lake. Daily.

Daniel Boone Home
County Z, Wentzville, 636-987-2221
Built by Boone and his son Nathan around 1803, this stone house is where Boone died in 1820; restored and authentically furnished; museum. Mid-March-mid-December: daily; rest of year: weekends.

HOTELS

★★Holiday Inn
900 Corporate Pkwy., Wentzville,
636-327-7001, 800-465-4329;
www.holiday-inn.com
138 rooms. Pets accepted, some restrictions. Restaurant, bar. Outdoor pool. $

WESTON

Before the Civil War, Weston was at its peak. Founded on whiskey, hemp and tobacco, it rivaled St. Louis as a commercial trade center and promised to become a major U.S. city. But disasters—fire, floods and the Civil War—ruined Weston's urban future. Today Weston, the first "district" west of the Mississippi entered into the National Register of Historic Sites, is a quiet town with more than 100 antebellum houses and other buildings.
Information: Information Center 502 Main St., 816-640-2909; www.ci.weston.mo.us

WHAT TO SEE AND DO

Historical Museum
601 Main St., Weston, 816-640-2977
On the site of the International Hotel built by stagecoach king and distillery founder Benjamin Holladay. Mid-March-mid-December, Tuesday-Sunday.

Snow Creek Ski Area
1 Snow Creek Dr., Weston, 816-386-2200;
www.skipeaks.com/sc_home
Two triple, double chairlift, rope tow; nine intermediate trails. Rentals; ski school, snow-making. Lodge, restaurant. Vertical drop 300 feet. Mid-December-mid-March, daily.

SPECIALTY LODGINGS

Inn at Weston Landing
526 Welt, Weston, 816-640-5788
Built atop the cellars of a former brewery, this inn has an Irish atmosphere and each room individually decorated.
4 rooms. Complimentary full breakfast. Restaurant. $

RESTAURANTS

★★America Bowman
500 Welt St., Weston, 816-640-5235
American, Irish menu. Lunch, dinner. Closed Monday. Bar. Mid-19th-century Irish pub atmosphere. $$

105

MISSOURI

NEBRASKA

IN LITTLE MORE THAN A CENTURY, NEBRASKA—PART OF WHAT WAS ONCE CALLED THE "great American desert"—has evolved from a vast prairie occupied by Native Americans and buffalo to a farming, ranching and manufacturing mainstay of America, with an enticing array of recreational and cultural attractions.

Spaniards visited the region first, but it was on the basis of explorations by Father Marquette and Louis Jolliet in 1673 that French fur traders and missionaries swept over the land, and France claimed it. Nevertheless, it was recognized as Spanish land until 1800, when it became a plaything of European politics and was sold by Napoleon to the United States as part of the Louisiana Purchase in 1803. Famous pathfinders like John C. Fremont, Kit Carson and the men who trapped for John Jacob Astor thought it a land unfit for cultivation.

Today, Nebraska is a "breadbasket" state, with an economy rooted in agriculture. But for the visitor, there is much more than corn, wheat and cows. As with Kansas to the south and South Dakota to the north, to traverse Nebraska from east to west is to trace a transition of terrain, climate and culture—from the tidy farms, sticky summers and small towns, along with the occasional big city, to a more unbridled landscape where cattle graze on vast tracts of rangeland patrolled by actual cowboys, where counties are bigger than some Northeastern states, and where the air dries out and the wind is almost always blowing as the land gradually slopes upward and becomes the high country stretching to the Rocky Mountains and the West.

At the eastern edge, by the Missouri River, is Omaha, the state's largest city. As one might expect in cattle country, it's a place to find a good steak, but if you're hunting for more adventurous cuisine, you'll find it. Home to a number of Fortune 500 companies as well as a major branch of the state university and the highly regarded Creighton University, Omaha offers its share of big-city sophistication.

Heading west on the interstate, you'll come to Lincoln, the state capital and site of the University of Nebraska main campus–and the fabled Cornhuskers football team and rabid army of red-clad fans who chew over the fortunes of their squad year-round.

Farther out, if you are traveling by Kearney on Interstate 80, one attraction you literally can't miss is the Great Platte River Road Archway, a structure that spans 300 feet over the highway and houses a multimedia exhibit that salutes Nebraska's pioneer spirit along with the state's progression into modern times. In the movie *As Good as It Gets,* Jack Nicholson's character pays a visit here.

Wherever you are in Nebraska, the history, whether of the Native population, the settlers from the East, or some of the tragic clashes between the two, is rich The landscape, whether bleak or lush, can be beautiful and is easily explored by car, bike, horse or foot.

★ SPOTLIGHT

★ Nebraska is the birthplace of the Reuben sandwich.

★ Nebraska has more miles of river than any other state.

FROM CRAZY HORSE TO CARHENGE

Vast, lightly populated and filled with raw beauty, the Sandhills country of western Nebraska takes visitors by surprise. Start in North Platte with a visit to Buffalo Bill Ranch State Historical Park, which preserves the Western icon's home on the range. Head north on Highway 83 to the Nebraska National Forest. At 90,000 acres, it's the largest hand-planted forest in the country. Continue north to Valentine, set along the Niobrara River, a favorite for canoeing. Drive west on Highway 20 to Merriman, site of the Sandhills Ranch State Historical Park (still a working ranch despite its name), then on to Chadron to visit the Museum of the Fur Trade. Continue west to Fort Robinson State Park, where Crazy Horse died. The nearby Pine Ridge and Oglala National Grassland are great spots for horseback riding, mountain biking and hiking. To return to civilization, take Highway 2 south from Crawford to Alliance, home to the famous Carhenge, a variation on England's Stonehenge. From Alliance, head south on Highway 385 to pick up the Oregon Trail route at Bridgeport, or return to North Platte on Highway 2 east and Highway 83 south. Approximately 550 miles.

AUBURN

WHAT TO SEE AND DO

Brownville
Hwy. 136, Auburn
Restored riverboat town of the 1800s. More than 30 buildings, many of which are open to the public.

Missouri River History Museum
Hwy. 136, Auburn, 402-825-3341
Located aboard the *Captain Meriwether Lewis,* a former Corps of Engineers dredge, this museum contains exhibits on river history. Memorial Day-Labor Day: daily; rest of year: weekends.

Indian Cave State Park
RR 1, Shubert, 402-883-2575
On approximately 3,400 acres, this park includes oak-covered Missouri River bluffs and the old St. Deroin town site, which has been partially reconstructed. Also here are ancient petroglyphs in Indian Cave; scenic overlooks of the river. Redbud trees bloom in profusion during spring.

Nemaha Valley Museum
1423 19th St., Auburn, 402-274-3203
Exhibits trace history of Nemaha County; period rooms; farm equipment. Tuesday-Sunday afternoons.

HOTELS

★**Auburn Inn**
517 J St., Auburn, 402-274-3143, 800-272-3143
36 rooms. Pets accepted, some restrictions. **$**

★**Palmer House**
1918 J St., Auburn, 402-274-3193, 800-272-3143
22 rooms. Pets accepted, some restrictions; fee. **$**

RESTAURANT

★**Wheeler Inn**
1905 J St., Auburn, 402-274-4931
American menu. Dinner. Closed Sunday; holidays. Bar. Casual attire. **$$**

NEBRASKA

★
★
★
★
★

CHADRON

Starting point of a sensational 1,000-mile horse race to Chicago in 1893, Chadron saw nine men leave in competition for a $1,000 prize. Doc Middleton, a former outlaw, was one of the starters, but John Berry beat him to the door of Buffalo Bill's Wild West Show in 13 days and 16 hours. The headquarters and a Ranger District office of the Nebraska National Forest and headquarters of the Oglala National Grasslands are located here. **Information: Chamber of Commerce, 706 W. Third St., 308-432-4401, 800-603-2937; www.chadron.com**

WHAT TO SEE AND DO

Chadron State Park
15951 Hwy. 385, Chadron, 308-432-6167
A park with approximately 950 acres, paddleboats, hiking, horseback riding, cross-country skiing and camping are available.

Museum of the Fur Trade
6321 Hwy. 20, Chadron, 308-432-3843
Displays depict the history of the North American fur trade from 1500-1900. Restored trading post (1837) and storehouse used by James Bordeaux, a French trader. Memorial Day-September: daily; rest of year: by appointment.

HOTELS

★Best Western West Hills Inn
1100 W. 10th St., Chadron, 308-432-3305, 877-432-3305; www.bestwestern.com
67 rooms. Pets accepted, some restrictions; fee. Complimentary continental breakfast. Fitness room. Indoor pool, whirlpool. **$**

★Super 8
840 W. Hwy. 20, Chadron, 308-432-4471; www.super8.com
45 rooms. Pets accepted. Indoor pool, whirlpool. **$**

CHIMNEY ROCK NATIONAL HISTORIC SITE

WHAT TO SEE AND DO
Pawnee Park
Hwy. 30, Columbus, 402-564-0914.

Swimming pool. Ball fields, tennis. Picnicking facilities, playground on 130 acres along Loup River. Quincentenary bell tower dedicated to Columbus's voyage to the new world.

HOMESTEADING ALONG THE MISSOURI RIVER

Wooded river bluffs, historic towns and Homestead National Monument are among the attractions of this drive through southeast Nebraska. Take Highway 77 from Lincoln south to Beatrice, the first of several charming small towns on this route. A few miles west of town, Homestead National Monument showcases a restored tallgrass prairie and explains the Homestead Act of 1862, which led to widespread settlement in the western United States. From Beatrice, drive east through the farmlands along Highway 136 to Auburn, a town known for its antique stores. Continue on to Brownville, which features a Missouri River History Museum aboard the dry-docked *Captain Meriwether Lewis*, and riverboat cruises aboard the *Spirit of Brownville*. From Brownville, backtrack to Auburn and head north on Highway 75 to Nebraska City, the birthplace of Arbor Day. Head west on Highway 34 north of Nebraska City to return to Lincoln. Approximately 180 miles.

COLUMBUS

Named by its founders for Ohio's capital, Columbus has become a center of industry, agriculture and statewide electrical power.
Information: Chamber of Commerce, 764 33rd Ave., 402-564-2769; www.ci.columbus.ne.us

Platte County Historical Society

2916 16th St., Columbus, 402-564-1856
See exhibits on local history, a period schoolroom, barbershop, research library and cultural center. April-mid-October, Friday-Sunday.

HOTELS

★★New World Inn and Conference Center

265 33rd Ave., Columbus, 402-564-1492, 800-433-1492; www.newworldinn.com

140 rooms. Restaurant, bar. Indoor pool, whirlpool. Airport transportation available. Indoor courtyard. **$**

★Super 8

3324 20th St., Columbus, 402-563-3456; www.super8.com
63 rooms. Pets accepted, some restrictions; fee. **$**

COZAD

Cozad is headquarters for a number of industries, as well as a shipping and agricultural center known for the production of alfalfa.
Information: Chamber of Commerce, 211 W. Eighth St., 308-784-3930.; www.ci.cozad.ne.us

WHAT TO SEE AND DO

Gallagher Canyon State Recreation Area

Hwys. 751 and 424, Cozad, 308-784-3907
Approximately 20 acres of park surround 400 acres of water. Fishing, boating, hiking. picnicking, camping. Standard hours, fees.

Robert Henri Museum and Historical Walkway

112 E. Eighth St., Cozad, 308-784-4154
This museum occupies the childhood home of artist Robert Henri, founder of the Ash Can School, as well as a former hotel built by Henri's father. Other historic buildings along the walkway include an original Pony Express station, a pioneer school and an early 20th-century church. Memorial Day-September: Tuesday-Saturday, also by appointment.

HOTELS

★★Circle S Best Value Inn

440 S. Meridian St., Cozad, 308-784-2290, 888-315-2378; www.bestvalueinn.com
49 rooms. Pets accepted, some restrictions; fee. Restaurant. Outdoor pool. **$**

CRAWFORD

The area around this community is rich in fossil beds. The Hudson-Meng Bison Kill Site is loaded with animal bones and other artifacts more than 10,000 year old.
Information: Chamber of Commerce, 308-665-1817; www.crawfordnebraska.com

WHAT TO SEE AND DO

Fort Robinson State Park

3200 Hwy. 20, Crawford, 308-665-2660; www.stateparks.com/fort_robinson.html

This fort was established in 1874 in the midst of Native American fighting (the Sioux leader, Crazy Horse, was killed here). Displays herds of buffalo. Park entry permit required.

FORT ROBINSON'S WORLD WAR II HISTORY

Nebraska might seem an unlikely place to encounter World War II history, but out in the northwestern corner of the state you can visit a fort that, having originally stood as an important outpost in the Indian Wars, served as camp for German and Axis POWs in 1943.

The fort compound had already come into wartime use as a K-9 Dogs for Defense training center. But as prisoner capacity in Great Britain became squeezed, Fort Robinson, located far from any city but alongside mainline railways and with opportunities for needed labor, was picked as a spot to hold captured enemy soldiers. The first to arrive in the facility–built to accommodate 3,000 men—were captured from Rommel's Tenth Panzer Division in North Africa. They traveled by train from Virginia. When they arrived at the camp, the men were searched for contraband; items such as maps, cameras and binoculars were confiscated. Somehow one German soldier had managed to travel with a Chihuahua in his coat pocket.

The prisoners worked at a variety of camp-based jobs and were paid 80 cents an hour, as mandated by the Geneva Conventions. But even though the war had caused a labor shortage in agriculture, the Fort Robinson prisoners were not pressed into farm work, whereas at Camp Scottsbluff, approximately 80 miles to the south, German and Italian POWs worked in sugar beet and bean fields.

110

NEBRASKA

★
★
★
★
★

Fort Robinson Museum
3200 W. Hwy. 20, Crawford,
308-665-2919
The museum is located in the former fort headquarters building and displays authentic costumes and weapons of Native Americans and soldiers. Other exhibit buildings include a 1874 guardhouse, 1904 harness repair, 1906 blacksmith and 1900 wheelwright shops, 1887 adobe officer quarters and 1908 veterinary hospital. Site of Red Cloud Indian Agency (1873–1877). Guided tours, Memorial Day-Labor Day. Museum, Memorial Day-Labor Day: daily; rest of the year: Monday-Friday. Maintained by the State Historical Society.

Trailside Museum
Main St., Crawford, 308-665-2929;
www.trailside.unl.edu
The newest exhibit at this museum is the fossils of two mammoths discovered in the nearby Little Badlands. The creatures locked tusks in battle and died intertwined. The museum also features exhibits of natural history from the Fort Robinson area and daily science field trips to Toadstool Park and fossil sites. Memorial Day-Labor Day: daily; May: Wednesday-Sunday. Operated by University of Nebraska State Museum.

Oglala National Grassland
16524 Hwy. 385, Chadron, 308-432-4475
This area includes nearly 95,000 acres of prairie grasses in the badlands of northwestern Nebraska, popular for hunting (in season), hiking and backpacking.

HOTELS
★★Fort Robinson Lodge
Crawford, 308-665-2900
53 rooms. Closed late November-mid-April. Restaurant. Indoor pool. Tennis. Access to facilities of state park. $

FREMONT

This town was named for John C. Fremont, a Union general in the Civil War who ran for president of the United States. In the town's early days, the crops were so bad that lots sold for 75 cents each. Finally, travelers on the Overland Trail brought enough trade that the town began to prosper and grow. Midland Lutheran College gives a collegiate atmosphere to an otherwise industrial town.

Information: Fremont Area Chamber of Commerce and Dodge County Convention and Visitors Bureau, 605 N. Broad St., 402-753-6414, 800-727-8323; www.visitdodgecountyne.org

WHAT TO SEE AND DO

Fremont and Elkhorn Valley Railroad
1835 N. Somers Ave., Fremont,
402-727-0615
Train rides to Nickerson and Hooper aboard vintage rail cars. Reservations recommended. Schedule varies.

Fremont Dinner Train
1835 N. Somers Ave., Fremont,
402-727-8321, 800-942-7245;
www.fremontrailroad.com
Two restored 1940s rail cars make 30-mile round trips through the Elkhorn Valley. Dinner and varied entertainment. Weekends, some holidays.

Louis E. May Historical Museum
1643 N. Nye Ave., Fremont, 402-721-4515
The 25-room house of Fremont's first mayor, built in 1874, features oak and mahogany paneling, art glass windows and rooms furnished in late 19th-century style. May-August and December: Wednesday-Sunday; April and September-October: Wednesday-Saturday; closed holidays.

HOTELS

★America's Best Value Inn
1649 E. 23rd St., Fremont, 402-721-1109;
www.bestvalueinn.com
48 rooms. Pets accepted; fee. Complimentary continental breakfast. Indoor pool, whirlpool. **$**

★★Wilderness Lodge and Comfort Center
1220 E. 23rd Ave., Fremont,
402-727-1110, 800-743-7666;
www.wildernesslodgecc.com
100 rooms. Pets accepted, some restrictions; fee. Restaurant, bar. Fitness room. Indoor pool, whirlpool. **$**

111

NEBRASKA

★
★
★

GRAND ISLAND

Named by French trappers for a large island in the Platte River, the town was moved five miles north in 1869 to its present location on the Union Pacific Railroad, which dominated Grand Island's early existence. Traditionally a trade center for a rich irrigated agriculture and livestock region, the city now has diversified industry, including meat and food processing, agricultural and irrigation equipment and mobile homes.

Information: Grand Island/ Hall County Convention and Visitors Bureau, 309 W. Second St., 308-382-4400, 800-658-3178; www.visitgrandisland.com

★
★
★
★
★

WHAT TO SEE AND DO

Crane Meadows Nature Center
9325 S. Alda Rd., Wood River,
308-382-1820
Educational center features exhibits and programs about the Platte River habitat. Five miles of public nature trails. Daily; closed holidays.

Mormon Island State Recreation Area
7425 S. Hwy. 281, Grand Island,
308-385-6211
Approximately 90 acres with 61 water acres on the Mormon Trail. Swimming, fishing, boating, picnicking. Tent and trailer sites.

Stuhr Museum of the Prairie Pioneer
3133 W. Hwy. 34, Grand Island,
308-385-5316
This museum situated on an island surrounded by a man-made lake, was designed by Edward Durell Stone. Daily; closed holidays.

Railroad Town
Hwy. 281 and Hwy. 34, Grand Island,
308-382-4400
Turn-of-the-century outdoor museum contains 60 original buildings, including three

houses, the cottage where Henry Fonda was born, schoolhouse, newspaper office, bank, post office, hotel, country church and more. May-mid-October, daily.

SPECIAL EVENTS

Husker Harvest Days
Cornhusker Army Ammunition Plant,
309 W. Second St., Grand Island,
www.huskerharvestdays.com
Agricultural exhibits, techniques, and equipment used in irrigation. Mid-September.

HOTELS

★Days Inn
2620 N. Diers Ave., Grand Island,
308-384-8624, 800-329-7466;
www.daysinn.com
63 rooms. Pets accepted; fee. Complimentary continental breakfast. **$**

★★Holiday Inn
2503 S. Locust St., Grand Island,
308-384-1330, 800-548-5542;
www.holiday-inn.com
197 rooms. Restaurant, bar. Children's pool, whirlpool. **$**

★★Howard Johnson
3333 Ramada Rd., Grand Island,
308-384-5150, 800-446-4656;
www.hojo.com
181 rooms. Pets accepted; fee. Complimentary continental breakfast. Restaurant, bar. Indoor pool, whirlpool. **$**

RESTAURANT
★Hunan
2249 N. Webb Rd., Grand Island,
308-384-6964
Chinese menu. Lunch, dinner. Closed holidays. Bar. **$$**

HASTINGS
Hastings came into being almost overnight when two railroad lines crossed. Within eight years of its founding, its population swelled to almost 3,000. After 75 years as a depot and supply center, the town turned out large quantities of ammunition during World War II and the Korean War.
Information: Convention and Visitors Bureau, 100 N. Shore Dr., 402-461-2370, 800-967-2189; www.visithastingsnebraska.com

WHAT TO SEE AND DO
Hastings Museum
1330 N. Burlington Ave., Hastings,
402-461-2399
Includes natural science, pioneer history, Native American lore and historical displays.. Daily; closed holidays. J. M. McDonald Planetarium, sky shows daily.

Willa Cather State Historic Site
413 N. Webster St., Red Cloud,
402-746-2653
Author Willa Cather grew up in Red Cloud, and her childhood home has been converted to a museum. Included are her letters, first editions of her books, photos and Cather family memorabilia. Daily; closed holidays. Other buildings include the Red Cloud depot, St. Juliana Falconieri Catholic Church, Grace Episcopal Church and *My Antonia* farmhouse. Tours of properties four times daily.

HOTELS
★★Quality Hotel and Convention Center
2205 Osborne Dr. E.,
Hastings, 402-463-6721, 888-465-4329;
www.choicehotels.com
100 rooms. Pets accepted. Restaurant, bar. Indoor pool, whirlpool. **$**

★Super 8
2200 N. Kansas Ave.,
Hastings, 402-463-8888;
www.super8.com
50 rooms. Pets accepted, some restrictions; fee. **$**

RESTAURANTS
★Bernardo's Steak House
1109 S. Baltimore,
Hastings, 402-463-4666.
Steak menu. Lunch, dinner. Closed holidays. Bar. Children's menu. **$**

★★Taylor's Steakhouse
1609 N. Kansas, Hastings, 402-462-8000;
www.taylorssteakhouseandcatering.com
Steak menu. Dinner. Closed Sunday; holidays. Bar. Children's menu. **$$$**

113

KEARNEY
Kearney (CAR-nee) is named for the frontier outpost Fort Kearny. It is one of the largest migratory bird flyways in the world, a temporary home for millions of species.
Information: Visitors Bureau, 1007 Second Ave., 308-237-3101, 800-652-9435;
www.kearneycoc.org

WHAT TO SEE AND DO

Fort Kearny State Historical Park
1020 V Rd., Kearney, 308-865-5305.
The first Fort Kearny was erected at Nebraska City in 1846; it was moved here in 1848 to protect the Oregon Trail. In the park are a restored 1864 stockade, sod blacksmith-carpenter shop, museum and interpretive center. Memorial Day-Labor Day: daily.

Museum of Nebraska Art
2401 Central Ave., Kearney, 308-865-8559
Collection of paintings, sculptures, drawings and prints created by Nebraskans or with Nebraska as the subject. Tuesday-Saturday, Sunday afternoons; closed holidays.

Trails and Rails Museum
710 W. 11th St., Kearney, 308-234-3041.
Visit a restored 1898 depot, 1880s freighters' hotel and 1871 country schoolhouse. Includes displays of pioneer trails and rails, steam engines and more. Memorial Day-Labor Day: daily; rest of year: by appointment.

University of Nebraska at Kearney
905 W. 25th St., Kearney, 308-865-8441.
This branch of the state university offers undergraduate, graduate and specialist degrees. Two art galleries and a planetarium are located on campus.

George W. Frank House
W. Hwy. 30, Kearney, 308-865-8284.
This three-story mansion, built in 1889, has a Tiffany window. June-August: Tuesday-Sunday.

HOTELS

★★Best Western Inn Of Kearney
1010 Third Ave., Kearney, 308-237-5185, 800-641-5437; www.bestwestern.com
62 rooms. Pets accepted, some restrictions; fee. Complimentary full breakfast. Restaurant. Fitness room. Outdoor pool, children's pool, whirlpool. $

★★Holiday Inn
110 S. Second Ave., Kearney, 308-237-5971; www.holiday-inn.com
163 rooms. Restaurant, bar. Fitness room. Indoor pool, whirlpool. $

★★Ramada Inn
301 Second Ave., Kearney, 308-237-3141, 800-652-1909; www.kearneyramada.com
209 rooms. Pets accepted; fee. Complimentary continental breakfast. Restaurant, bar. Indoor pool, children's pool, whirlpool. $

RESTAURANTS

★★Alley Rose
2013 Central Ave., Kearney, 308-234-1261.
Lunch, dinner. Closed Sunday; holidays. Bar. Children's menu. $$

★★Grandpa's Steak House
13 Central Ave., Kearney, 308-237-2882.
Steak menu. Lunch, dinner. Closed holidays. Bar. Children's menu. $$

114

NEBRASKA

LEXINGTON
Originally a frontier trading post and settlement along the Oregon Trail, completion of the Union Pacific Railroad brought more settlers to this farmland. Lexington is known as the antiques center of Nebraska.
Information: Lexington Area Chamber of Commerce, 709 E. Pacific Ave., 308-324-5504, 888-966-0564; www.ci.lexington.ne.us

WHAT TO SEE AND DO

Dawson County Historical Museum

805 N. Taft St., Lexington, 308-324-5340

Exhibits include Dawson County history gallery, furnished rural schoolhouse, 1885 Union Pacific depot, 1903 locomotive, farm equipment and 1919 experimental biplane. Collection also includes quilts and prehistoric Native American artifacts. Art gallery and archives. Monday-Saturday, closed holidays.

SPECIAL EVENTS

Antique and Craft Extravaganza

Dawson County Fairgrounds, Lexington, 308-324-5504

More than 275 antiques, craft and flea market dealers. Labor Day weekend.

HOTELS

★First Interstate Inn

2503 Plum Creek Pkwy, Lexington, 308-324-5601, 800-462-4667; www.firstinns.com

52 rooms. Pets accepted; fee. Complimentary continental breakfast. Outdoor pool. **$**

★Super 8

104 E. River Rd., Lexington, 308-324-7434, 800-800-8000; www.super8.com

47 rooms. Fitness room. **$**

LINCOLN

The second-largest city in Nebraska, Lincoln feuded with Omaha, the territorial seat of government, for the honor of being capital of the new state. When the argument was settled in Lincoln's favor in 1867, books, documents and office furniture were moved in covered wagons late one night to escape the armed band of Omaha boosters. As a young lawyer in the 1890s, William Jennings Bryan went to Congress from Lincoln; in 1896, 1900 and 1908 he ran unsuccessfully for president.

The unicameral (one-house legislature) form of government in Nebraska, which was set up by an amendment to the state constitution in 1934 (mostly by the efforts of Nebraska's famous senator, George W. Norris), is of great interest to students of political science. Supporters say it works efficiently and avoids delays and deadlocks common to two-house legislatures.

Information: Convention and Visitors Bureau, 1135 M St., 402-434-5335, 800-423-8212; www.lincoln.org

SPOT★ LIGHT

★LINCOLN WAS NAMED FOR THE 16TH PRESIDENT TWO YEARS AFTER HIS ASSASSINATION.

★LINCOLN MUNICIPAL AIRPORT IS A SPACE SHUTTLE EMERGENCY LANDING SITE.

★TV TALK SHOW HOST JOHNNY CARSON ATTENDED UNIVERSITY OF NEBRAKSA.

WHAT TO SEE AND DO

Folsom Children's Zoo
1222 S. 27th St., Lincoln, 402-475-6741;
www.lincolnzoo.org
Exotic animals, contact areas, botanical gardens. April-mid-August: daily. Train and pony rides.

Lincoln Children's Museum
1420 P St., Lincoln, 402-477-0128;
www.lincolnchildrensmuseum.org
A variety of cultural and scientific exhibits invite exploration and involve the senses. Tuesday-Sunday; closed holidays.

Museum of Nebraska History
131 Centennial Mall N., Lincoln,
402-471-4754; www.nebraskahistory.org
History of Nebraska summarized in exhibits covering events from prehistoric times through the 1950s. Native American Gallery, period rooms. Tuesday-Sunday; closed holidays.

National Museum of Roller Skating
4730 South St., Lincoln, 402-483-7551;
www.rollerskatingmuseum.com
Skates, costumes and photographs documenting the sport and industry from 1700 to the present; also archives dealing with world and national competitions since 1910. The only museum in the world devoted solely to roller skating. Monday-Friday; closed holidays.

Pioneers Park
3201 S. Coddington Ave., Lincoln,
402-441-7895
Hiking, bike trails, bridle path; golf course, picnicking, playgrounds. Nature preserve, outdoor amphitheater. Daily.

State Capitol
1445 K St., Lincoln, 402-471-0448
Designed by Bertram Goodhue, the most dominant feature of this building is the central tower, which rises 400 feet. Ground was broken in 1922 for this third capitol building at Lincoln and was completed 10 years later. Sculpture by Lee Lawrie includes reliefs and friezes depicting the history of law and justice, great philosophers, symbols of the state and a bronze statue of the Sower (32 feet) atop

the tower dome. The great hall, rotunda and legislative chambers are decorated in tile and marble murals, tapestries and wood-inlaid panels. Guided tours. Daily; closed holidays.

Executive Mansion
1425 H St., Lincoln, 402-471-3466;
www.lincoln.org
The state governor's mansion features Georgian Colonial architecture. Guided tours. Thursday afternoons; closed holidays.

Lincoln Monument
201 N. Seventh, Lincoln, 402-434-5348
This standing figure of Abraham Lincoln was designed by the sculptor Daniel Chester French, who also produced the seated statue for Henry Bacon's Lincoln Memorial in Washington, D.C. Architectural setting by Bacon.

Statehood Memorial—Thomas P. Kennard House
1627 H St., Lincoln, 402-471-4764
This 1869 house is the restored residence of Nebraska's first secretary of state. Monday-Friday, by appointment; closed holidays.

Strategic Air & Space Museum
28210 W. Park Hwy., Ashland,
402-944-3100;
www.strategicairandspace.com
Features a permanent collection of 33 aircrafts and six missiles relating to the history of SAC and its importance in the preservation of world peace. Interactive children's gallery, theater, museum store. Daily; closed holidays.

University of Nebraska
501 N. 14th St., Lincoln, 402-472-7211;
www.unl.edu
This state university of more than 33,000 students has research-extension divisions throughout the state. Following Cornhuskers football is a treasured state pasttime.

Great Plains Art Museum
1155 Q St., Lincoln, 402-472-6220
Works by Remington, Russell and other artists are among the nearly 700 pieces of this

NEBRASKA

★
★
★
☆
☆

collection. Also featured are 4,000 volumes of Great Plains and Western Americana. Tuesday-Sunday; closed between exhibits.

University of Nebraska State Museum
14th and U streets, Lincoln, 402-472-2642; www-museum.unl.edu
Displays of fossils (dinosaurs and mounted elephants), rocks and minerals, ancient life, Nebraska plants and animals. Native American exhibits; changing exhibits. Daily; closed holidays.

SPECIAL EVENTS
July Jamm
12 and N. streets, Lincoln, 402-434-6900
Art show, music festival. Late July.

Nebraska State Fair
1800 State Fair Park Dr., Lincoln, 402-473-4109; www.statefair.org
Large fair with livestock, food, contests, games. Late August.

HOTELS
★★Best Western Villager Courtyard & Gardens
5200 O St., Lincoln, 402-464-9111; www.bestwestern.com
186 rooms. Pets accepted. Complimentary continental breakfast. Restaurant, bar. Fitness room. Outdoor pool, whirlpool. $

★★Holiday Inn
141 N. Ninth St., Lincoln, 402-475-4011; 800-432-0002; www.holiday-inn.com
233 rooms. Restaurant, bar. Indoor pool, whirlpool. $

★Woodfin Suites
200 S. 68th Place, Lincoln, 402-483-4900, 888-433-6183; www.woodfinsuitehotels.com
120 rooms. Pets accepted; fee. Complimentary full breakfast. Fitness room. Outdoor pool, whirlpool. Tennis. $

★★★The Cornhusker
333 S. 13th St., Lincoln, 402-474-7474, 800-793-7474; www.thecornhusker.com
Continental style meets Midwestern friendliness at Lincoln's luxurious Cornhusker Hotel. A Nebraska landmark since 1926, today's Cornhusker has sophisticated decor, fine dining, exceptional amenities and dedicated service. The tenth-floor Executive Level offers an upgraded experience. Hand-painted murals and fiber-optic starlight help make the Terrace Grille a pleasant setting for continental cuisine.
290 rooms. WiFi. Restaurant, bar. Fitness room. Indoor pool. Airport transportation available. Business center. $$

RESTAURANTS
★★Billy's
1301 H St., Lincoln, 402-474-0084
American menu. Lunch, dinner. Closed Sunday; holidays. Bar. In a historic house. $$

★Yia Yia
1423 O St., Lincoln, 402-477-9166
Pizza. Lunch, dinner. Closed Sunday; holidays. Bar. Outdoor seating. No credit cards accepted. $

MCCOOK
McCook began as the small settlement of Fairview. The Lincoln Land Company and the Burlington & Missouri Railroad gave the town its name and ensured its growth.
Information: Chamber of Commerce, 107 Norris Ave., 308-345-3200, 800-657-2179; www.aboutmccook.com

WHAT TO SEE AND DO
Museum of the High Plains
423 Norris Ave., McCook, 308-345-3661
Pioneer and Native American artifacts; World War II prisoner of war paintings;
apothecary shop; fossils; flour mill; oil industry exhibit; special exhibits. Tuesday-Sunday afternoons; closed holidays.

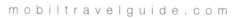

Senator George W. Norris State Historic Site
706 Norris Ave., McCook, 308-345-8484
Restored house of former senator (1861-1944); original furnishings; museum depicts events in his life. Wednesday-Saturday; closed holidays.

SPECIAL EVENTS
Heritage Days
Norris Park, McCook, 308-345-3200
Entertainment, parade, arts and crafts fair, carnival. Last full weekend in September.

Red Willow County Fair and Rodeo
Fairgrounds, W. Fifth and O Streets, McCook, 308-345-3200
Late July.

HOTELS
★★**Best Western Chief Motel**
612 W. B St., McCook, 308-345-3700, 866-641-5437; www.bestwestern.com
111 rooms. Pets accepted, some restrictions. Complimentary continental breakfast. Restaurant. Fitness room. Indoor pool, whirlpool. **$**

NEBRASKA CITY
Nebraska City began as a trading post but grew larger and wilder as the Missouri River and overland traffic brought bullwhackers, muleskinners and riverboat men with bowie knives and pistols in their belts. Located on the Missouri River, Nebraska City ships grain and agricultural products worldwide.
Information: Chamber of Commerce, 806 First Ave., 402-873-3000, 800-514-9113; www.nebraskacity.com

★
★
★
★
★

WHAT TO SEE AND DO
Arbor Lodge State Historical Park
2300 Second Ave., Nebraska City, 402-873-7222
More than 72 acres of wooded grounds surround the 52-room, neo-colonial mansion of J. Sterling Morton (the originator of Arbor Day and the secretary of agriculture under Grover Cleveland) and summer residence of his son Joy Morton (the founder of Morton Salt Company). Picnicking. Mansion, April-December, daily. Park grounds daily.

Mayhew Cabin and Historic Village Foundation
2012 Fourth Corso, Nebraska City, 402-873-3115; www.johnbrownscave.com
Original log cabin and cave where slaves were hidden before and after the Civil War. April-November: Wednesday-Sunday.

Wildwood Historic Home
420 S. Steinhart Park Rd., Nebraska City, 402-873-6340
A 10-room 1869 house with mid-Victorian furnishings, this house has a formal parlor; antique lamps and fixtures. The original brick barn is now an art gallery. April-November: Monday-Saturday, also Sunday afternoons.

SPECIAL EVENTS
Applejack Festival
Nebraska City, 402-873-3000
Celebration of the apple harvest. Parade, antique and craft show, classic car show, football game. Third weekend in September.

Arbor Day Celebration
2300 Second Ave., Nebraska City, 402-873-3000
Tree-planting ceremonies in Arbor Lodge State Historical Park; parade, arts festival, fly-in, breakfast. Last weekend in April.

HOTELS
★**Apple Inn**
502 S. 11th St., Nebraska City, 402-873-5959, 800-659-4446; www.appleinn.net

65 rooms. Pets accepted, some restrictions; fee. Complimentary continental breakfast. Outdoor pool. **$**

RESTAURANTS
★★Embers Steakhouse
1102 Fourth Corso, Nebraska City, 402-873-6416
Steak menu. Lunch, dinner. Bar. Children's menu. **$$**

NORFOLK
German families from Wisconsin were the first to till the rich soil around Norfolk. The town's livestock business and expanding industries have brought prosperity, making Norfolk the chief marketplace of northeastern Nebraska.
Information: Madison County Convention and Visitors Bureau, 402-371-2932, 888-371-2932; www.norfolk.ne.us

WHAT TO SEE AND DO
Cowboy Trail
Hwy. 81 and Tahazorika Rd., Norfolk, 402-371-4862
This 321-mile trail follows the former Chicago and North Western railroad line from Norfolk to Chadron. Includes 13,878 feet of handrailed bridges. Trail is suitable for hiking and mountain biking, with horseback riding allowed alongside the trail.

HOTELS
★★Norfolk Country Inn
1201 S. 13th St., Norfolk, 402-371-4430, 800-233-0733; www.norfolkcountryinn.com
127 rooms. Pets accepted. Restaurant, bar. Outdoor pool. **$**

★★Ramada Inn
1227 Omaha Ave., Norfolk, 402-371-7000; www.ramada.com
98 rooms. Pets accepted; fee. Restaurant, bar. Indoor pool. **$**

★Super 8
1223 W. Omaha Ave., Norfolk, 402-379-2220, 800-800-8000; www.super8.com

66 rooms. Pets accepted, some restrictions; fee. Complimentary continental breakfast. **$**

RESTAURANTS
★★Brass Lantern
1018 S. Ninth St., Norfolk, 402-371-2500
Steak menu. Lunch, dinner. Closed holidays. Bar. Children's menu. **$$**

★★Prenger's
116 E. Norfolk Ave., Norfolk, 402-379-1900
American menu. Lunch, dinner. Closed holidays. Bar. Children's menu. **$$**

★★★The Uptown Café
801 10th St., Stanton, 402-439-5100
Visitors to this restaurant in the middle of the Wild West may be surprised by the refined food and good wine selection. Famed for its support of local artists and musicians, the dining room is filled with paintings and live music.
Seafood menu. Lunch, dinner, late-night. Bar. **$$**

NORTH PLATTE

North Platte, Buffalo Bill Cody's hometown, is the retail, railroad and agricultural hub of west central Nebraska.

Information: North Platte/Lincoln County Convention and Visitors Bureau, 219 S. Dewey, 308-532-4729, 800-955-4528; www.ci.north-platte.ne.us

WHAT TO SEE AND DO

Buffalo Bill Ranch State Historical Park
2921 Scouts Rest Ranch Rd.,
North Platte, 308-535-8035; www.
visitnebraska.org
The 18-room house, barn and outbuildings of William F. Cody's ranch include an interpretive film and displays of buffalo. Memorial Day-Labor Day: daily; October-April: Monday-Friday.

Fort McPherson National Cemetery
I-80, exit 190, Maxwell
Soldiers and scouts of Native American and later wars are buried here.

Lincoln County Historical Museum
2403 N. Buffalo Bill Ave., North Platte,
308-534-5640
Several authentically furnished rooms and exhibits, including a World War II canteen, depict the life and history of Lincoln County. In back is the re-creation of a railroad village with a restored depot, house, church, schoolhouse, log house, and barn. Memorial Day-Labor Day: daily; rest of year: by appointment.

SPECIAL EVENT

"NEBRASKAland DAYS" Celebration
509 E. Fourth St., North Platte,
308-532-7939
Parades, entertainment, food, and the famous PRCA Rodeo. Mid-late June.

HOTELS

★Best Western Chalet Lodge
920 N. Jeffers St., North Platte,
308-532-2313, 866-641-5437;
www.bestwestern.com
38 rooms. Pets accepted; fee. Complimentary continental breakfast. Outdoor pool. $

★Hampton Inn
200 Platte Oasis Pkwy.,
North Platte, 308-534-6000, 800-426-7866;
www.hamptoninn.com
111 rooms. Complimentary continental breakfast. Indoor pool, whirlpool. $

★★Royal Colonial Inn
1402 S. Jeffers St., North Platte,
308-534-3630, 800-624-4643;
www.royalcolonialinn.com
140 rooms. Pets accepted, some restrictions; fee. Complimentary continental breakfast. Restaurant, bar. Outdoor pool. $

★Super 8
220 Eugene Ave., North Platte,
308-532-4224, 800-800-8000;
www.super8.com
113 rooms. Pets accepted, some restrictions; fee. Complimentary continental breakfast. Fitness room. $

RESTAURANTS

★Golden Dragon
120 W. Leota, North Platte, 308-532-5588
Chinese menu. Lunch, dinner. Closed holidays. $$

NEBRASKA

OGALLALA

Developed as a shipping point on the Union Pacific Railroad for the great western cattle herds, Ogallala was the goal of the cattle-driving cowboys who rode day and night with their "eyelids pasted open with tobacco." Many of them are buried in a genuine Boot Hill Cemetery, between 11th and 12th Streets on a 100-foot rise above the South Platte River, where there have been no burials since the 1880s.

Information: Chamber of Commerce, 204 East A St., 308-284-4066, 800-658-4390; www.ogallala.com

WHAT TO SEE AND DO

Ash Hollow State Historical Park
Hwy. 26, Ogallala, 308-778-5651
Approximately 1,000 acres on the Oregon Trail. The hills, caves and springs of Ash Hollow have sustained humans from prehistoric times through the pioneer days. Hiking, picnicking. Interpretive center, restored school.

Crescent Lake National Wildlife Refuge
10630 Road 181, Oshkosh, 308-762-4893
A nesting and migratory bird refuge comprising more than 45,000 acres with numerous pothole lakes. Birds found in the refuge include Canadian geese, great blue herons, American bitterns, prairie chickens, prairie falcons and long-billed curlews.

Front Street
519 E. First St., Ogallala, 308-284-4066
Cowboy museum, general store, saloon, arcade, restaurant. Nightly shows in Crystal Palace during summer.

Lake McConaughy State Recreation Area
1500 Hwy. 61 N., Ogallala, 308-284-3542
Approximately 5,500 acres on Nebraska's largest lake. Swimming, fishing, boating, picnicking, camping.

Lake Ogallala State Recreation Area
1500 Hwy. 61 N., Ogallala, 308-284-3542
Approximately 300 acres on a 320-acre lake. Fishing; boating, camping. Standard fees.

Mansion on the Hill
1004 N. Spruce St., Ogallala
This 1890s mansion contains period furniture, pioneer household items. Memorial Day-Labor Day: daily.

HOTELS

★★Best Western Stagecoach Inn
201 Stagecoach Trail, Ogallala, 308-284-3656, 800-662-2993; www.bestwestern.com
100 rooms. Pets accepted; fee. Complimentary continental breakfast. Restaurant, bar. Indoor pool, outdoor pool, children's pool, whirlpool. Airport transportation available. $

★Comfort Inn
110 Pony Express Lane, Ogallala, 308-284-4028, 877-424-6423; www.comfortinn.com
49 rooms. Complimentary continental breakfast. Indoor pool, whirlpool. $

RESTAURANTS

★★Hill Top Inn
197 Kingsley Dr., Ogallala, 308-284-4534
Dinner. Closed Monday; holidays. Bar. Children's menu. $$

121

NEBRASKA

★
★
★
★
★

OMAHA

The largest city in Nebraska, Omaha is named for the Native Americans who lived here until they signed a treaty with the federal government on June 24, 1854. Opportunists across the Missouri River in Council Bluffs, Iowa, who had been waiting for the new territory to open, rushed to stake out property, triggering a real estate boom. Omaha also saw the trial of Standing Bear, chief of the Ponca Tribe, which established the precedent that Native Americans were entitled to constitutional rights and protections.

During early boom times, steamboats docked in Omaha daily, bringing gold-seekers and emigrants to be outfitted for the long journey west. Local merchants further prospered when Omaha was named the eastern terminus for the Union Pacific. The first rail was laid in 1865. Public buildings rose on the prairie; schools, plants and stockyards flourished in the 1870s and 1880s. Fighting tornadoes, grasshopper plagues, floods and drought, the people built one of the farm belt's great commercial and industrial cities.

Today, Omaha continues to be a major transportation and agribusiness center, but is also a recognized leader in telecommunications, insurance and manufacturing as well as the home of five Fortune 500 companies. Omaha is also the headquarters of STRATCOM, the Strategic Air Command, one of the vital links in the national defense chain. Information: **Greater Omaha Convention and Visitors Bureau, 6800 Mercy Rd., 402-444-4660, 866-937-6624; www.visitomaha.com**

★
★
★
★
★

SPOT★ LIGHT

★UNION PACIFIC RAILROAD HAS BEEN HEADQUARTERED IN OMAHA SINCE 1862.

★WARREN BUFFET, THE WORLD'S THIRD RICHEST PERSON, LIVES IN OMAHA.

★FAMOUS RESIDENTS INCLUDE MARLON BRANDO, NICK NOLTE AND FRED ASTAIRE.

WHAT TO SEE AND DO

Durham Western Heritage Museum
Omaha Union Station, 801 S. 10th St., Omaha, 402-444-5071; www.dwhm.org
Restored Art Deco railroad depot is now a history museum. Exhibits on Omaha history from 1880 to 1954; Byron Reed coin collection; traveling temporary exhibits. Tuesday-Sunday; closed holidays.

General Crook House
5730 N. 30th St., Omaha, 402-455-9990

Built in 1878 to serve as the residence of the commander of the Department of the Platte. Originally called Quarters I, Fort Omaha, the house soon came to be known by the name of its first occupant, General George Crook. Italianate architecture; many antiques from the Victorian era; Victorian garden in summer. Guided tours by appointment. Daily; closed holidays.

Gerald Ford Birth Site
32nd and Woolworth Ave., Omaha,

402-444-5955
Model of the original house and White House memorabilia. Betty Ford Memorial Rose Garden. Daily.

Great Plains Black History Museum
2213 Lake St., Omaha, 402-345-2212
Housed in a building designed in 1907 by prominent Nebraska architect Thomas R. Kimball, the museum preserves the history of African Americans and their part in the heritage of Omaha and Nebraska since the territorial period of the 1850s. Includes rare photographs, relics, historical displays; films. Monday-Friday.

Heartland of America Park
Eighth and Douglas Streets, Omaha, 402-444-5920
A 31-acre site features picnic facilities, arbors and waterfalls. The park's 15-acre lake has a computer-driven fountain that has a colored light show at night. Excursion boat rides on *The General Marion:* Memorial Day-Labor Day, Wednesday-Sunday. Gene Leahy Mall, bounded by Douglas and Farnam, 10th and 14th streets N. P. Dodge Memorial Park, John Pershing Dr. Elmwood Park, Dodge and 60th Streets. Memorial Park, Dodge and 63rd Streets across street from Elmwood Park. World War II memorial, rose garden, walking and jogging paths.

Henry Doorly Zoo
3701 S. 10th St., Omaha, 402-733-8401; www.omahazoo.org
More than 18,500 animals, many rare, are on display in a 110-acre park. Exhibits include an aquarium, indoor rainforest, walk-through aviary, white tigers, and polar bears. Daily, closed holidays.

Historic Bellevue
112 W. Mission Ave., Bellevue, 402-293-3080, 800-467-2779
Restored buildings include the first church in the Nebraska territory (1856); old depot (1869); settlers' log cabin (circa 1830); and Fontenelle Bank (1856). Sarpy County Historical Museum (2402 SAC Place) has displays concerning the history of the county

and changing exhibits Tuesday-Sunday; closed holidays.

Joslyn Art Museum
24th and Dodge Streets, Omaha, 402-342-3300; www.joslyn.org
Museum building of Art Deco design with collections of art, ancient through modern, including European and American paintings, sculpture; art of the Western frontier, Native American art; traveling exhibitions. Guided tours, lectures, workshops, films, gallery talks, concerts. A 30,000-volume art reference library; museum shop. Tuesday-Sunday; closed holidays.

Mormon Trail Center at Winter Quarters
3215 State St., Omaha, 402-453-9372
The winter of 1846-1847 took the lives of more than 600 Mormon emigrants who camped near here. A monument commemorates their hardship. Films and pioneer exhibits in visitor center.

Old Market
11th and Howard Sts., extending to 10th St. and W. to 13th, Omaha, 402-341-1877
Art galleries, antique shops, restaurants. Revitalization of old warehouse district; some of Omaha's oldest commercial buildings line the market's brick-paved streets.

Omaha Children's Museum
500 S. 20th St., Omaha, 402-342-6163; www.ocm.org
Self-directed exploration and play for children and families; constantly changing series of hands-on exhibits in science, the arts and humanities, health and creative play. Tuesday-Sunday; closed holidays.

Platte River State Park
14421 346th St., Louisville, 402-234-2217
These 413 acres are located on rolling bluffs overlooking the Platte River. Swimming pool; paddleboats. Hiking, horseback riding; tennis courts, archery range, recreational fields. Cross-country skiing.

Ak-Sar-Ben Aquarium
21502 W. Hwy. 31, Gretna, 402-332-3901

NEBRASKA

★
★
★
★
☆
☆

OMAHA'S OLD MARKET

One of the few downtown areas that preserves Omaha's original Victorian-era architecture, the Old Market Area is a five-block-square shopping, dining and gallery district that's the heart and soul of the city center. Window-shop, stop for coffee, pop into art-filled boutiques—this neighborhood is made for strolling. Bounded by Farnam and Jones Streets and 10th and 13th Streets, the Old Market Area was originally the food-processing center for the region: Swanson Food, Anheuser Busch and other stalwarts of the food and beverage industry once occupied these buildings. Food is still one of the finest reasons to visit the Old Market Area. Find provisions for a picnic at one of Omaha's best bakeries, Delice European Bakery and Coffee Bar (1206 Howard), and pick up cheese and wine at La Buvette Wine and Grocery (511 S. 11th St.). On Wednesdays and Saturdays in summer and fall, stop for fresh local produce at the farmer's market, held on 11th Street between Jackson and Howard.

Directly south of the Old Market Area on 10th Street is the Durham Western Heritage Museum (801 S. 10th St.), housed in the architecturally stunning Union Station, an Art Deco gem from Omaha's past. The museum has vintage cars and railroad equipment, and a period soda fountain is still in operation.

Walk north on 10th Street five blocks to reach Gene Leahy Mall, a 10-acre park with a lake that serves as a reflecting pond for the modern high-rise architecture of Omaha. Trails wind through the park, linking formal flower gardens, a playground for children, a bandstand and public art displays. To the east, the Leahy Mall connects to Heartland of America Park and Fountain, which is bounded by Eighth Street and the Missouri River. The highlight of the park is its lake, with a fountain that shoots streams of water 300 feet into the air. The *General Marion* tour boat navigates the lake to take visitors closer to the fountain. At night, the water display is accompanied by pulsing lights.

Return to the Leahy Mall along Douglas Street, which leads into the modern city center. At 24th Street, turn north one block to the Joslyn Art Museum (2200 Dodge St.), Nebraska's premier center for the visual arts. The museum building is itself a work of art, a fanciful Art Deco structure faced with shimmering pink marble. The permanent collection consists of American and European art from the 19th and 20th centuries. A highlight is the cache of works from Karl Bodmer, a German watercolorist who traveled up the Missouri River in the 1830s, capturing the pristine landscapes, Native Americans and wildlife before white pioneer settlement.

★
★
★
★
☆

This modern facility features more than 50 species of fish native to Nebraska, as well as a terrarium, the World Herald Auditorium, a natural history classroom and orientation and display areas.

Two Rivers State Recreation Area
27702 F St., Waterloo, 402-359-5165
More than 600 acres with a water area of 320 acres. Swimming; trout fishing, boat-

ing. Picnicking, concession. Camping late April-October.

Kountze Planetarium
68th and Dodge Streets, Omaha, 402-554-3722
Planetarium shows display galaxies, stars, planets and other celestial phenomena. Observatory, first Friday, Saturday each month.

SPECIAL EVENTS

River City Round-up
Fairgrounds, 6800 Mercy Rd.,
Omaha, 402-554-9610
Celebration of agriculture and western heritage includes parade, barbecues, trail rides. Late September.

HOTELS

★★Best Western Redick Plaza Hotel
1504 Harney St., Omaha,
402-342-1500, 888-342-5339;
www.bestwestern.com
89 rooms. Complimentary full breakfast. Restaurant, bar. Fitness room. Airport transportation available. **$**

★★Days Inn
1811 Hillcrest Dr., Bellevue,
402-292-3800, 800-292-7277;
www.daysinn.com
126 rooms. Pets accepted; fee. Complimentary full breakfast. Restaurant, bar. Indoor pool, children's pool, whirlpool. **$**

★★Doubletree Guest Suites Omaha
7270 Cedar St., Omaha,
402-397-5141, 800-222-8733;
www.doubletree.com
189 rooms, all suites. Restaurant. Fitness room. Indoor pool, whirlpool. Airport transportation available. Indoor tropical courtyard. **$**

★★Doubletree Hotel
1616 Dodge St., Omaha,
402-346-7600, 800-222-8733;
www.doubletree.com
413 rooms. Restaurant, bar. Fitness room. Indoor pool, whirlpool. Airport transportation available. Business center. **$**

★★Embassy Suites
555 S. 10th St., Omaha,
402-346-9000, 800-362-2779;
www.embassysuitesomaha.com
249 rooms, all suites. Pets accepted, some restrictions; fee. Complimentary continental breakfast. Restaurant, bar. Fitness room. Indoor pool, whirlpool. **$$**

★Hampton Inn
9720 W. Dodge Rd., Omaha,
402-391-5300; www.hamptoninn.com
129 rooms. Complimentary continental breakfast. **$**

★★Hilton Garden Inn
1005 Dodge St., Omaha, 402-341-4400,
800-445-8667; www.hilton.com
178 rooms. Restaurant. Fitness room. Indoor pool, whirlpool. **$**

★La Quinta Inn
3330 N. 104th Ave., Omaha, 402-493-1900;
www.laquinta.com
130 rooms. Pets accepted. Outdoor pool. **$**

★★★Marriott Omaha
10220 Regency Circle, Omaha, 402-399-9000; www.marriott.com
This hotel offers two restaurants, a lounge, an indoor and outdoor pool, health club, and many more amenities. It is located near the Joslyn Art Museum, Old Market, golf courses and tennis facilities.
301 rooms. Restaurant, bar. Fitness room. Indoor pool, outdoor pool, whirlpool. **$**

RESTAURANTS

★Bohemian Café
1406 S. 13th St., Omaha, 402-342-9838
American, Eastern European menu. Lunch, dinner. Closed holidays. **$$**

★★Busty le Doux's
1014 Howard St., Omaha, 402-346-5100
Cajun menu. Lunch, dinner. Closed holidays. Bar. Outdoor seating. **$$**

★★★Cafe de Paris
1228 S. Sixth St., Omaha, 402-344-0227
As the name suggests, this is an exceptional French bistro with a menu that does not stray from the classics. A knowledgeable staff and sommelier add to the experience. French menu. Dinner. Closed Sunday-Monday; holidays. Bar. Jacket required. Reservations recommended. **$$$**

★★★French Café
1017 Howard St., Omaha, 402-341-3547;

125

★
★
★
★
★

www.frenchcafe.com

Elegant French dishes, continually refreshed with contemporary ingredients, have earned this restaurant a good reputation. Peppersteak is a signature dish, and the roasted rack of pork is popular. The wine cellar is substantial.American, French menu. Lunch, dinner, Sunday brunch. Closed Monday; holidays. Bar. **$$$**

★★★Gorat's Steak House
4917 Center St., Omaha, 402-551-3733; www.goratssteakhouse.com

An Omaha landmark for more than 60 years, this steakhouse specializes in classics with thick cuts of filet mignon and more. Enhance the old school experience with a traditional side dish such as escargot, doused in butter, or chilled shrimp cocktail.
Steak menu. Lunch, dinner. Closed Sunday; holidays. Bar. Children's menu. Reservations recommended. **$$$**

★★Indian Oven
1010 Howard St., Omaha, 402-342-4856
Northern Indian menu. Lunch, dinner. Closed Sunday; holidays. Bar. Reservations recommended. Outdoor seating. **$$**

★Johnny's Café
4702 S. 27th St., Omaha, 402-731-4774; www.johnnyscafe.com

Steak menu. Lunch, dinner. Closed Sunday; holidays. Bar. Children's menu. **$$**

★Mc Fosters Natural Kind Café
302 S. 38th St., Omaha, 402-345-7477; www.mcfosters.com

American, seafood menu with natural-foods emphasis. Lunch, dinner. Closed holidays. Bar. Children's menu. Casual attire. Outdoor seating. **$$**

★★★Signature's
1616 Dodge St., Omaha, 402-346-7600
Located at the top of the Doubletree Hotel, this restaurant offers a panoramic view of the city's skyline. A continental concept, the menu draws on influences from all over the world.
Seafood menu. Breakfast, lunch, dinner, late-night. Bar. **$$**

★Trini's
1020 Howard St., Omaha, 402-346-8400
Mexican, seafood menu. Lunch, dinner. Closed Sunday; holidays. **$**

★★★V. Mertz
1022 Howard St., Omaha, 402-345-8980; www.vmertz.com

Located just off the brick-walled Old Market Passageway, this cozy restaurant offers a quiet atmosphere. The menu, consisting of continental dishes, changes weekly; the wine list is expansive. Jacket and tie are recommended for men.
American menu. Lunch, dinner. Bar. **$$**

SCOTTSBLUFF
Scottsbluff is the trading center for a large area of western Nebraska and eastern Wyoming.
Information: Scottsbluff-Gering United Chamber of Commerce, 1517 Broadway, 308-632-2133, 800-788-9475; www.scottsbluffgering.net

WHAT TO SEE AND DO
Agate Fossil Beds National Monument
301 River Rd., Harrison, 308-668-2211
An approximately 2,700-acre area with two self-guided nature trails, a visitor center with exhibits of the fossils of animals that roamed the area between 19 and 21 million years ago, and exhibits of Plains Native Americans. Visitor center, daily; closed holidays. Park all year.

Chimney Rock National Historic Site
Hwy. 26, Bridgeport, 308-586-2581; www.nps.gov/chro

A landmark of the Oregon Trail, Chimney Rock rises almost 500 feet above the south bank of the North Platte River. Starting as a cone-shaped mound, it becomes a narrow 150-foot column towering above the landscape. For early travelers, many of whom sketched and described it in their journals,

Chimney Rock marked the end of the prairies. It became a National Historic Site in 1956.

Riverside Zoo
1600 S. Beltline W., Scottsbluff, 308-630-6236; www.riversidezoo.org
More than 97 species of both native and exotic animals in a lush park setting. Walk-through aviary, white tiger, moose woods. Daily, weather permitting.

Scotts Bluff National Monument
190276 Hwy. 92 W., Gering, 308-436-4340; www.nps.gov/scbl
This 800-foot bluff in western Nebraska was a landmark to pioneers who traveled the California/Oregon Trail by wagon trains. Historians often speak of this natural promontory in the North Platte Valley, which was originally named me-a-pa-te, "hill that is hard to go around," by the Plains Native Americans. Many people, including fur traders, Mormons and gold seekers, came this way. Westward-bound pioneers, Pony Express riders and the first transcontinental telegraph all passed through Mitchell Pass (within Monument boundaries) to skirt this pine-studded bluff. The Oregon Trail Museum at the monument's visitor center (daily; closed Christmas) depicts the story of westward migration along the trail. A paved road and hiking trail provide access to the summit for a view of the North Platte Valley and other landmarks such as Chimney Rock.

West Nebraska Arts Center
106 E. 18th St., Scottsbluff, 308-632-2226
Changing gallery shows in all media throughout the year showcasing the finest artists in the region. Daily; closed holidays.

HOTELS

★Candlelight Inn
1822 E. 20th Place, Scottsbluff, 308-635-3751, 800-424-2305; www.candlelightscottsbluff.com
60 rooms. Complimentary continental breakfast. Fitness room. Airport transportation available. $

★Comfort Inn
1902 21st Ave., Scottsbluff, 308-632-7510, 877-424-6423; www.comfortinn.com
46 rooms. Pets accepted; fee. Complimentary continental breakfast. Fitness room. Indoor pool, whirlpool. $

SIDNEY
In 1867, Sidney was established as a division point on the Union Pacific Railroad. Fort Sidney was established shortly thereafter, providing military protection for railroad workers and immigrants. Many relics of the Fort Sidney era remain and have been restored. Sidney, the seat of Cheyenne County, is also a peaceful farm, trading and industrial center.
Information: Cheyenne County Chamber of Commerce, 740 Illinois St., 308-254-5851, 800-421-4769; www.sidney-nebraska.com

WHAT TO SEE AND DO
Cabela's
115 Cabela Dr., Sidney, 308-254-5505; www.cabelas.com
Sidney is the corporate headquarters for one of the world's largest outdoor gear outfitters. The 73,000-square-foot building displays more than 60,000 products as well as 500 wildlife mounts. Other attractions in the showroom include an 8,000-gallon aquarium, art gallery, gun library, restaurant and "Royal Challenge," a twice-life-size bronze sculpture of two battling elk. Daily.

Fort Sidney Post Commander's Home.
1108 Sixth Ave., Sidney, 308-254-2150
One of the original buildings of old Fort Sidney, this house was used in the 19th century to protect railroad workers during the Native American wars and has been authentically restored. Memorial Day-Labor Day, daily, afternoons.

HOTELS

★Comfort Inn
730 E. Jennifer Lane, Sidney,
308-254-5011; www.comfortinn.com
55 rooms.. Complimentary continental breakfast.**$**

★Days Inn
3042 Silverberg Dr., Sidney,
308-254-2121; www.daysinn.com
47 rooms. Pets accepted, some restrictions; fee. Complimentary continental breakfast. Indoor pool, whirlpool. **$**

SOUTH SIOUX CITY
This community is an extension of neighboring Sioux City, Iowa.
Information: Visitors Bureau, 2700 Dakota Ave., 402-494-1307, 800-793-6327; www.visitsouthsiouxcity.com

WHAT TO SEE AND DO

Ponca State Park
R.R. 2, Ponca, 402-755-2284.
Approximately 1,400 acres. Panoramic views of the Missouri River Valley. Swimming pool, fishing, boating, hiking, horseback riding, cross-country skiing, picnicking, camping.

HOTELS

★★Marina Inn Conference Center
Fourth and B Streets, South Sioux City,
402-494-4000, 800-798-7980;
www.marina-inn.com
182 rooms. Pets accepted; fee. Restaurant, bar. Indoor pool, whirlpool. Airport transportation available. **$**

YORK
This town originated as a stop on the Oregon Trail. It's now a thriving agricultural community.
Information: York County Visitors Center, 116 S Lincoln Ave., 402-362-5531, 888-733-9675; www.yorkchamber.org

WHAT TO SEE AND DO

Anna Bemis Palmer Museum
211 E. Seventh St., York, 402-363-2630.
Items and displays relating to the history of the city, York County and the state of Nebraska. Monday-Friday; closed holidays.

HOTELS

★Best Western Palmer Inn
2426 S. Lincoln Ave., York,
402-362-5585, 800-452-3185;
www.bestwestern.com
41 rooms. **$**

★Days Inn
3710 S. Lincoln Ave., York,
402-362-6355; www.daysinn.com
39 rooms. Complimentary continental breakfast. Indoor pool, whirlpool. **$**

RESTAURANT

★★★Chances R
124 W. Fifth, York, 402-362-7755
This restaurant, decorated with early 20th century antiques, specializes in home-cooked classics. Expect to sample classics such as crispy fried chicken and creamy mashed potatoes.
American menu. Breakfast, lunch, dinner, late-night, Sunday brunch. Closed holidays. Bar. Children's menu. Valet parking. **$$$**

NEBRASKA

★
★
★
★
★

NORTH DAKOTA

IN BISMARCK THERE IS A STATUARY GROUP, *PIONEER FAMILY*, AND BEHIND IT, GLEAMING white against the sky, towers the famous skyscraper capitol. One symbolizes the North Dakota of wagon trains and General Custer. The other symbolizes modern North Dakota—a place where a thousand oil wells have sprouted, dams harness erratic rivers, and vast natural resources have been found.

This is a fascinating land of prairies, rich river valleys, small cities, huge ranches and vast stretches of wheat. Bordering Canada for 320 miles to the north, North Dakota shares straight-line borders with Montana to the west and South Dakota to the south. The Red River of the North forms its eastern boundary with Minnesota. The Garrison Dam has changed much of the internal geography of the state's western areas, converting the Missouri River, known as "Big Muddy," into a broad waterway with splendid recreation areas bordering the reservoir Lake Sakajawea. To the southwest stretch the Badlands in all their natural grandeur, and the open range about which Theodore Roosevelt wrote so eloquently in his *Ranch Life and the Hunting Trail.*

At various times, Spain, France and England claimed what is now North Dakota as part of their empires. French Canadian fur trappers were the first Europeans to explore the land. After the Louisiana Purchase, explorers Lewis and Clark crossed Dakota, establishing Fort Mandan. The Dakota Territory was organized on March 2, 1861, but major settlement of what later became North Dakota followed after the entry of the Northern Pacific Railroad in the early 1870s.

This is the state in which to trace 19th-century frontier history, to stand at the center of the continent, to see Native American dances and outdoor dramas, or to watch the 10 million migratory waterfowl that soar across the sky each spring and fall.

★ SPOTLIGHT

★ Theodore Roosevelt National Park is considered one of the darkest spots in North America and the best place in the world to view the Northern Lights.

★ Entertainer Lawrence Welk was born in Strasburg, North Dakota.

★ Dakota is a Sioux word that means "friend."

THE FREE-FLOWING MISSOURI RIVER

There's very little of the free-flowing Missouri River left in North Dakota—only one portion, from Garrison Dam to Bismarck, resembles the broad prairie river as seen by explorers Meriwether Lewis and William Clark. This route explores a section of Missouri River wetlands, allowing modern-day explorers the chance to see the cottonwood forests and wetlands that once stretched along the Missouri, before hydroelectric dams tamed the river.

From Mandan, travel north on Highway 25, which follows the Missouri's western banks. The route passes through farmland and then drops onto a broad, arid basin, with the green, cottonwood-fringed Missouri in the distance. If you don't mind traveling a few miles on gravel roads, turn off Highway 25 east toward the community of Price. Follow the road north along the banks of the river. A number of wildlife refuges string along the river—you may see wild turkeys, deer or bald eagles.

At Hensler, turn west on Highway 200A to visit Fort Clark State Historic Site. Fort Clark was built in 1830 by the American Fur Company as a trading post near a Mandan Indian earthlodge village. A second fort, Primeaus Post, was built on the site in the early 1850s and operated in competition with Fort Clark for most of that decade. Artists Karl Bodmer and George Catlin visited the site, as did German Prince Maximilian, John James Audubon and more than 50 steamboats per year. Many of Bodmer's paintings were of the people and village of Fort Clark.

Continue west along Highway 200A. At Stanton, follow County Highway 37 north to the Knife River Indian Village National Historic Site. One of the largest Hidatsa villages was located at the confluence of the Missouri and the Knife rivers, where this new interpretive center and earthlodge reconstruction are now found. More than 50 earthlodge remains suggest that Native Americans lived in this location for nearly 8,000 years. The circular depressions at the three village sites are up to 40 feet in diameter and are a silent testimony to the people that lived here.

Continue north to join Highway 200 and follow it across the Garrison Dam, the third-largest earth-filled dam in the United States. The dam backs up the Missouri River 175 miles to the west in 378,000-acre Lake Sakajawea. Continue to Highway 83, then head south, zipping past the coal strip mines at Underwood. At Washburn, leave the freeway and follow signs to the Fort Mandan Historic Site, where volunteers have reconstructed Lewis and Clark's log fort. The Lewis and Clark Expedition spent the winter of 1804-1805 here in a cottonwood blockade above the Missouri River. It was here that they met French-Canadian Toussaint Charbonneau, who would serve as their interpreter, and his young Shoshone wife, Sacagawea. This reconstruction of Fort Mandan is downstream from the original site, which has been swallowed by the river. The triangular fort is modest and small, considering that there were 40-odd members of the expedition living here. Also at the park are a visitor center, gift shop and picnic area along the river.

Return to Highway 83 and travel south for seven miles, then exit at Highway 1804 and follow this scenic route south along the free-flowing Missouri's eastern banks to Bismarck. Approximately 162 miles.

NORTH DAKOTA

BISMARCK

On the east bank of the Missouri, near the geographic center of the state and within 150 miles of the geographic center of the continent, North Dakota's capitol flourished as a steamboat port called "the Crossing." As the terminus of the Northern Pacific Railway, Bismarck gained new importance and was named for the Chancellor of Germany to attract German capital for building transcontinental railroads. General Custer came to Bismarck to take command of the nearby newly constructed Fort Abraham Lincoln and in 1876 rode out to his fatal rendezvous with Sitting Bull. In 1883, Bismarck became the capital of the Dakota Territory, and in 1889, the seat of the new state.

Information: Bismarck-Mandan Convention and Visitors Bureau, 1600 Burnt Boat Dr., 701-222-4308, 800-767-3555; www.bismarckmandancvb.com

131

SPOT★LIGHT

★THE 19-STORY ART DECO CAPITOL BUILDING IS THE LARGEST IN THE CITY.

★THE CITY WAS NAMED AFTER GERMAN CHANCELLOR OTTO VON BISMARCK IN AN EFFORT TO ATTRACT GERMAN SETTLERS TO THE AREA.

WHAT TO SEE AND DO

North Dakota State Capitol
600 E. Boulevard Ave., Bismarck, 701-328-2480

Constructed in 1933 on a $2 million budget after the original building burned in 1930, this state capitol building stands out from its traditionally domed peers. The 19-story Art Deco limestone tower is one of only four vertically oriented capitols in the United States (along with those in Nebraska, Louisiana and Florida). Beyond its distinctive exterior, the Skyscraper of the Prairies is capped with an observation deck, features lavish interiors fashioned from wood, stone and metal from all over the globe and a cavernous Great Hall running to the legislative quarters. Tours are available on weekdays in the summer.

Also on the grounds are the former Governors' Mansion, now restored and featuring historic displays, and the North Dakota Heritage Center, a regional history museum with an impressive collection of Plains Indians artifacts. Outdoors are two notable sculptures, one of Lewis and Clark guide Sacagawea, and another dubbed The Pioneer Family by Avard Fairbanks.

Ward Earthlodge Village Historic Site
4480 Fort Lincoln Rd., Bismarck, 701-222-6455

Mandan Indians once occupied this bluff above the Missouri River, living in dome-shaped homes built of logs and earth. By the time Lewis and Clark passed through the region, the village was deserted. Depressions remain where the houses once stood, and the site is now part of the city park system. Interpretive signs explain how the village was constructed and elements of Mandan cultural life. Spectacular views from the bluff. For more information, contact Bismarck Parks and Recreation. Daily dawn-dusk.

SPECIAL EVENTS
United Tribes Powwow
3315 University Dr., Bismarck,
701-255-3285;
www.unitedtribespowwow.com
Among the most attended powwows in the United States, this annual event is one of the top cultural happenings in North Dakota. Some 1,500 Native American dancers and drummers, representing more than 70 tribes and clothed in traditional garb, perform at the Lone Star Arena at United Tribes Technical College. You'll find singing, dancing and drumming competitions, as well as a softball tournament, a parade, an intertribal summit, a pageant and plenty of food. Early September.

HOTELS
★★Best Western Ramkota Hotel
800 S. Third St., Bismarck, 701-258-7700, 800-780-7234; www.bestwestern.com
306 rooms. Pets accepted, some restrictions; fee. High-speed Internet access. Restaurant, bar. Fitness room. Indoor pool, children's pool, whirlpool. Airport transportation available. $

★

★

★

☆

☆

★Expressway Inn
200 E. Bismarck Expy., Bismarck, 701-222-2900, 800-456-6388;
www.expresswayinnandsuites.com
163 rooms. Pets accepted; fee. Complimentary continental breakfast. High-speed, wireless Internet access. Fitness room. Outdoor pool, whirlpool. Airport transportation available. $

★Fairfield Inn
135 Ivy Ave., Bismarck,
701-223-9293, 800-228-2800;
www.fairfieldinn.com
63 rooms. Complimentary continental breakfast. High-speed, wireless Internet access. Indoor pool, whirlpool. $

★★Kelly Inn-Bismarck
1800 N. 12th St., Bismarck.
701-223-8001, 800-635-3559;
www.kellyinns.com
101 rooms. Pets accepted, some restrictions. High-speed Internet access. Restaurant, bar. Fitness room. Indoor pool, whirlpool. Airport transportation available. $

★★Radisson Hotel Bismarck
605 E. Broadway Ave., Bismarck,
701-255-6000, 800-333-3333;
www.radisson.com-bismarcknd_downtown
215 rooms. Pets accepted. High-speed Internet access. Restaurant, bar. Fitness room. Indoor pool, whirlpool. Airport transportation available. Business center. $

★Ramada Limited Suites
3808 E. Divide Ave., Bismarck,
701-221-3030, 800-295-3895;
www.ramada.com
66 rooms. Pets accepted; fee. Complimentary continental breakfast. High-speed, wireless Internet access. Fitness room. Indoor pool, whirlpool. $

RESTAURANTS
★Meriwether's
1700 River Rd., Bismarck, 701-258-0666
American menu. Lunch, dinner, Sunday brunch. Bar. Children's menu. Casual attire. Outdoor seating. $$

★★Peacock Alley
422 E. Main St., Bismarck, 701-255-7917
American, seafood menu. Lunch, dinner, brunch. Bar. Children's menu. Casual attire. $$

DEVILS LAKE

Located near the shore of Devils Lake, this city offers some of the best fishing in North Dakota. The opening of the federal land office here in 1883 sparked the growth of the city.

Information: Devils Lake Area Chamber of Commerce, Hwy. 2 E., 701-662-4903, 800-233-8048; www.devilslakend.com

WHAT TO SEE AND DO

Devils Lake
Devils Lake, six miles south of town

This lake gets its name from the Indian name Miniwaukan, which means "bad water." Bolstered by legends of drowned warriors, the name evolved into Devils Lake. Fishing, boating; hunting, golfing, biking, snowmobiling, picnicking, camping.

Fort Totten State Historic Site
Hwy. 20, Devils Lake, 701-766-4441

Built in 1867 to protect the overland route to Montana, this was the last outpost before 300 miles of wilderness. One of the best preserved military forts west of the Mississippi; 16 original buildings. Pioneer Daughters Museum; interpretive center, commissary display; videotape program of the site's history. Summer dinner theater. Self-guided tours. Memorial Day-Labor Day, daily; rest of year, by appointment.

HOTELS

★Fireside Inn
215 Hwy. 2 E., Devils Lake, 701-662-6760, 888-266-3948; www.comfortinn.com

87 rooms. Pets accepted; fee. Complimentary continental breakfast. Indoor pool, whirlpool. Business center. $

★★Totten Trail Historic Inn
Fort Totten State Historic Site, 701-766-4787; www.tottentrailinn.com

10 rooms. Closed October-April. Complimentary full breakfast. $

133

FARGO

Fargo, the largest city in North Dakota, was named for William G. Fargo of the Wells-Fargo Express Company. It's the hometown of baseball great Roger Maris, and a museum filled with his personal memorabilia is located in West Acres Mall.

With blackjack legal in North Dakota, Fargo has taken the lead in promoting its gaming tables. There are approximately 30 casinos in the city, making it a major tourist attraction for the three-state region including Minnesota and South Dakota. Charities and nonprofit organizations run the casinos and collect all profits above expenses. The 1996 dark comedy *Fargo* took its name from the city, gently poking fun at the residents' thick northern accents and Scandinavian heritage, but most of the movie actually takes place in Minnesota.

Information: Fargo-Moorhead Convention and Visitors Bureau, 2001 44th St. S.W., 701-282-3653, 800-235-7654; www.fargomoorhead.org

SPOT★ LIGHT

★FARGO IS SHOWN ONLY IN THE FIRST SCENES OF THE FILM OF THE SAME NAME.

★BASEBALL GREAT ROGER MARIS HAILED FROM FARGO.

★IN THE 1880S, FARGO WAS A DIVORCE CAPITAL DUE TO LENIENT LAWS.

HOTELS

★AmericInn
1423 35th St. S.W., Fargo,
701-234-9946, 800-634-3444;
www.americinnfargo.com
61 rooms. Pets accepted; fee. Complimentary continental breakfast. Wireless Internet. Fitness room. Indoor pool, whirlpool. Business center. $

★★Best Western Fargo Doublewood Inn
3333 13th Ave. S., Fargo,
701-235-3333, 800-433-3235;
www.bestwestern.com
172 rooms. Pets accepted, some restrictions; fee. Wireless Internet. Restaurant, bar. Indoor pool, whirlpool. Airport transportation available. Business center. Casino. $

★★Best Western Kelly Inn
3800 Main Ave., Fargo,
701-282-2143, 800-580-1234;
www.bestwestern.com
133 rooms. Complimentary continental breakfast. Internet. Restaurant, bar. Fitness room. Indoor pool, outdoor pool, children's pool, whirlpool. Business center. Casino. $

★Comfort Suites
1415 35th St. S., Fargo,
701-237-5911, 800-228-5150;
www.choicehotels.com
66 rooms, all suites. Pets accepted. Complimentary continental breakfast. WiFi. Indoor pool, whirlpool. Business center. $

★Country Inn & Suites By Carlson
3316 13th Ave., Fargo,
701-234-0565, 888-201-1746;
www.countryinns.com

99 rooms. Pets accepted, some restrictions; fee. Complimentary continental breakfast. Wireless Internet. Fitness room. Indoor pool, whirlpool. Airport transportation available. Business center. $

★Fairfield Inn
3902 Ninth Ave. S.W., Fargo,
701-281-0494, 800-228-2800;
www.fairfieldinn.com
63 rooms. Complimentary continental breakfast. Wireless Internet. Indoor pool, whirlpool. $

★Hampton Inn
3431 14th Ave. S.W., Fargo,
701-235-5566, 800-426-7866;
www.hamptoninn.com
75 rooms. Complimentary continental breakfast. High-speed Internet access. Indoor pool, whirlpool. Business center. $

★★Holiday Inn
3803 13th Ave. S., Fargo,
701-282-2700, 877-282-2700;
www.holiday-inn.com
308 rooms. Pets accepted, some restrictions. Two restaurants, bar. Fitness room. Indoor pool, children's pool, whirlpool. Airport transportation available. Business center. $

★Holiday Inn Express
1040 40th St. S., Fargo,
701-282-2000, 800-465-4329;
www.hiexpress.com
77 rooms. Pets accepted; fee. Complimentary continental breakfast. Internet. Indoor pool, whirlpool. Airport transportation available. $

134

NORTH DAKOTA

★Kelly Inn-Fargo

4207 13th Ave. S.W., Fargo,
701-277-8821, 800-635-3559;
www.kellyinnfargo.com

59 rooms. Pets accepted, some restrictions. Complimentary continental breakfast. Wireless Internet. Indoor pool, whirlpool. Business center. **$**

★★Radisson Hotel Fargo

201 Fifth St. N., Fargo,
701-232-7363, 800-333-3333;
www.radisson.com-fargond

151 rooms. Pets accepted, some restrictions; fee. Internet. Restaurant, bar. Fitness room. Indoor pool, whirlpool. Airport transportation available. Business center. **$**

★Sleep Inn

1921 44th St. S.W., Fargo,
701-281-8240, 800-424-6423;
www.sleepinnfargo.com

61 rooms. Pets accepted, some restrictions. Complimentary continental breakfast. Wireless Internet access. Fitness room. Indoor pool, children's pool, whirlpool. Airport transportation available. Business center. **$**

RESTAURANTS

★★Mexican Village

814 Main Ave., Fargo, 701-293-0120

Mexican menu. Lunch, dinner. Closed holidays. Children's menu. Casual attire. **$**

GRAND FORKS

Grand Forks stands at the point where the Red River of the North and Red Lake River form a fork. Socially, culturally, and commercially the town is closely allied with its cousin city across the river, East Grand Forks, Minnesota. First a French fur trading post, Grand Forks later developed as a frontier river town. The arrival of the railroad and cultivation of nearby farmland brought about another change in its personality. The University of North Dakota plays a dominant role in the city's culture and economy. Grand Forks Air Force Base is 14 miles west on Highway 2.

Information: Convention and Visitors Bureau, 4251 Gateway Dr., 701-746-0444, 800-866-4566; www.grandforkscvb.org

WHAT TO SEE AND DO

Grand Forks County Historical Society

2405 Belmont Rd., Grand Forks,
701-775-2216; www.grandforkshistory.com

This historical society maintains the Campbell House, the historic pioneer cabin of agricultural innovator Tom Campbell. Original log cabin portion dates from 1879. Also on the grounds are a log post office (1870), one-room schoolhouse and Myra Carriage Museum, which houses a collection of late 19th- and early 20th-century artifacts from surrounding area. May-October: daily 1-5 p.m.

135

NORTH DAKOTA

Turtle River State Park
3084 Park Ave., Arvilla, 701-594-4445;
www.ndparks.com-parks-trsp.htm
Located in a green valley carved out by the gently winding Turtle River, this 784-acre park is a big recreational draw in the Grand Forks area. Because the river is stocked with rainbow trout, angling is a popular pursuit, and there are hiking and biking trails, as well as cross-country ski routes and a sledding hill. For overnighters, a dozen duplex rental cabins, with running water but without kitchens, and 125 campsites are available.

University of North Dakota
Grand Forks, west end of University Ave., 701-777-3304, 800-225-5863;
www.und.edu
The *Eternal Flame of Knowledge,* an immense steel-girded sphere, commemorates Old Main and past presidents. North Dakota Museum of Art; Chester Fritz Library houses artwork. Tours.

HOTELS
★★**Best Western Town House**
710 First Ave. N., Grand Forks, 701-746-5411, 800-867-9797;
www.bestwestern.com
101 rooms. Pets accepted, some restrictions; fee. Wireless Internet. Restaurant, bar. Indoor pool, whirlpool. Airport transportation available. Casino. **$**

★**C'Mon Inn**
3051 32nd Ave., Grand Forks, 701-775-3320, 800-255-2323;
www.cmoninn.com
80 rooms. Complimentary continental breakfast. Internet. Fitness room. Indoor pool, whirlpool. **$**

★**Comfort Inn**
3251 30th Ave. S., Grand Forks, 701-775-7503, 800-424-6423;
www.comfortinn.com
65 rooms. Pets accepted, some restrictions; fee. Complimentary continental breakfast. Wireless Internet. Indoor pool, whirlpool. **$**

★**Fairfield Inn**
3051 S. 34th St., Grand Forks, 701-775-7910, 800-228-2800;
www.fairfieldinn.com
62 rooms. Complimentary continental breakfast. Internet. Indoor pool, whirlpool. **$**

★★**Holiday Inn**
1210 N. 43rd St., Grand Forks, 701-772-7131, 800-465-4329;
www.holidayinn.com
148 rooms. Wireless Internet. Restaurant, bar. Fitness room. Indoor pool, children's pool, whirlpool. Airport transportation available. Casino. **$**

★**Lakeview Inns And Suites Grand Forks**
3350 S. 32nd Ave., Grand Forks, 701-775-5000, 877-355-3500;
www.lakeviewhotels.com
86 rooms. Complimentary continental breakfast. Wireless Internet. Indoor pool, whirlpool. **$**

★★**Ramada Inn**
1205 N. 43rd St., Grand Forks, 701-775-3951, 888-298-2054;
www.ramada.com
100 rooms. Pets accepted, some restrictions. Wireless Internet. Restaurant, bar. Fitness room. Indoor pool, children's pool, whirlpool. Airport transportation available. Business center. Casino. **$**

RESTAURANTS
★★**GF Goodribs**
4223 N. 12th Ave., Grand Forks, 701-746-7115
Steak menu. Lunch, dinner, Sunday brunch. Closed holidays. Bar. Children's menu. Casual attire. **$$**

JAMESTOWN

Settlers and businessmen arrived after soldiers and railroad workers established Jamestown as a transportation center guarded by Fort Seward. When farmers discovered they could pay for their rich land with two years' worth of crops, the area developed as a prosperous agricultural town. The James River, the longest unnavigable river in the world, flows through the area. On the northeastern edge of town is Jamestown College, founded 1883.

Information: Jamestown Promotion and Tourism Center, 212 Third Ave. N.E., 701-252-4835, 800-222-4766; www.jamestownnd.com

WHAT TO SEE AND DO

Frontier Village
Jamestown, 701-252-6307

The big lure here is the "Worlds Largest Buffalo," a 60-ton concrete sculpture jutting out of the plains. The adjacent village is also a good place to get a glimpse of North Dakota's pioneer past. About a dozen historic structures were relocated here to spare them from the wrecking ball, including a one-room schoolhouse, a barbershop, and a train depot. May-September, daily. Also on-site are the National Buffalo Museum, the home of White Cloud, an albino buffalo.

Whitestone Hill Battlefield State Historic Site
Kulm, 701-396-7731

Probably triggered by the 1862 Sioux uprising in Minnesota, the September 1863 Battle of Whitestone Hill marked the beginning of a war between the U.S. Cavalry and the Plains Sioux that lasted for more than 20 years. Granite monument of bugler, graves of soldiers; small museum. Mid-May-mid-September: Thursday-Monday.

HOTELS

★Comfort Inn
811 S.W. 20th St., Jamestown, 701-252-7125; www.comfortinn.com

52 rooms. Pets accepted. Complimentary continental breakfast. Indoor pool, whirlpool. $

★★Dakota Inn
Highway 281 S., Jamestown, 701-252-3611, 800-726-7924

120 rooms. Pets accepted; fee. Restaurant, bar. Indoor pool, whirlpool. $

★★Gladstone Select Hotel
111 Second St. N.E., Jamestown, 701-252-0700, 800-641-1000; www.selectinn.com

111 rooms. Pets accepted; fee. Restaurant, bar. Fitness room. Indoor pool, whirlpool. $

MANDAN

The Mandan tribe originally farmed this area, and today the agricultural tradition persists in the dairy and dry farms that surround the city. Lignite, a soft coal, is mined in this region. Mandan has been an important railroad city since tracks crossed the Missouri River the year the city was founded.

Information: Bismarck-Mandan Convention and Visitors Bureau, 1600 Burnt Boat Dr., Bismarck, 701-222-4308, 800-767-3555; www.bismarckmandancvb.com

WHAT TO SEE AND DO

Cross Ranch Nature Preserve
The Nature Conservancy, 1401 River Rd., Center, 701-794-8741

This 6,000-acre nature preserve has mixed grass prairies, Missouri River floodplain forest, and upland woody draws. Bison herd. Hiking and self-guided nature trails. Daily.

Fort Abraham Lincoln State Park
4480 Fort Lincoln Rd., Mandan, 701-663-9571

137

★
★
★
★
★

Historic site marks the fort which Custer commanded prior to his "last stand." Reconstructed fort buildings (tours, Memorial Day-Labor Day), and Mandan earthlodge village. Fishing, hiking, cross-country skiing, snowmobiling, picnicking, playground, concession, camping. Visitor center, amphitheater, museum, summer interpretive program.

HOTELS

★★Best Western Seven Seas Inn & Conference Center
2611 Old Red Trail, Mandan,
701-663-7401, 800-597-7327;
www.bestwestern.com
103 rooms. Pets accepted. Internet. Restaurant, bar. Indoor pool, whirlpool. Business center. $

THE LITTLE MISSOURI BADLANDS

Medora sits at the base of the dramatic Little Missouri Badlands, a deeply eroded gorge that exposes millions of years of sedimentary deposits in colorful horizontal striations. Medora itself is a fascinating historical town—Teddy Roosevelt lived near here in the 1880s, as did the flamboyant Marquis de Mores, a French nobleman who journeyed to the Dakota Territory to live out his cowboy fantasies. Before setting out to explore bluffs that rise behind the town, be sure to visit the Chateau de More, the luxurious frontier home built by the Marquis. When it was constructed in 1883, this 26-room mansion was the finest and most modern private home for hundreds of miles.

The Maah Daah Hey Trail is 100 miles long and connects the northern and southern sections of the Theodore Roosevelt National Park, passing through the Little Missouri National Grassland. The following hike covers four miles at the trail's southern extreme and explores the scenic badlands above Medora, passing through the fascinating and ruggedly beautiful badlands ecosystem. The area is home to prairie wildlife including pronghorn antelope, coyotes, white-tail deer, prairie dogs and rattlesnakes.

Begin at Sully Creek State Park, two miles south of Medora (the Maah Daah Hey Trail is also popular with mountain bikers, so you'll share the trail). The trail crosses the Little Missouri River, which is ankle-deep and easily waded in summer, and follows the river valley through stands of cottonwood, willow and silver sage. The path then begins to climb up the face of a badland mesa, eventually reaching a plateau. From a rocky escarpment, enjoy a magnificent overlook onto Medora and the Little Missouri River breaks. Continue north on the trail through prairie grassland to a side path, the Canyon Trail, which drops steeply down a rugged canyon wall to a prairie dog town. Follow the trail north, through a self-closing gate, to where the Canyon Trail rejoins the Maah Daah Hey. From here, hikers can return to Medora along a gravel road or continue north through more badlands landscape to the South Unit of the Theodore Roosevelt National Park headquarters.

NORTH DAKOTA

MEDORA

This village is a living museum of two of the most colorful characters of the badlands frontier—young, bespectacled Theodore Roosevelt and the hot-blooded, visionary Marquis de Mores. The Marquis, a wealthy Frenchman, established the town and named it for his wife, daughter of a New York banker. He built a packing plant and icehouses, aiming to slaughter cattle on the range and ship them to metropolitan markets in refrigerated railroad cars. The plan fizzled, but not before the mustachioed Frenchman left his stamp on the community.

Roosevelt came here in 1883 and won respect as part owner of the Maltese Cross and Elkhorn ranches and as organizer and first president of the Little Missouri Stockmen's Association. Information: Chamber of Commerce, 701-623-4910; www.medorand.com

WHAT TO SEE AND DO
Chateau de Mores State Historic Site
Hwy. 10, Medora, 701-623-4355
This site commemorates the life of Antoine de Vallombrosa, the Marquis de Mores. The Marquis dabbled with a stagecoach line, an experiment with refrigerated railroad cars, and a beef packing plant. Remaining are the ruins of a packing plant, a 26-room, two-story frame mansion filled with French furnishings, a library, servants' quarters and relic room displaying the Marquis's saddles, guns, boots, coats and other possessions. An interpretive center is on the grounds. The site is not heated. Station-guided tours mid-May-mid-September, daily; rest of year, by appointment.

HOTELS
★Americinn Medora
75 E. River Rd. S., Medora, 701-623-4800; www.americinn.com
56 rooms. Pets accepted, some restrictions; fee. Complimentary continental breakfast. Indoor pool, whirlpool. $

THEODORE ROOSEVELT NATIONAL PARK
This national park is a monument to 26th president Theodore Roosevelt, who was the nation's champion of the conservation of natural resources. Roosevelt, who came to the badlands in September 1883 to hunt buffalo and other big game, became interested in the open-range cattle industry and purchased an interest in the Maltese Cross Ranch near Medora. He returned the next year and established another ranch, the Elkhorn, about 35 miles north of Medora. The demands of his political career and failures at raising cattle eventually forced him to abandon his ranching ventures.

This park preserves the magnificent badlands landscape as Roosevelt knew it. Wind and water have carved from a thick series of flat-lying sedimentary rocks curiously sculptured formations, tablelands, buttes, canyons and rugged hills. Thick, dark layers of lignite coal, which are sometimes fired by lightning and burn slowly for many years, are exposed in eroded hillsides. The fires often bake adjacent clay layers into a red, brick-like substance called scoria, or clinker.

Elk and bison have been reintroduced and thrive here and can be easily seen throughout the park. There are several large prairie dog towns, and mule and whitetail deer are abundant. Wild horses can be seen in the South Unit, and the area is populated with hawks, falcons, eagles and other more common species.

The park is divided into three units. The South Unit is accessible from I-94 at Medora, where there is a visitor center (daily) and Roosevelt's Maltese Cross cabin. The Elkhorn Ranch Site on the Little Missouri River can be reached only by rough dirt roads, and visitors should check in with rangers at the Medora Visitor Center before venturing out (701-623-4466). The North Unit is accessible from US 85, near Watford City and has a visitor center. An additional visitor center is located at Painted Canyon Scenic Overlook on I-94 (April-October: daily). The park is open all year; visitor centers are closed holidays.

Information: Park headquarters, 701-623-4466; www.nps.gov/thro

NORTH DAKOTA

★
★
★
★
★

MINOT

Minot's advance from tepee and tarpaper to a supersonic-age city has been so vigorous that it calls itself the "Magic City." Where buffalo bones were once stacked by plainscombers stands a city rich from agriculture, lignite coal reserves, oil pools, industries and railroad yards on both sides of the Mouse River. Minot is the commercial center of a radius that sweeps into Canada. Minot State University is located here.

Information: Convention and Visitors Bureau, 1020 S. Broadway, 701-857-8206, 800-264-2626; www.visitminot.org

WHAT TO SEE AND DO

Roosevelt Park and Zoo
1219 Burdick Expy. E., Minot,
701-857-4166
Includes 90 acres of formal lawns and sunken gardens. On the grounds are a swimming pool, water slide and bathhouse. Lifeguards on duty. Late May-early September, daily.

Scandinavian Heritage Center
Broadway and 11th Ave.,
Minot, 701-852-9161;
www.minotparkdistrict.org/scand.shtml
A 230-year-old house from Sigdal, Norway; Danish windmill; flag display; statues of famous Scandinavians. Daily; Memorial Day-Labor Day: weekends.

HOTELS

★Best Western Kelly Inn
1510 26th Ave. S.W., Minot,
701-852-4300, 800-735-5868;
www.bestwesternminot.com
100 rooms. Pets accepted, some restrictions. Complimentary continental breakfast. Internet. Bar. Indoor pool, whirlpool. $

★Comfort Inn
1515 22nd Ave. S.W., Minot,
701-852-2201, 800-228-5150;
www.comfortinn.com
140 rooms. Pets accepted, some restrictions. Complimentary continental breakfast. Indoor pool, whirlpool. $

★★Holiday Inn
2200 Burdick Expy. E., Minot,
701-852-2504, 800-465-4329;
www.holiday-inn.com
172 rooms. Pets accepted, some restrictions. Internet. Two restaurants, two bars. Fitness room. Indoor pool, whirlpool.

140

NORTH DAKOTA

VALLEY CITY

The railroad and the first settlers arrived here simultaneously to establish a community then known as Worthington. Later, as the seat of Barnes County, this town in the deeply forested Sheyenne River Valley changed to its present name. The grain fields and dairy farms of the surrounding area are the town's main industry.

Information: Valley City Area Chamber of Commerce, 205 N.E. Second St., 701-845-1891; www.hellovalley.com

WHAT TO SEE AND DO

Fort Ransom State Park
5981 Walt Hjelle Pkwy., Fort Ransom,
701-973-4331, 800-807-4723;
www.ndparks.com-Parks-frsp.htm
This former frontier Army post has a historic farm that re-creates the life of early homesteaders. The Sodbuster Days festival is held the second weekends in July and September. An arts and crafts festival is the held last weekend in September. Downhill ski resort. Camping, picnic areas, hiking, cross-country skiing, and snowmobiling.

HOTELS

★**Wagon Wheels Inn**
455 Winter Show Rd., Valley City,
701-845-5333
88 rooms. Indoor pool, whirlpool. **$**

RESTAURANTS

★**Dutton's Parlour**
256 Central Ave. N., Valley City,
701-845-3390
American menu. Breakfast, lunch. **$**

WILLISTON

This city, which was first called Little Muddy, began as a small supply center for ranchers. As the area grew, farming and petroleum, discovered here in the early 1950s, had an impact on the local economy.
Information: Convention & Visitors Bureau, 10 Main St., 701-774-9041, 800-615-9041; www.willistonndtourism.com

WHAT TO SEE AND DO

Fort Buford State Historic Site
15349 39th Lane N.W., Williston,
701-572-9034
Established in 1866 near the merging point of the Missouri and Yellowstone Rivers, Fort Buford served as the distribution point for government annuities to peaceful natives in the vicinity. During the war with the Sioux in the 1870s and 1880s, the post became a major supply depot for military field operations. The fort was the site of the surrender of Sitting Bull in 1881. Original features include a stone powder magazine, the post cemetery, and a museum. Mid-May-mid-September: daily; rest of year, by appointment.

Fort Union Trading Post National Historic Site
15550 Hwy. 1804, Williston,
701-572-9083; www.nps.gov-fous
The American Fur Company built this fort in 1829 at the junction of the Yellowstone and Missouri Rivers. During the next three decades, it was one of the most important trading depots on the western frontier. In 1867, the government bought the fort, dismantled it, and used the materials to build Fort Buford two miles away. Much of the fort has been reconstructed. A National Park Service visitor center is located in the Bourgeois House. Guided tours and interpretive programs are available in summer. Daily.

Lewis and Clark State Park
4904 119th Rd. N.W.,
Williston, 701-859-3071;
www.ndparks.com-parks-lcsp.htm
Situated on a northern bay in Lake Sakakawea—a man-made body of water created by damming the Missouri River—this state park is so named because the Lewis and Clark expedition camped nearby twice, on their 1805 westward journey in search of the fabled Northwest Passage and on the return trip east the next year. Today, the park is popular because of its marina, a jumping-off point for boaters and anglers. Of the fish lurking below, the most remarkable are immense paddlefish, prehistoric-looking beasts once thought to be extinct, and endangered pallid sturgeon, which grow up to six feet in length. A good trail system allows for hiking and cross-country skiing.

Lewis and Clark Trail Museum
Hwy. 85, Alexander, 701-828-3595.
Located on the first leg of the Corps of Discovery's westward route (south of Williston and the Missouri River in Alexander), this museum covers not only Lewis and Clark but also early homesteaders in North Dakota. The most notable exhibit is a scale model of Fort Mandan, where the party stayed during the winter of 1804-1805. Memorial Day-Labor Day: daily.

141

NORTH DAKOTA

★
★
★
★
★

OKLAHOMA

PROBABLY EVERY STATE IS MISUNDERSTOOD IN ITS OWN WAY. BUT MAYBE OKLAHOMA HAS a special claim. Is it the vast dusty terrain from which impoverished farmers fled during the Great Depression? Is it the good-ol'-boy land of "Okie from Muskogee" that Merle Haggard celebrated in song, or the romantic land of the stylized cowboy culture as sung to in the musical *Oklahoma!*? Is it Southern—bordered, as it is, by Arkansas (on the east)? Is it a northern annex of Texas? (The twang of the Lone Star state is certainly audible here.) Or does it belong to the West, with its neatly rectangular panhandle touching New Mexico and Colorado?

The area that was to become the state of Oklahoma was practically unknown to Americans at the time of the Louisiana Purchase of 1803. Believing those unsettled lands to be of little value, the government set them aside as "Indian Territory" in 1830, assigning a portion to each of the Five Civilized Tribes. Thousands of Creeks, Choctaws, Chickasaws, Seminoles and Cherokees were forced to leave the Southeastern U.S. and move to Oklahoma. About one-fourth of those forced west over this "Trail of Tears" died on the way of hunger, disease, cold and exhaustion. Today Oklahoma has the largest Native American population in the United States.

As the nation moved west, settlers squatted in the Indian Territory, wanting the land for development. On April 22, 1889, portions of the land were opened for settlement. In the next few years all unassigned Oklahoma land was opened by a series of six "runs." People who jumped the gun were called "Sooners," giving the state its nickname, the "Sooner State." Close to 17 million acres of land were settled in this way; the last lottery, a form of run, took place on August 16, 1901. Previously unsettled tracts became cities within eight hours.

Oklahoma produces many millions of barrels of oil a year, and you might see churning derricks almost anywhere, including beside runways of the Oklahoma City airport. The state has vast expanses of lightly settled country—forests and green fields in the eastern part; ranchland and prairie in the drier west. Some people would be surprised to learn that Oklahoma has mountains, but in the southeastern corner of the state (Kiamichi Country), there are seven ranges. Northeast Oklahoma has both rolling hills and flat prairie, along with several large lakes and plenty of state parks. The southwestern part of the state is true Great Plains and Chisolm Trail territory and has several major museums that explore the region's heritage and history, which started with the Kiowa, Comanche, Apache, the original inhabitants and then saw the impact of settlers and clashes between newcomers and natives.

★ SPOTLIGHT

★ More Native American tribes are headquartered in Oklahoma than in any other state.

★ The shopping cart was invented in Ardmore, Oklahoma.

★ Cimarron County is bordered by Oklahoma, Texas, New Mexico, Coloroado and Kansas—more than any other county in the country.

★ The word Oklahoma is a combination of two Choctaw words meaning "red man."

ALTUS

In the spring of 1891, a flood on Bitter Creek forced a group of settlers to flee to higher ground, taking with them what possessions they could. Gathered together to escape destruction, they founded a town and called it Altus because one of them said the word meant "high ground." On the border between the high plains and the southland, Altus lies between winter wheat on the north and cotton on the south. Nearby Altus Air Force Base is the home of the 97th Air Mobility Wing.

Information: Chamber of Commerce, 123 Commerce, 580-482-0210; www.cityofaltus.org

WHAT TO SEE AND DO

Museum of the Western Prairie

1100 Memorial Dr., Altus, 580-482-1044; www.okhistory.org/ museums/westernprairie.html

Exhibits depict all aspects of pioneer living in southwestern Oklahoma. Tuesday-Saturday.

SPECIAL EVENTS

Great Plains Stampede Rodeo

580-482-0210

Professional Rodeo Cowboys Association-sanctioned rodeo; special events. Late August.

HOTELS

★Best Western Altus

2804 N. Main St., Altus, 580-482-9300; www.bestwestern.com

100 rooms. Pets accepted, some restrictions; fee. Complimentary continental breakfast. Fitness room. Indoor pool, outdoor pool. Business center. **$**

★★Ramada Inn

2515 E. Broadway St., Altus, 580-477-3000; www.ramada.com

20 rooms. Pets accepted; fee. Restaurant, bar. Indoor pool. **$**

ALVA

Founded in 1893 as a land office for the largest land run in Oklahoma following the opening of the Cherokee strip, this small northwestern town is home to Northwestern Oklahoma State University.

Information: Chamber of Commerce, 410 College Ave., 580-327-1647, 888-854-2262; www.alvaok.net

WHAT TO SEE AND DO

Alabaster Caverns

Hwy. 50A, Freedom, 580-621-3381

On approximately 200 acres, Alabaster is said to be the largest known natural gypsum cavern in the world. Tours daily.

Great Salt Plains

Hwy. 38, Jet, 580-626-4731

Approximately 840 acres with a 9,300-acre lake. Swimming, fishing, boating, nature trails, picnic area, playground, camping areas, cabins. Daily.

Little Sahara

Hwy. 281, 580-824-1471

Park with approximately 1,600 acres. Sand dunes. Picnicking, playground.

HOTELS

★Ranger Inn

420 E. Oklahoma Blvd., Alva, 580-327-1981; www.rangerinnmotel.com

41 rooms. Pets accepted, some restrictions. **$**

★
★
★
★
★

ARDMORE

The Arbuckle Mountains are a few miles north of this southern Okalhoma town. The community is close to Wichita and the Texas border.

Information: Chamber of Commerce, 410 W. Main, 580-223-7765
www.ardmore.org

WHAT TO SEE AND DO

Greater Southwest Historical Museum

35 Sunset Dr., Ardmore, 580-226-3857. This museum details the history of the area, with displays of oil and agricultural machinery, military memorabilia and a re-creation of a pioneer community. Tuesday-Saturday, Sunday afternoon.

HOTELS

★Days Inn

2614 W. Broadway St., Ardmore,

580-226-1761; www.daysinn.com 47 rooms. Pets accepted; fee. Complimentary continental breakfast. $

★★Holiday Inn

2705 W. Broadway Dr., Ardmore, 580-223-7130, 800-465-4329; www.holiday-inn.com

169 rooms. Pets accepted, some restrictions; fee. Restaurant. Fitness room. Outdoor pool, children's pool. $

OKLAHOMA

EXPLORING OKLAHOMA'S STATE PARKS

Begin your tour of southeastern and eastern Oklahoma at the small town of Broken Bow, located at the edge of the Ouachita National Forest. About six miles east of town on Highway 70 is the 1880s home of Choctaw Chief Jefferson Gardner. Nearby Beavers Bend State Park is one of the most gorgeous places in this part of the country. Lake Broken Bow, at 14,200 acres, offers park visitors 180 miles of pretty, wooded shoreline, as well as bass fishing, paddleboating, canoeing and swimming. The park is also adjacent to Mountain Fork River, popular for its trout fishing and canoe trips; on land, you can do horseback riding, miniature golf, and golf on Cedar Creek Golf Course. Stay overnight here, or continue on for an overnight at Lake Wister.

Continue north on scenic Highway 259 through the tree-covered Kiamichi Mountains and you'll enter the Ouachita National Forest. If you turn west on Oklahoma Highway 1, you'll be on the spectacular Talimena Scenic Drive, which makes a 54-mile reach between Talihina, Oklahoma and Mena, Arkansas. Have the camera ready to capture the vistas from various look-out spots on the sides of the road; look to the north to see the beautiful Winding Stair Mountains. At Talihina, go four miles southwest on Highway 271 to Talimena State Park, a prime spot for picnicking. Back on Highway 259, continue north and pick up Highway 59 north to Lake Wister State Park, a pretty, wooded spread of 33,428 acres that showcase 4,000-acre Lake Wister. Some of the park's 15 cabins have fireplaces. Less than three miles northeast of Highway 59 and Highway 270, Heavener Runestone State Park features gigantic stone tablets carved with runic alphabet characters. Nobody knows how it happened, but the markings are thought to have been made by Vikings around 1012 A.D.

Finish a driving tour at Tallequah, capital city of the Cherokee Nation. Destinations here include the Cherokee Heritage Center and the restored 1889 Cherokee National Female Seminary, at Northeastern State University.

RESTAURANTS
★★Fireside Dining
Hwy. 77, Lake Murray State Park,
580-226-4070

American menu. Dinner. Closed Sunday-Monday. Children's menu. **$$**

ATOKA
This small south Oklahoma town was named for a leader of the Choctaw Nation. A small Civil War battle took place here in 1864.
Information: Chamber of Commerce, 580-889-2410; www.atokacity.org

WHAT TO SEE AND DO
Boggy Depot State Park
Park Lane, Atoka, 580-889-5625.
This park has approximately 420 acres with picnicking, playgrounds and camping areas. Daily.

HOTELS
★★Best Western Atoka Inn
2101 S. Mississippi Ave., Atoka,
580-889-7381, 800-780-7234;
www.bestwestern.com
54 rooms. Pets accepted, some restrictions; fee. Restaurant. Outdoor pool. Airport transportation available. **$**

BARTLESVILLE
The Bartlesville area is proud of its Western and Native American heritage, which involves three tribes—the Cherokee, Delaware and Osage. Oklahoma's first electricity was produced here in 1876 when Jacob Bartles, an early settler, hitched a dynamo to the Caney River. Oil, first tapped in the area in 1897, is the economic base of the city. Bartlesville has become internationally known for its distinguished, modern architecture, a building trend initiated by the H. C. Price family which made its fortune in oil. The town boasts a number of both public and private buildings by Frank Lloyd Wright and Bruce Goff.
Information: Bartlesville Area Chamber of Commerce, 201 S. Keeler, 918-336-8708, 800-364-8708; www.bartlesville.com

WHAT TO SEE AND DO
Frank Phillips Mansion
1107 S. Cherokee Ave., Bartlesville,
918-336-2491
Built in 1909 by the founder of the Phillips Petroleum Company, this Neoclassical house has been restored to the 1930s period. The interior includes imported woods, marble, Oriental rugs and original furnishings. Listed on the National Register of Historic Places. Wednesday-Sunday.

Nellie Johnstone Oil Well
Johnstone Park, 300 N. Cherokee, Bartlesville
Replica of the first commercial oil well in the state. An 83-acre park with a low water dam on the Caney River. Fishing, picnicking, playgrounds, children's rides.

Late May-Labor Day: daily; closed July 4. Park, daily.

Price Tower
510 Dewey Ave., Bartlesville,
918-336-4949; www.pricetower.org
Designed by Frank Lloyd Wright, this 221-foot office building was built for pipeline construction pioneer H. C. Price as headquarters for his company. The building design is based on a diamond module of 30/60-degree triangles. Although Wright designed many skyscrapers, Price Tower was his only tall building to be completed. Guided tours Tuesday-Saturday.

145

OKLAHOMA

★
★
★
★
★

Tom Mix Museum
721 N. Delaware, Dewey, 918-534-1555
Exhibits and memorabilia of silent movie star Tom Mix, the first "King of the Cowboys." Displays of his cowboy gear; stills from his films. Tuesday-Sunday.

Woolaroc
Hwy. 23, Bartlesville., 918-336-0307; www.woolaroc.org
Complex covering 3,600 acres with wildlife preserve for herds of American bison, longhorn cattle, Scottish Highland cattle, elk, deer and other native wildlife. Paintings by Russell, Remington and other great Western artists are at the museum; exhibits on the development of America; artifacts of several Native American tribes, pioneers, and cowboys. The Native American Heritage Center has multimedia shows, authentic Native American crafts, art displays and a nature trail (1 1/2 miles). Picnic area. Late May-early September: Tuesday-Sunday; rest of year: Wednesday-Sunday.

HOTELS
★★Best Western Weston Inn
222 S.E. Washington Blvd.,
Bartlesville,918-335-7755, 800-780-7234; www.bestwestern.com

109 rooms. Pets accepted; fee. Complimentary continental breakfast. Restaurant. Outdoor pool. $

★★★Inn at Price Tower
510 Dewey Ave., Bartlesville,
918-336-1000; www.innatpricetower.com
This contemporary hotel is located in the Frank Lloyd Wright-designed Price Tower. The tower suites, decorated in mid-century modern style, are two-story and offer views of the prairie.
21 rooms. Complimentary continental breakfast. Restaurant, bar. Business center. $$$

RESTAURANTS
★Murphy's Original Steak House
1625 S.W. Frank Phillips Blvd.,
Bartlesville, 918-336-4789.
Steak menu. Lunch, dinner. Closed Monday. $$

★★Sterling's Grille
2905 E. Frank Phillips Blvd.,
Bartlesville, 918-335-0707.
Seafood, steak menu. Lunch Sunday-Friday, dinner. Bar. Children's menu. Outdoor seating. Three separate rooms with different motifs. $$

BROKEN BOW
This southeastern Oklahoma town is located near several state parks, including Broken Bow Lake. Timber and tourism are the area's main industries.
Information: Chamber of Commerce, 113 W. Martin Luther King, 580-584-3393, 800-528-7337; www.brokenbowchamber.com

WHAT TO SEE AND DO
Beavers Bend Resort State Park
Hwy. 259A, Broken Bow, 580-494-6300
This 3,522-acre mountainous area is crossed by the Mountain Fork River and includes the Broken Bow Reservoir. Swimming, bathhouse, fishing, boating, nature trail, picnic areas, playground, grocery, restaurant, camping, cabins. Nature center. Daily.

HOTELS
★★The Charles Wesley Motor Lodge
302 N. Park Dr., Broken Bow,
580-584-3303; www.charleswesleymotorlodge.com
50 rooms. Pets accepted, some restrictions; fee. Restaurant. Outdoor pool. $

CHICKASHA

Established to serve as a passenger and freight division point for the Rock Island and Pacific Railroad in 1892, this town site was on land originally given to the Choctaw in 1820. It became part of the Chickasaw Nation in 1834. It was incorporated in 1907, when the Oklahoma and Indian territories were joined to form the 46th state.

Information: Chamber of Commerce, 221 W. Chickasha Ave., 405-224-0787; www.chickasha-cc.com

WHAT TO SEE AND DO

Lake Chickasha
Hwy. 62, Chickasha
Swimming, waterskiing, fishing, hunting. Picnic areas. Camping.

SPECIAL EVENTS

Festival of Light
Ninth St., Chickasha, 405-224-9627
Lighted displays; 16-story Christmas tree; crystal bridge; shopping. Thanksgiving-December 31.

Grady County Fair
Grady County Fairgrounds, Chickasha, 405-224-2216
Third week in August.

HOTELS

★★Best Western Inn
2101 S. Fourth St., Chickasha, 405-224-4890, 877-489-0647; www.bestwestern.com
148 rooms. Pets accepted, some restrictions; fee. Restaurant, bar. Indoor pool, whirlpool. $

CLAREMORE

Claremore is most famous as the birthplace of Will Rogers. He was actually born about halfway between this city and Oologah but claimed Claremore as his home because, he said, "nobody but an Indian could pronounce Oologah." Rogers County, of which Claremore is the seat, was named not for Will Rogers but for his father, Clem.

Information: Claremore Area Chamber of Commerce, 419 W. Will Rogers Blvd., 918-341-2818; www.claremore.org

WHAT TO SEE AND DO

Lynn Riggs Memorial
121 N. Chickasaw Ave., Claremore
Houses the author's personal belongings, sculpture of Riggs, original manuscripts and the original "surrey with the fringe on top" from *Oklahoma!* Monday-Friday.

Will Rogers Birthplace and Dog Iron Ranch
9501 E. 380 Rd., Oologah, 918-275-4201
Home where the actor and cowboy was born on November 4, 1879. Daily.

Will Rogers Memorial
1720 W. Will Rogers Blvd., Claremore, 918-341-0719
Mementos, murals, saddle collection, dioramas, theater, films, tapes and a research library are located here. Jo Davidson's statue of Rogers stands in the foyer. The memorial is on 20 acres once owned by the humorist. Garden with Rogers' tomb. Daily.

SPECIAL EVENTS

Will Rogers Stampede PRCA Rodeo
Will Rogers Stampede Arena, Claremore. 918-640-1603
Late June.

HOTELS

★★Best Western Will Rogers Inn
940 S. Lynn Riggs Blvd., Claremore, 918-341-4410, 800-644-9455; www.bestwestern.com
52 rooms. Pets accepted. Restaurant, bar. Outdoor pool. $

OKLAHOMA

★
★
★
★
★

RESTAURANTS
★★Hammett House
1616 W. Will Rogers Blvd.,
Claremore, 918-341-7333;
www.hammetthouse.com
American menu. Lunch, dinner. Closed
Monday. Children's menu. **$$**

DUNCAN
Once a cattle town on the old Chisholm Trail, Duncan has become an oil services and
agricultural center. It was here that Erle P. Halliburton developed his oil well cementing
business, which now operates all over the world.
Information: Chamber of Commerce, 911 Walnut Ave., 580-255-3644;
www.duncanchamber.com

WHAT TO SEE AND DO
Chisholm Trail Museum
1000 Chisolm Trail Pkwy., Duncan,
580-252-6692
Interactive displays demonstrating the history of the Chisholm Trail. Daily.

Stephens County Historical Museum
Fuqua Park, Hwy. 81 and Beech Ave.,
Duncan, 580-252-0717
Houses pioneer and Native American artifacts, antique toys, gem and lapidary display; Plains Indian exhibit. Tuesday, Thursday-Saturday; closed holidays.

HOTELS
★★Holiday Inn
1015 N. Hwy. 81, Duncan, 580-252-1500;
www.holiday-inn.com
138 rooms. Pets accepted, some restrictions; fee. Restaurant, bar. Indoor pool, children's pool. **$**

DURANT
Long a farm and livestock-producing town in Oklahoma's Red River Valley, Durant
has become a recreation center since the completion of Lake Texoma. Home of Southeastern Oklahoma State University, Durant has many mansions, magnolia trees and
gardens.
Information: Chamber of Commerce, 215 N. Fourth St., 580-924-0848; www.durant.org

WHAT TO SEE AND DO
Fort Washita
Hwy. 199, Durant, 580-924-6502
Originally built in 1842 to protect the Five
Civilized Tribes from the Plains Indians;
used during the Civil War as a Confederate
supply depot; remains of 48 buildings are
visible. Daily.

Three Valley Museum
Main St., Durant, 580-920-1907
Museum housed in the Choctaw Nation
Headquarters building; contains turn-of-
the-century artifacts, art and beadwork.
Monday-Saturday, also by appointment;
closed holidays.

SPECIAL EVENTS
Oklahoma Shakespearean Festival
Southeastern Oklahoma State University,
Durant, 580-924-0121
Musicals; children's show, teen cabaret;
dinner theater. Late June-July.

HOTELS
★★Best Western Markita Inn
2401 W. Main St., Durant,
580-924-7676, 800-780-7234;
www.bestwestern.com
62 rooms. Restaurant. Outdoor pool, whirlpool. Airport transportation available. **$**

★Comfort Inn
2112 W. Main St., Durant, 580-924-8881;
www.choicehotels.com

62 rooms. Pets accepted, some restrictions; fee. Complimentary continental breakfast. **$**

ELK CITY

This was once a stopping point for cattlemen driving herds from Texas to railheads in Kansas. Centrally located on historic Route 66, Elk City lies near the center of the Anadarko Basin, where extensive natural gas exploration takes place.
Information: Chamber of Commerce, 1016 Airport Industrial Rd., 580-225-0207, 800-280-0207; www.elkcitychamber.com

WHAT TO SEE AND DO
Old Town Museum
2717 W. Third St., Elk City, 580-225-2207
Turn-of-the-century house has Victorian furnishings, Native American artifacts, Beutler Brothers Rodeo memorabilia and more. Tuesday-Sunday.

HOTELS
★★Holiday Inn
101 Meadow Ridge, Elk City, 580-225-6637; www.holiday-inn.com
151 rooms. Pets accepted, some restrictions. Complimentary full breakfast. Restaurant, bar. Fitness room. Indoor pool, whirlpool. **$**

RESTAURANTS
★Country Dove
610 W. Third, Elk City, 580-225-7028
American menu. Lunch. Closed Sunday. **$**

★Lupe's
905 N. Main St., Elk City, 580-225-7109
American, Mexican menu. Lunch Monday-Friday, dinner. Closed Sunday. Bar. Children's menu. **$$**

★
★
★
★
★

ENID

Like many Oklahoma cities, Enid was born of a land rush. When the Cherokee Outlet (more popularly known as the Cherokee Strip) was opened to settlement on September 16, 1893, a tent city sprang up. It is now a prosperous community and a center for farm marketing and oil processing. Just south of town is Vance Air Force Base, a training base for jet aircraft pilots.
Information: Chamber of Commerce, 210 Kenwood Blvd., 580-237-2494, 800-299-2443; www.enidchamber.com

WHAT TO SEE AND DO
Homesteader's Sod House
Hwy. 8, Cleo Springs, 580-463-2441
This two-room sod house built by Marshall McCully in 1894 is said to be the only original example of this type of structure still standing in Oklahoma. Period furnishings; farm machinery. Tuesday-Sunday.

Museum of the Cherokee Strip
507 S. Fourth St., Enid, 580-237-1907

Artifacts covering the Oklahoma history of the Plains Indians, the Land Run of 1893 and events from 1900-present. Tuesday-Saturday.

SPECIAL EVENTS
Cherokee Strip Celebration
111 W. Purdue Ave., Enid, 580-237-1907
This city-wide festival commemorates the opening of the Cherokee Strip to settlers. Includes entertainment, parade, rodeo, arts and crafts, food. Mid-September.

HOTELS

★★Best Western Inn
2818 S. Van Buren St., Enid, 580-242-7110,
800-378-6308; www.bestwestern.com
99 rooms. Pets accepted; fee. Restaurant,
bar. Fitness room. Indoor pool, whirlpool.
$

★★Days Inn
2901 S. Van Buren St., Enid, 580-237-6000;
www.daysinn.com
100 rooms. Pets accepted; fee. Restaurant,
bar. Fitness room. $

RESTAURANTS

★★Sage Room
1927 S. Van Buren St., Enid, 580-233-1212
Seafood menu. Dinner. Closed Sunday.
Children's menu. $$$

GROVE

This tourism-fueled community is located in the Ozark foothills on Grand Lake.
The town got its start as a trading center for French fur trappers and as a community for resettled Cherokees.
Information: www.groveok.org

WHAT TO SEE AND DO

Cherokee Queen I boat cruises
11350 Hwy. 59 N., Grand Lake,
918-786-4272.
Narrated cruise on Grand Lake O' the Cherokees; entertainment, refreshments.

Har-Ber Village
4404 W. 20th St., Grove, 918-786-6446
Reconstructed old-time village with 90 buildings and shops typical of a pioneer town. March-November: daily.

Lendonwood Gardens
1308 W. 13th St., Grove, 918-786-2938
Houses one of the largest collections of chamaecyparis in the United States, plus rhododendrons, day lilies and azaleas. Gardens include the Display Garden, English Terrace Garden and Japanese Garden. Daily.

HOTELS

★★Shangri-La Resort and Conference Center
57401 E. Hwy. 125 S., Afton,
918-257-4204, 800-331-4060;
www.shangrilaok.com
101 rooms. Restaurant, bar. Fitness room. Indoor pool, whirlpool. Tennis. $

OKLAHOMA

★
★
★
★
★

GUTHRIE

Guthrie was founded in just a few hours during the great land rush. Prior to the run, only a small-frame railroad station and a partially completed land registration office stood on the site. A few hours later, perhaps 20,000 inhabited the tent city on the prairie. Oklahoma's territorial and first state capital, Guthrie now has the most complete collection of restored Victorian architecture in the United States, with 1,400 acres of the city listed on the National Historic Register. Included are 160 buildings in the central business district and the center of town, and numerous Victorian mansions. The town is being restored to the 1907-1910 era, including the expansive Guthrie Railroad Hotel and the former opera house, the Pollard Theatre. Some who have called Guthrie home at one time or another are Tom Mix, Lon Chaney, Will Rogers, Carry Nation and O. Henry.
Information: Chamber of Commerce, 212 W. Oklahoma, 405-282-1947;
www.guthrieok.com

WHAT TO SEE AND DO

Oklahoma Territorial Museum
406 E. Oklahoma Ave., Guthrie,
405-282-1889;
www.oklahomaterritorialmuseum.org
Exhibits and displays of life in territorial Oklahoma during the turn of the century. Adjacent is the Carnegie Library (1902-1903), site of inaugurations of the last territorial and the first state governor. Tuesday-Saturday.

Scottish Rite Masonic Temple
900 E. Oklahoma Ave., Guthrie,
405-282-1281
This multimillion-dollar Classical Revival building is said to be the largest structure used for Masonic purposes. The building contains the original state capitol, 13 artistic rooms and 200 stained-glass windows. Surrounding it is a 10-acre park. Monday-Friday.

State Capital Publishing Museum
301 W. Harrison, Guthrie, 405-282-4123
Located in the four-story State Capital Publishing Company Building (1902). Houses a collection of original furnishings, vintage letterpress equipment; exhibits featuring the history of the first newspaper in the Oklahoma Territory and period printing technology. Thursday-Saturday.

SPECIAL EVENTS

Territorial Christmas
Guthrie, 405-282-1947
Seven miles of lights outline architecture in the Historic District; streets are filled with persons clad in turn-of-the-century style clothes, horse drawn vehicles; window displays echo 1890-1920 era. Friday after Thanksgiving-late December.

HOTELS

★★Best Western Territorial Inn
2323 Territorial Trail, Guthrie,
405-282-8831, 800-780-7234;
www.bestwestern.com
84 rooms. Pets accepted, some restrictions. Restaurant, bar. Outdoor pool. $

RESTAURANTS

★Stables Cafe
223 N. Division, Guthrie, 405-282-0893
American menu. Lunch, dinner. Closed holidays. Children's menu. $$

151

IDABEL

The western portion of the Ouachita National Forest is located to the east of Idabel. Although predominantly evergreen, the deciduous growth—a mixture of oak, gum, maple, sycamore, dogwood and persimmon—makes the forest notable for its magnificent fall color.
Information: Chamber of Commerce, 13 N., Central, 580-286-3305; www.idabelchamber.com

WHAT TO SEE AND DO

Museum of the Red River
812 Lincoln Rd., Idabel, 580-286-3616.
Interpretive exhibits of historic and prehistoric Native Americans; local archaeology; changing exhibits. Tuesday-Sunday.

HOTELS

★★Holiday Inn
Hwy. 70 W., Idabel, 580-286-6501;
www.holiday-inn.com
99 rooms. Pets accepted; fee. Restaurant. $

★
★
★
★
★

KREBS

This community of 2,000 is known throughout the state for its Italian restaurants. The locally beloved Choc beer, first brewed at Pete's Place restaurant during Prohibition, is made and sold here.

RESTAURANTS

★★Isle Of Capri

150 S.W. Seventh, Krebs, 918-423-3062
American, Italian menu. Lunch Monday, Thursday. Dinner. Closed Sunday. Bar. Children's menu. $$

★★Pete's Place

120 S.W. Eighth St., Krebs, 918-423-2042; www.petes.org
Italian menu. Dinner. Children's menu. $$

LAWTON

Last of the many Oklahoma cities that sprang up overnight, Lawton had its land rush on August 6, 1901. It is now the state's third-largest city. Much of the city's prosperity is due to Fort Sill, established in 1869, and to the Goodyear Tire plant headquartered here, the world's largest. The Wichita Mountains provide a dramatic backdrop to the city.
Information: Chamber of Commerce, 629 S.W. C Ave., 580-355-3541;
www.lawtonfortsillchamber.com

★ WHAT TO SEE AND DO

★ Fort Sill Military Reservation

Hwy. 277., Lawton, 580-442-2521
A 94,268-acre army installation, U.S. Army Field Artillery Center and School. Geronimo, war leader of the Apaches, spent his final years here and is buried in the post's Apache cemetery. Daily.

Fort Sill National Historic Landmark and Museum

437 Quanah Rd., Fort Sill, 580-442-5123
Forty-three buildings built of native stone during the 1870s, many of which are still being used for their original purpose. Monday-Saturday 8:30 a.m.-4:30 p.m.

Old Post Chapel

Lawton, 580-442-5123
One of the oldest houses of worship still in use in the state. Monday-Saturday; services on Sunday.

Museum of the Great Plains

Elmer Thomas Park, 601 Ferris Blvd., Lawton, 580-581-3460; www.museumgreatplains.org
Displays on Native Americans, fur trade, exploration, cattle industry and settlement of the area. Daily.

Wichita Mountains Wildlife Refuge

Hwy. 115, Cache
This 59,060-acre refuge has 12 man-made

lakes. Nonmotorized boating permitted on four lakes, trolling motors on three lakes; picnicking, camping only at Doris Campground; limited backcountry camping by reservation only. Quanah Parker Visitor Center, March-November: Friday-Sunday. Self-guided trails. Longhorn cattle, herds of buffalo, elk, deer and other wildlife can be viewed from several wildlife/scenic viewing areas. Daily.

HOTELS
★Days Inn
3110 N.W. Cache Rd., Lawton, 580-353-3104; www.daysinn.com
95 rooms. Pets accepted; fee. Complimentary continental breakfast. Indoor pool, outdoor pool, whirlpool. $

★★Ramada Inn
601 N. Second St., Lawton, 580-355-7155, 888-298-2054; www.ramada.com
98 rooms. Pets accepted; fee. Check-out noon. Restaurant, bar. $

RESTAURANTS
★★Fishermen's Cove
Hwy. 49, Lawton, 580-529-2672
Seafood menu. Lunch Sunday only, dinner. Closed Monday-Tuesday;. Children's menu. $$

★★Salas
111 W. Lee Blvd., Lawton, 580-357-1600.
Mexican, American menu. Lunch, dinner. Closed Monday-Tuesday. $$

MCALESTER
This town is named for James J. McAlester, who came to Indian Territory in 1870 armed with a geologist's notebook describing some coal deposits and a fine sense of commercial strategy. He set up a tent store where the heavily traveled Texas Road crossed the California Trail and later married a Native American woman, which made him a member of the Choctaw Nation with full rights. In 1911 he became lieutenant governor of the state.
Information: McAlester Area Chamber of Commerce & Agriculture, 10 S. Third St., 918-423-2550; www.mcalester.org

WHAT TO SEE AND DO
McAlester Scottish Rite Temple
305 N. Second St., McAlester, 918-423-6360
Unusual copper dome containing multicolored lenses makes this a landmark when lighted. One of its most illustrious members was Will Rogers who took degrees in 1908. Tours, Monday-Friday, by appointment; closed holidays.

Robber's Cave State Park
2450 S.E. Regional Lane, McAlester, 918-465-2565
Approximately 8,200 acres including lakes, alpine forests and an outlaw cave. Swimming, bathhouse, fishing, boating; hiking and horseback riding trails, picnicking, playground, restaurant, grocery, camping, cabins. Amphitheater. Daily.

HOTELS
★★Best Western Inn of Mcalester
1215 George Nigh Expy., McAlester, 918-426-0115, 800-780-7234; www.bestwestern.com
61 rooms. Pets accepted. Complimentary continental breakfast. Restaurant. Outdoor pool. $

★★Days Inn
1217 S. George Nigh Expy., McAlester, 918-426-5050, 800-329-7466; www.daysinn.com
100 rooms. Pets accepted, some restrictions; fee. Restaurant, bar. Indoor pool, whirlpool. Near Municipal Airport. $

RESTAURANTS
★Giacomo's
501 S. George Nigh Expy.,

153

OKLAHOMA

★
★
★
☆
☆

McAlester,
918-423-2662

American, Italian menu. Lunch, dinner. Closed Sunday-Monday. Children's menu. $$

MIAMI

Situated on the headwaters of Grand Lake, Miami has many recreational facilities.
Information: Chamber of Commerce, 111 N. Main, 918-542-4481; www.miamiok.org

WHAT TO SEE AND DO

Coleman Theatre Beautiful
103 N. Main St., Miami, 918-540-2425;
www.colemantheatre.org
Built as a vaudeville theater and movie palace in 1929, this structure features a Spanish Mission Revival exterior and Louis XV interior with gold-leaf trim and carved mahogany staircases. The original Wulitzer pipe organ has been restored. Tours, Tuesday-Saturday, also by appointment.

HOTELS

★★Best Western Inn Of Miami
2225 E. Steve Owens Blvd., Miami,
918-542-6681, 877-884-5422;
www.bestwestern.com
80 rooms. Pets accepted. Restaurant, bar. Outdoor pool. Airport transportation available. $

MUSKOGEE

Located near the confluence of the Verdigris, Grand and Arkansas rivers, Muskogee was a logical site for a trading center. Southward on the old Texas Road, over which families moved to Texas, and northward, over which cattle were driven to market, the town's location was commercially ideal. The railroad superseded the rivers in transportation importance, however, almost before the town was settled.

Today Muskogee is a diversified agricultural and industrial center, a town dotted with 32 small parks and the gateway to the eastern lakes area. The port of Muskogee is part of the McClellan-Kerr Arkansas River Navigation System, handling barges that go through the inland waterway system from Pittsburgh and Minneapolis to Houston and New Orleans.

The area's surroundings made it a logical location for the U.S. Union Agency for the Five Civilized Tribes (Cherokee, Chickasaw, Choctaw, Creek and Seminole). The agency is in located in the Old Union Building.
Information: Convention & Tourism, 425 Boston Ave., 918-684-6464, 888-687-6137; www.muskogee.org

WHAT TO SEE AND DO

Five Civilized Tribes Museum
Honor Heights Park,
1101 Honor Heights Dr., Muskogee,
918-683-1701
Art and artifacts of the Cherokees, Chickasaws, Choctaws, Creeks and Seminoles; displays relating to their history and culture. March-December: daily; rest of year: Tuesday-Saturday.

Fort Gibson Historic Site
907 N. Garrison, Fort Gibson,
918-478-4088

Established as the state's first military post in 1824, the park includes 12 reconstructed or restored buildings on a 55-acre site; period rooms depict army life in the 1830s and 1870s. Fort Gibson National Cemetery is 1 1/2 miles east. Mid-April-mid-October: Tuesday-Sunday 10 a.m.-5 p.m.; rest of year: Thursday-Sunday 10 a.m.-5 p.m.

Honor Heights Park
Muskogee, 918-684-6302
A 120-acre park with azalea, rose and chrysanthemum gardens; nature walks, lakes, waterfall. Picnicking. Daily.

OKLAHOMA

★
★
★
★
★

HOTELS

★Days Inn
900 S. 32nd St., Muskogee,
918-683-3911, 800-329-7466;
www.daysinn.com
43 rooms. Pets accepted; fee. Complimentary continental breakfast. Outdoor pool. **$**

★★Ramada Inn
800 S. 32nd St., Muskogee, 918-682-4341;
www.ramada.com
142 rooms. Pets accepted; fee. Restaurant, bar. Fitness room. Indoor pool, whirlpool. **$**

RESTAURANTS

★Okies
219 S. 32nd St., Muskogee, 918-683-1056.
American menu. Lunch, dinner. Bar. Children's menu. **$$**

NORMAN

Norman was founded on April 22, 1889, in the famous land rush known as the Oklahoma land run. The run opened what was once the Indian Territory to modern-day settlement. A year later the University of Oklahoma was founded. The city now offers numerous restaurants, museums, shopping areas, parks and hotels, as well as convention, conference and symposium sites. The University of Oklahoma, once mostly known as a football powerhouse, has been transformed into a respected academic and research institution.
Information: Convention & Visitors Bureau, 224 W. Gray St., 405-366-8095, 800-767-7260; www.visitnorman.com

WHAT TO SEE AND DO

University of Oklahoma
1000 Asp Ave., Norman, 405-325-1188,
800-234-6868; www.ou.edu
This campus is home to 25,000 students and has more than 225 buildings. The University of Oklahoma Press is a distinguished publishing house. On campus are the Fred Jones Jr. Museum of Art (Tuesday-Sunday; 405-325-3272); Oklahoma Museum of Natural History (405-325-4712); Rupel Jones Theater (405-325-4101); University Research Park. (Museums closed holidays) OU Visitor Center, Jacobson Hall, 550 Parrington Oval.

SPECIALTY LODGINGS

Holmberg House Bed and Breakfast
766 Debarr Ave., Norman,
405-321-6221, 877-621-6221;
www.holmberghouse.com
4 rooms. Complimentary full breakfast. Built in 1914 by the first dean of the University of Oklahoma's College of Fine Arts. **$**

Montford Inn Bed & Breakfast
322 W. Tonhawa St., Norman,
405-321-2200, 800-321-8969;
www.montfordinn.com
Surrounded by gardens, this hotel is also near the college campus and many restaurants.
16 rooms. Complimentary full breakfast. **$**

RESTAURANTS

★Cafe Plaid
333 W. Boyd St., Norman, 405-360-2233;
www.cafeplaid.com
American, Deli menu. Breakfast, lunch, brunch. Children's menu. Casual attire. **$**

★★★Legend's
1313 W. Lindsey St., Norman, 405-329-8888; www.legendsrestaurant.com
Owner Joe Sparks has presided over this American-continental restaurant for 40 years. It's a favorite of university faculty. The intimate dining room is filled with original artwork and features a broad menu of pastas, steaks and daily seafood specials. American menu. Lunch, dinner, Sunday brunch. Bar. Outdoor seating. **$$**

★Vista Sports Grill
111 N. Peters, Norman, 405-447-0909;
www.vistasportsgrill.com
American menu. Lunch, dinner. Bar. Children's menu. Casual attire. **$$**

★
★
★
★
★

OKLAHOMA CITY

What is now the site of Oklahoma's capital was barren prairie on the morning of April 22, 1889. Unassigned land was opened to settlement that day, and by nightfall the population numbered 10,000. No city was ever settled faster than during this famous run.

The city sits atop one of the nation's largest oil fields—there are even wells on the lawn of the Capitol. First discovered in 1928, the field was rapidly developed throughout the city. It still produces large quantities of high-gravity oil. Oil well equipment manufacture became one of the city's major industries. Tinker Air Force Base is southeast of the city.

Information: Convention & Visitors Bureau, 189 W. Sheridan, 405-297-8912, 800-225-5652; www.okccvb.org

SPOT★ LIGHT

★THE PARKING METER WAS INVENTED IN OKLAHOMA CITY.

★THE STATE CAPITOL BUILDING IS THE ONLY CAPITOL IN THE WORLD TO HAVE AN OIL WELL UNDER IT.

WHAT TO SEE AND DO

45th Infantry Division Museum
2145 N.E. 36th St., Oklahoma City, 405-424-5313.

Exhibits include state military history from its beginnings in the early Oklahoma Territory through World War II and Korea to the present National Guard; Desert Storm exhibit; uniforms, vehicles, aircraft, artillery and an extensive military firearms collection with pieces dating from the American Revolution; memorabilia and original cartoons by Bill Mauldin. Tuesday-Sunday.

Aquaticus
2101 N.E. 50th, Oklahoma City, 405-424-3344

This marine-life science facility contains a comprehensive collection of aquatic life; shark tank; adaptations and habitat exhibits; underwater viewing. Daily.

Civic Center Music Hall
201 N. Walker, Oklahoma City, 405-297-2584

Home of the Oklahoma City Philharmonic, Canterbury Choral Society, Ballet Oklahoma and Lyric Theatre of Oklahoma. Entertainment choices include Broadway shows and popular concerts.

Frontier City
11501 N.E. Expy, Oklahoma City, 405-478-2412

A 65-acre Western theme park; including more than 75 rides, shows and attractions;

entertainment; shops, restaurants. Memorial Day-late August: daily; Easter-Memorial Day and late August-October: weekends only.

Garden Exhibition Building and Horticulture Gardens
3400 N.W. 36th St., Oklahoma City, 405-943-0827
Azalea trails; butterfly garden; rose, peony, and iris gardens; arboretum; the conservatory has one of the country's largest cactus and succulent collections.

Harn Homestead and 1889er Museum
1721 N. Lincoln Blvd., Oklahoma City, 405-235-4058; www.harnhomestead.com
Historic homestead claimed in Land Run of 1889; 1904 farmhouse furnished with pre-statehood objects. Three-story stone and cedar barn; one-room schoolhouse; working farm. Monday-Friday; closed holidays.

Myriad Botanical Gardens
301 W. Reno, Oklahoma City, 405-297-3995
A 17-acre botanical garden in the heart of the city's redeveloping central business district. Features a lake, amphitheater, botanical gardens and seven-story Crystal Bridge Tropical Conservatory.

National Cowboy Hall of Fame and Western Heritage Center
1700 N.E. 63rd St., Oklahoma City, 405-478-2250; www.nationalcowboymuseum.org
Major art collections depict America's Western heritage; Rodeo Hall of Fame; landscaped gardens. Daily 9 a.m.-5 p.m.

Oklahoma City Museum of Art
415 Coach Dr., Oklahoma City, 405-236-3100; www.okcmoa.com
Permanent collection of 16th-20th-century European and American paintings, prints, drawings, photographs, sculpture and decorative arts. Tuesday-Sunday.

Oklahoma City National Memorial
N.W. Fifth St. and N. Robinson Ave., Oklahoma City, 405-235-3313; www.oklahomacitynationalmemorial.org
A series of monuments honors the men, women and children killed by a bomb at the Murrah Federal Building on April 19, 1995. The Gates of Time memorial represents the moment of the blast; the Field of Empty Chairs pays tribute to the 168 lives lost in the bombing. The Survivor Tree is an American elm tree that withstood the blast. Museum Monday-Saturday; Sunday

157

OKLAHOMA

OKLAHOMA CITY THEN AND NOW

Single-day events have shaped both the past and present of this settlement in the American heartland. Oklahoma City was born on April 22, 1889, when the area known as the Unassigned Lands in Oklahoma Territory was opened for settlement. A cannon was fired at noon that day, signaling a rush of thousands of settlers who raced into the two million acres of land to make their claims on the plains.

Just over a century later, the city was the site of the April 19, 1995 bombing of the Alfred P. Murrah Federal Building by American terrorist Timothy McVeigh. Today, this event is memorialized at the Oklahoma City National Memorial. Begin at the Gates of Time, twin monuments that frame the moment of destruction: 9:02 a.m. The east gate represents 9:01 a.m. and the west gate 9:03 a.m. The Field of Empty Chairs consists of 168 bronze-and-stone chairs arranged in nine rows, representing the lives lost and the floor each victim was on at the time of the blast. Smaller chairs memorialize the 19 children killed. The area also includes an orchard and reflecting pool.

afternoon. Also a reflecting pool, orchard and children's area. Daily.

Oklahoma City Zoo
2101 N.E. 50th, Oklahoma City,
405-424-3344; www.okczoo.com
This zoo is home to more than 2,000 animals representing 500 species. Daily.

Oklahoma Firefighters Museum
2716 N.E. 50th St., Oklahoma City,
405-424-3440
See antique fire equipment dating to 1736. Also, the first fire station (1869) in Oklahoma was reassembled here. Daily.

Oklahoma History Center
2401 N. Laird Avenue,
Oklahoma City, 405-522-5248;
www.okhistorycenter.org
Located on 18 acres across from the Capital building, the History Center is a self-guided exploration of Oklahoma from past to present. Outside the museum, the Red River Journey offers visitors a walking tour of the Red River Valley. The grounds also include an outdoor oilfield exhibit with drilling derricks, a portable derrick and machinery associated with Oklahoma oil explorations. Monday-Sunday.

Oklahoma National Stockyards
2501 Exchange Ave., Oklahoma City,
405-235-8675; www.onsy.com
One of the world's largest cattle markets, this stockyard features auctions of cattle, hogs and sheep. Monday-Tuesday.

International Photography Hall of Fame and Museum
2100 N.E. 52nd St., Oklahoma City,
405-424-4055.
Permanent and traveling exhibits; one of world's largest photographic murals. Daily.

Kirkpatrick Science and Air Space Museum
2100 N.E. 52nd St., Oklahoma City,
405-602-6664

Includes a hands-on science museum, Air Space Museum, Kirkpatrick Galleries, gardens/greenhouse; Kirkpatrick Planetarium (shows change quarterly). Daily.

Red Earth Indian Center
2100 N.E. 52nd St., Oklahoma City,
405-427-5228; www.redearth.org
Exhibits and educational programs encourage appreciation of Native American cultures. Daily.

State Capitol
2300 N. Lincoln Blvd.,
Oklahoma City, 405-521-3356
Greco-Roman, neoclassical building designed by S. A. Layton and Wemyss Smith. An oil well beneath the Capitol building reaches 1 1/4 miles underground. After pumping oil from 1941 to 1986, it is now preserved as a monument. The legislature meets annually for 78 days beginning on the first Monday in February. Tours daily.

SPECIAL EVENTS
Ballet Oklahoma
7421 N. Classen, Oklahoma City,
405-843-9898; www.balletoklahoma.com
Productions are staged October-April.

Festival of the Arts
Downtown, Hudson Ave., Oklahoma City.
405-270-4848
International foods, entertainment, children's learning and play area; craft market; artists from many states display their work. Six days in late April.

International Finals Rodeo
333 Gordon Cooper Blvd.,
Oklahoma City, 405-948-6700
The International Pro Rodeo Association's top 15 cowboys and cowgirls compete in seven events to determine world championships.

Oklahoma City Philharmonic Orchestra
Civic Center Music Hall, 201 N. Walker,
Oklahoma City, 405-297-2584

158

OKLAHOMA

Concerts are held weekly from mid-September through May.

State Fair of Oklahoma
333 Gorden Cooper Blvd.,
Oklahoma City, 405-948-6700
Livestock, crafts, art exhibits; Native American ceremonial dances; carnival, parades. Arena and grandstand attractions. September.

HOTELS

★Baymont Inn Oklahoma City South
8315 S. I-35 Service Rd.,
Oklahoma City, 405-631-8661,
877-229-6668; www.baymontinns.com
122 rooms. Complimentary continental breakfast. High-speed, wireless Internet access. Outdoor pool. **$**

★★Best Western Saddleback Inn
4300 S.W. Third St., Oklahoma City,
405-947-7000, 800-228-3903;
www.bestwestern.com/saddlebackinn
220 rooms. Pets accepted, some restrictions; fee. Complimentary full breakfast. High-speed, wireless Internet access. Restaurant, bar. Fitness room. Outdoor pool, whirlpool. Business center. **$**

★★Courtyard Oklahoma City Downtown
4301 Highline Blvd., Oklahoma City,
405-946-6500, 800-321-2211;
www.courtyard.com
149 rooms. High-speed Internet access. Restaurant. Fitness room. Outdoor pool, whirlpool. Airport transportation available. Business center. **$**

★★★Crowne Plaza Hotel
2945 N.W. Expy, Oklahoma City,
405-848-4811, 800-774-1500;
www.crowneplaza.com
Located in the business district of Oklahoma City, this hotel offers easy access to city attractions. Granite bathrooms with closets, dark wood furniture and club chairs with ottomans are found in guest rooms. The Spa Select bedding package includes an amenity bag of lavender linen spray, an eye pillow and a CD of soothing music.

MUSIC TO BROADWAY'S EARS: *OKLAHOMA!*

Oklahoma is lucky to have one of the most popular Broadway musicals celebrating its name in the title. *Oklahoma!*, the first musical collaboration by Richard Rodgers and Oscar Hammerstein II, was different. It had a plot. The songs and dances emerged logically from the plot and the thoughts and emotions of the characters helped carry the story line, which atypically for the time, had its share of dark moments and serious themes. The dancing was more folk-ballet style than kick-line. Even the rural setting of the play was unusual—most musicals were set in urban confines, with sophisticated, affluent characters, not farmhands.

When it opened on Broadway in 1943, critics thought *Oklahoma!* wouldn't make it to a second performance. Scouts who saw the show in out-of-town tryouts were said to deliver a verdict along the lines of "No girls, no gags, no chance." In the tryout stage, the show had a different title—*Away We Go!* Rogers and Hammerstein changed the title to *Oklahoma!* and adding the exuberant song of the same name as the show's closing number. The rousing song thrilled the audience, which gave a standing ovation. The next day, the once-doubting critics could not find enough praise for the show, and *Oklahoma!* was on its to theatrical immortality. It set a record of more than 2,000 performances over five years at St. James Theatre, and is still performed at theaters across the country.

159

OKLAHOMA

★

★

★

★

☆

215 rooms. Pets accepted; fee. Wireless Internet access. Restaurant, bar. Fitness room. Outdoor pool, whirlpool. Business center. **$**

★★Embassy Suites
1815 S. Meridian Ave., Oklahoma City, 405-682-6000, 800-362-2779; www.embassysuites.com
236 rooms, all suites. Pets accepted, some restrictions; fee. Complimentary full breakfast. Wireless Internet access. Restaurant, bar. Children's activity center. Fitness room. Indoor pool, whirlpool. Airport transportation available. Business center. **$$**

★Governors Suites Hotel
2308 S. Meridian Ave., Oklahoma City, 405-682-5299, 888-819-7575; www.govsuitesokc.com
50 rooms. Complimentary full breakfast. High-speed, wireless Internet access. Fitness room. Outdoor pool, whirlpool. Airport transportation available. **$**

★★Holiday Inn
6200 N. Robinson Ave., Oklahoma City, 405-843-5558, 800-682-0049; www.holiday-inn.com
200 rooms. Pets accepted, some restrictions; fee. High-speed Internet access. Restaurant, bar. Fitness room. Indoor pool, whirlpool. Airport transportation available. Business center. **$**

★★★Marriott Waterford
6300 Waterford Blvd., Oklahoma City, 405-848-4782, 800-992-2009; www.marriott.com
Located in Oklahoma City's tony Waterford community, the hotel is 15 minutes from downtown and the airport. Enjoy a drink in the waterfront lounge or take a swim in the outdoor pool. Volleyball and squash facilities are also available. Rooms feature pillow-top mattresses and crisp white linens, and granite bathrooms have jetted tubs and Bath and Body Works amenities.
197 rooms. High-speed, wireless Internet access. Restaurant, bar. Fitness room, spa.

Outdoor pool, whirlpool. Business center. **$$**

★★★Renaissance Oklahoma City Convention Center Hotel
10 N. Broadway, Oklahoma City, 405-228-8000, 800-468-3571; www.renaissancehotels.com
Located in downtown Oklahoma City at the corner of Broadway and Sheridan, the Renaissance Oklahoma City is a 15-story tower that is connected to the adjacent Cox Convention Center by a sky bridge. It's close to the restored Bricktown area, with its shops, restaurants, amusements and River Walk. A 13-story atrium dominates the center of the hotel and the lobby is filled with lush landscaping that includes koi ponds and a waterfall.
311 rooms. High-speed Internet access. Restaurant, bar. Fitness room, spa. Indoor pool, whirlpool. Airport transportation available. Business center. **$$**

★★★The Sheraton Oklahoma City
1 N. Broadway Ave., Oklahoma City, 405-235-2780, 800-285-2780; www.sheraton.com
This downtown hotel is connected to the Cox Convention Center as well as many shops and businesses by an underground concourse. Contemporary styling is the theme, from the lobby with its leather sofas and modern art collection to the oversized guest rooms with long working desks with ergonomic chairs, black-and-white photographs, and brown and black granite bathrooms. An outdoor pool, sun deck and fitness center are available, and pets are welcomed with bowls, treats and beds.
396 rooms. Pets accepted, some restrictions. High-speed, wireless Internet access. Restaurant, bar. Fitness room, spa. Outdoor pool. Business center. **$$**

RESTAURANTS
★★Aria Grill
1 N. Broadway, Oklahoma City, 405-235-2780; www.sheraton.com
American menu. Breakfast, lunch, dinner. Bar. Children's menu. Business casual attire. Valet parking. **$$$**

★
★
★
★
★

★★★Bellini's Ristorante & Grill
6305 Waterford Blvd.,
Oklahoma City, 405-848-1065;
www.bellinis.net

This casual restaurant has the ambience of an Italian piazza. Modern art hangs on the dark wood-paneled walls, and tables are set with black cloths. Everything from pizza to steak, seafood and pasta dishes are featured on the extensive menu. Offers a view of lakeside sunset.
American menu, Italian menu. Lunch, dinner, Sunday brunch. Bar. Children's menu. Reservations recommended. Outdoor seating. **$$**

★Bricktown Brewery
1 N. Oklahoma Ave., Oklahoma City,
405-232-2739; www.bricktownbrewery.com

American menu. Lunch, dinner, late-night. Bar. Children's menu. Casual attire. **$$**

★★Cafe 501
501 S. Boulevard St., Edmond,
405-359-1501.
International menu. Lunch, dinner. Children's menu. **$$**

★★Castle Falls
820 N. MacArthur Blvd., Oklahoma City,
405-942-6133; www.castlefalls.com
German menu. Dinner. Closed Monday-Wednesday, Sunday. Bar. Children's menu. Outdoor seating. **$$**

★★Cattleman's Steakhouse
1309 S. Agnew St., Oklahoma City,
405-236-0416;
www.cattlemensrestaurant.com
Steak menu. Breakfast, lunch, dinner, late-night, brunch. Children's menu. Casual attire. **$$**

★★★The Coach House
6437 Avondale Dr., Oklahoma City,
405-842-1000; www.tch-ok.com
The seasonally changing menu at this restaurant features local produce and meats, with rack of lamb as a signature dish. The cuisine is supported by an extensive wine list. Subdued lighting, double linen table cloths, fine stemware and flatware, and copper chargers give the restaurant an elegant, formal feel.
American menu. Lunch, dinner. Closed Sunday. Children's menu. Business casual attire. Reservations recommended. **$$$**

★County Line
1226 N.E. 63rd St., Oklahoma City,
405-478-4955; www.countyline.com
Barbecue menu. Lunch, dinner. Bar. Children's menu. Casual attire. **$$**

★★Deep Fork Grill
5418 N. Western Ave.,
Oklahoma City, 405-848-7678;
www.deepforkgrill.com
Steak, seafood menu. Lunch, dinner, brunch. Bar. Children's menu. Business casual attire. Reservations recommended. Valet parking. **$$**

★★Eddy's of Oklahoma City
4227 N. Meridian Ave.,
Oklahoma City, 405-787-2944;
www.eddyssteakhouseokc.com
Steak menu. Dinner. Closed Sunday-Monday. Children's menu. Business casual attire. Reservations recommended. **$$**

★Gopuram Taste Of India
4559 N.W. 23rd St., Oklahoma City,
405-948-7373;
www.members.aol.com/gopuram
Indian menu. Lunch, dinner. Children's menu. Casual attire. **$$**

★★★JW's Steakhouse
3233 N.W. Expy, Oklahoma City,
405-842-6633; www.marriott.com
This steakhouse in the Oklahoma City Marriott has dark wood paneling and red leather chairs and banquettes. Serving dinner only, JW's has the full steakhouse look, and specializes in classics such as filet mignon and prime rib.
Steak menu. Dinner, late-night. Children's menu. Business casual attire. Reservations recommended. Valet parking. **$$$**

OKLAHOMA

★
★
★
★
★

★★Kona Ranch Steakhouse
1037 S. Meridian, Oklahoma City,
405-681-1000.
Steak menu. Lunch, dinner. Bar. Children's
menu. Casual attire. $$

★★★La Baguette Bistro
7408 N. May Ave., Oklahoma City,
405-840-3047; www.labaguettebistro.com
Just northwest of downtown, this bistro
offers an authentic experience. The owners/
chefs hail from France, and serve simple
but authentic bistro fare (including baguette
sandwiches) in an L-shaped dining room.
French menu. Breakfast, lunch, dinner,
brunch. Bar. Casual attire. $$

★★Las Palomas
2329 N. Meridian, Oklahoma City,
405-949-9988.
Mexican menu. Lunch, dinner. Children's
menu. Casual attire. $

★★Sushi Neko
4318 N. Western Ave.,
Oklahoma City, 405-528-8862;
www.sushineko.com
Japanese menu. Lunch, dinner, late-night.
Closed Sunday. Bar. Children's menu.
Casual attire. Reservations recommended.
Valet parking. Outdoor seating. $$

OKMULGEE

The capital of the Creek Nation was established in 1868 and operates at the Creek Indian
Complex. The Creeks gave the town its name, which means "bubbling water." Within
Okmulgee County nearly five million pounds of wild pecans are harvested annually. The
city is the home of Oklahoma State University/Okmulgee, one of the country's largest resi-
dential-vocational training schools.

Information: Chamber of Commerce, 112 N. Morton, 918-756-6172;
www.tourokmulgee.com

WHAT TO SEE AND DO
Creek Council House Museum
106 W. 6th St., Okmulgee, 918-756-2324
Museum houses a display of Creek tribal
history. Tuesday-Saturday.

SPECIAL EVENTS
Pecan Festival
6th and Morton, Okmulgee,
918-756-6172, 800-355-5552
This festival holds the Guinness World
Record for biggest pecan pie ever baked,
and a pie approximately 40 feet in diameter
is baked every year for the festival's par-
ticipants. A carnival, arts, crafts and vari-
ous forms of entertainment round out the
offerings. First weekend in June.

HOTELS
★★Best Western Okmulgee
3499 N. Wood Dr., Okmulgee,
918-756-9200, 800-552-9201;
www.bestwestern.com
50 rooms. Pets accepted; fee. Complimen-
tary continental breakfast. Restaurant, bar.
Outdoor pool. $

★Henryetta Inn and Dome
810 E. Trudgeon St., Henryetta,
918-652-2581, 800-515-3663
85 rooms. Pets accepted, some restrictions;
fee. Restaurant, bar. Fitness room. Indoor
pool. $

PERRY

Settled during the opening of the Cherokee Outlet, this town was once called Hell's Half-Acre. It's home to a Carnegie library, a public library built with money donated by Andrew Carnegie.

Information: Chamber of Commerce, 300 Sixth St.. 580-336-4684; www.perrychamber.fullnet.net

WHAT TO SEE AND DO

Cherokee Strip Museum

2617 W. Fir, Perry, 580-336-2405
This museum includes a schoolhouse (circa 1895), pioneer artifacts and documents depicting the era of the 1893 land run. Tuesday-Saturday.

SPECIAL EVENT

Cherokee Strip Celebration

Courthouse Lawn, Perry, 580-336-4684
This festival commemorates the opening of the Cherokee Strip to settlers. Parade, entertainment, rodeo, contests, Noble County Fair. Mid-September.

HOTELS

★★Best Western Cherokee Strip Motel

2903 Hwy. 77 W., Perry, 580-336-2218; www.bestwestern.com
88 rooms. Pets accepted, some restrictions; fee. Restaurant, bar. Indoor pool. $

PONCA CITY

Ponca City was founded in a single day in the traditional Oklahoma land-rush manner. Although located in the Cherokee Strip, the town was named for the Ponca tribe. Ponca City is a modern industrial town surrounded by cattle and wheat country.

Information: Ponca City Tourism, 580-763-8092, 866-763-8092; www.poncacitynews.com

WHAT TO SEE AND DO

Kaw Lake

Hwy. 2, Ponca City, 580-762-5611
Located on the Arkansas River, the shoreline of this lake covers 168 miles. Water sports, fishing, boating, hunting. Recreation and camping areas located one mile off Highway 60. Daily.

Marland Mansion Estate

901 Monument Rd., Ponca City, 580-767-0420
A 55-room mansion built in 1928 by E. W. Marland, an oil baron, Oklahoma governor and philanthropist. Modeled after the Davanzati Palace in Florence, Italy, the estate features elaborate artwork and hand-painted ceilings. Tours, daily.

Marland's Grand Home

1000 E. Grand Ave., Ponca City, 580-767-0427
This structure houses an Indian Museum and a Daughters of the American Revolution Memorial Museum. Tuesday-Saturday.

HOTELS

★★Holiday Inn

2215 N. 14 St., Ponca City, 580-762-8311, 800-465-4329; www.holiday-inn.com
138 rooms. Pets accepted, some restrictions. Restaurant, bar. Fitness room. Outdoor pool. $

163

OKLAHOMA

★
★
★
★
★

POTEAU

Rich in ancient history and pioneer heritage, Poteau is located in an area of timber and high hills. The nearby peak of Cavanal Hill provides a spectacular view of the entire Poteau River Valley. Poteau lies approximately 15 miles north of the Ouachita National Forest.
Information: Chamber of Commerce, 201 S. Broadway St., 918-647-9178; www.poteau-ok.com

WHAT TO SEE AND DO

Heavener Runestone
Hwy 59, Poteau, 918-653-2241
Scientists belive the Scandinavian cryptograph in eight runes carved into Poteau Mountain were inscribed by Vikings in 800 A.D. Other runes from the Scandinavian alphabet of the third through 10th centuries have been found engraved on several stones in the area. Daily.

Kerr Museum
1507 S. McKenna St., Poteau,
918-647-8221
The home of former Senator Robert S. Kerr, this museum contains material detailing the history and development of eastern Oklahoma including natural history, pioneer, Choctaw and special exhibits. Tuesday-Sunday afternoons, also by appointment.

Spiro Mound Archeological State Park
Spiro Mounds Rd., Spiro, 918-962-2062
A 138-acre site with 12 earthen mounds dating from 600 A.D. to 1450 A.D. A reconstructed Native American house and excavated items are on display in the interpretive center. Summer: Tuesday-Sunday; winter: Wednesday-Sunday.

ROMAN NOSE STATE PARK

Information: www.oklahomaparks.com

WHAT TO SEE AND DO

Roman Nose State Park
Hwy. 8, Watonga. 580-623-7281
Named after Chief Henry Roman Nose of the Cheyenne, this is a 750-acre area with a 55-acre man-made lake stocked with bass, crappie, bluegill, rainbow trout and catfish. Facilities include a swimming pool, bathhouse, fishing, boating, paddleboats, golf, tennis, picnicking, playgrounds, concession and a lodge.

HOTELS

★★Roman Nose Resort
Hwy. 8A, Watonga,
580-623-7281, 800-654-8240;
www.oklahomaparks.com
57 rooms. Pets accepted, some restrictions. Restaurant. Children's activity center. Outdoor pool. Tennis. $

SEQUOYAH STATE PARK

Information: www.oklahomaparks.com

WHAT TO SEE AND DO

Sequoyah State Park
Hwy. 51, Tahlequah, 918-772-2046
These approximately 2,800 acres in Oklahoma's Cookson Hills were once a bandits' hideout. The park is on Fort Gibson Reservoir, created by the dam of the same name. This 19,100-acre reservoir shifts its level less than most hydroelectric power lakes in Oklahoma and is stocked with bass, catfish, and crappie.

HOTELS
★Indian Lodge
3370 Hwy. 51, Wagoner,
918-485-3184; www.indianlodge.net
25 rooms. Closed November-March. Outdoor pool. **$**

★★Western Hills Guest Ranch
19808 Park #10, Wagoner, 918-772-2545,
800-368-1486
18 rooms. Pets accepted, some restrictions. Restaurant, bar. Children's activity center. Outdoor pool, children's pool. Tennis. On Fort Gibson Reservoir. **$**

SHAWNEE

The history of Shawnee is that of Oklahoma in miniature. In the center of the state, it stands on what was originally Sac and Fox land, which was also claimed at various times by Spain, France and England. It was opened by a land rush on September 22, 1891. Oil was struck in 1926. Shawnee is the home of Oklahoma Baptist University. Jim Thorpe, the great Native American athlete, and Dr. Brewster Higley, the physician who wrote "Home on the Range," lived here. Astronaut Gordon Cooper was born and raised in Shawnee.
Information: Chamber of Commerce, 131 N. Bell, 405-273-6092; www.shawneenet.com

WHAT TO SEE AND DO
Mabee-Gerrer Museum of Art
1900 W. MacArthur Dr., Shawnee,
405-878-5300
This art gallery features works by 19th- and 20th-century European and American artists as well as works from the Middle Ages and the Renaissance. Museum features artifacts of Egyptian, Babylonian, Grecian, Roman, Persian, Chinese, African and Polynesian civilizations as well as North, Central and South American native civilizations. Tuesday-Sunday.

Seminole Nation Museum
524 S. Wewoka Ave., Wewoka,
405-257-5580

The museum traces the Seminoles' history from their removal from Florida over the Trail of Tears to the establishment of the capital in Oklahoma. Displays include a collection of Native American peace medals; replicas of a Chick (Florida Seminole house) and artifacts from the pioneer through the oil boom days of the 1920s. Art gallery with Native American paintings and sculpture. Tuesday-Sunday.

HOTELS
★★Ramada Inn
4900 N. Harrison Blvd., Shawnee,
405-275-4404, 800-298-2054;
www.ramada.com
106 rooms. Pets accepted; fee. Restaurant, bar. Indoor pool. **$**

165

OKLAHOMA

STILLWATER

Stillwater was born overnight in the great land run of 1889. The settlement was less than a year old when, on Christmas Day 1890, the territorial legislature established Oklahoma State University (formerly Oklahoma A & M).

Information: Convention & Visitors Bureau, 409 S. Main St., 405-743-3697, 800-991-6717; www.come2stillwater.com

WHAT TO SEE AND DO

Lake Carl Blackwell
11000 W. Hwy. 51C, Stillwater, 405-372-5157

A 19,364-acre recreation area operated by Oklahoma State University. Swimming, water-skiing, fishing, boating, sailing, hunting, picnic areas, campgrounds, cabins. Fees for various activities.

Oklahoma State University
Washington St. and Universtiy Ave., Stillwater, 405-744-9341; www.osu. okstate.edu

On a campus of 840 acres with an additional 4,774 acres of experimental university farms statewide., this university has more than 20,000 students. On campus is the Noble Research Center for Agriculture and Renewable Natural Resources, an education/research complex with an emphasis on the biological sciences. Buildings include Old Central, the oldest collegiate building in the state built in 1894 of pink brick, as well as attractive modified Georgian buildings of red brick with slate roofs.

HOTELS

★★Best Western Stillwater
600 E. McElroy Rd., Stillwater, 405-377-7010, 800-353-6894; www.bestwestern.com

122 rooms. Pets accepted, some restrictions. Restaurant, bar. Fitness room. Indoor pool, whirlpool. Business center. **$**

★★Holiday Inn
2515 W. Sixth Ave., Stillwater, 405-372-0800; www.holiday-inn.com

141 rooms. Pets accepted. Restaurant, bar. Indoor pool, whirlpool. Business center. **$**

OKLAHOMA

TAHLEQUAH

Tribal branches of the Cherokee met here in 1839 to sign a new constitution forming the Cherokee Nation. They had been driven by the U.S. Army from North Carolina, Alabama, Tennessee and Georgia over the Trail of Tears. The Cherokee were the only tribe with a constitution and a body of law written in their own language, using a written alphabet which had been created by Sequoyah. These talented people published the first newspaper in Indian Territory and in 1885 established the first commercial teleline in Oklahoma. The Southwestern Bell TeleCompany, to which it was later sold, established a monument to this remarkable enterprise on the Old Courthouse Square.

Information: Tahlequah Area Chamber of Commerce, 123 E. Delaware St., 918-456-3742, 800-456-4860; www.tahlequahok.com

WHAT TO SEE AND DO

Cherokee Heritage Center
21192 S. Keeler Dr., Tahlequah, 918-456-6007
A National Museum of Cherokee artifacts, this center features a reconstructed 1890 rural village. Daily.

SPECIAL EVENTS

Trail of Tears
Tsa-La-Gi Amphitheater, Tahlequah. 918-456-6007.
A professional cast presents a musical drama depicting the history of the Cherokee Tribe. Monday-Saturday evenings. Mid-June-Labor Day.

Cherokee National Holiday
Tahlequah, 918-456-0671
Celebration of Constitutional Convention. Championship cornstalk bow and arrow shoot, powwow. Labor Day weekend.

Illinois River Balloon Fest
Airport, Tahlequah, 918-456-3742
Balloon race, balloon glow, arts and crafts, carnival, skydiving exhibition, food. Mid-August.

HOTELS

★★Tahlequah Motor Lodge
2501 S. Muskogee Ave., Tahlequah, 918-456-2350, 800-480-8705
53 rooms. Complimentary full breakfast. Restaurant. Indoor pool, whirlpool. $

TENKILLER FERRY LAKE

Information: www.oklahomafishingguides.com

WHAT TO SEE AND DO

Tenkiller Ferry Lake
Hwy. 64, Talequah, 918-489-5643
The shores of this lake are lined with cliffs, rock bluffs and wooded slopes. The Tenkiller Ferry Dam on the Illinois River is 197 feet high and backs up the stream for 34 miles, creating more than 130 miles of shoreline. There are 12,900 acres of water surface. The lake has marinas, lodges and boat docks; the lower Illinois River is famous for its striped bass fishing.

HOTELS

★★Fin & Feather Resort
RR 1, Gore, 918-487-5148; www.finandfeatherresort.com
83 rooms. Closed October-Easter. Pets accepted, some restrictions; fee. Restaurant. Indoor pool with retractable roof, children's pool, whirlpool. $

167

OKLAHOMA

TULSA

Not an oil derrick is visible to visitors, yet Tulsa is an important energy city. Oil and gas fields surround it, and offices of energy companies are prevalent: more than 600 energy firms employ 30,000 people. This is the second largest city in Oklahoma, and its atmosphere is cosmopolitan.

With the completion of the Arkansas River Navigation System, Tulsa gained a water route to the Great Lakes and the Gulf of Mexico. The Port of Catoosa, three miles from the city and located on the Verdigris River, is at the headwaters of the waterway and is now America's westernmost inland water port.

Information: Convention & Visitors Bureau, 616 S. Boston Ave., 918-585-1201, 800-558-3311; www.visittulsa.com

OKLAHOMA

SPOT★ LIGHT

★ROUTE 66 WAS CONCEIVED BY TULSA BUSINESSMAN CYRUS AVERY.

★THE CITY IS IN THE HEART OF TORNADO ALLEY AND HAS FREQUENT TWISTERS.

★COUNTRY SINGER GARTH BROOKS CALLS TULSA HOME.

WHAT TO SEE AND DO

Arkansas River Historical Society Museum
Tulsa Port of Catoosa, 5350 Cimarron Rd., Catoosa, 918-266-2291
Located in the Port Authority Building, this museum has pictorial displays and operating models that trace the history of the 1,450-mile Arkansas River and McClellan-Kerr Navigation System. Monday-Friday.

Bell's Amusement Park
3901 E. 21st., Tulsa, 918-744-1991; www.bellsfamilyfun.com
Rides include a large wooden roller coaster, log ride, sky ride and bumper boats, plus two miniature golf courses and an arcade.

June-August: daily; April-May and September: weekends.

Boston Avenue United Methodist Church
1301 S. Boston Ave., Tulsa, 918-583-5181
Designed and built in 1929 by Adah Robinson, this Art Deco structure was the first large-scale use of the style in a church. It features a 225-foot tower and many lesser towers decorated with bas-relief pioneer figures. The sanctuary is ornamented with Italian mosaic reredos. Monday-Friday.

Creek Council Oak Tree
18th and Cheyenne, Tulsa
A landscaped plot housing the Council Oak, this tree stands as a memorial to the Lochapokas Creek tribe.

Gilcrease Museum

1400 Gilcrease Museum Rd., Tulsa,
918-596-2700; www.gilcrease.org

Founded by Thomas Gilcrease, an oil man
of Creek descent, this museum has a collection of Native Americans and artifacts
from 12,000 years ago-present. The library
houses about 90,000 items, including the
earliest known letter sent to Europe from
the New World. Daily.

The Tulsa Zoo

5701 E. 36th St., Tulsa, 918-669-6200;
www.tulsazoo.com

More than 200 varieties of animals are
housed within 68 acres of landscaped
grounds. The zoo features Native American
artifacts, geological specimens, dinosaur
replicas, live plants and animals. Daily.

Oxley Nature Center

6700 Mohawk Blvd., Tulsa, 918-669-6644;
www.oxleynaturecenter.org

This 800-acre wildlife sanctuary has numerous nature trails. Daily.

Philbrook Museum of Art

2727 S. Rockford Rd., Tulsa,
918-749-7941, 800-324-7941;
www.philbrook.org

Exhibits include Italian Renaissance, 19th-
century English, American and Native
American paintings; Native American baskets and pottery; Chinese jades and decorative material; Southeast Asian tradeware;
African sculpture. Housed in an Italian
Renaissance-revival villa on 23 acres; formal and sculpture gardens. Tuesday-Sunday;
closed holidays.

Sherwin Miller Museum of Jewish Art

2021 E. 71st St., Tulsa, 918-294-1366;
www.jewishmuseum.net

The Southwest's largest collection of Juda-
ica contains objects representative of Jewish history, art, ceremonial events and daily
life from around the world. Monday-Friday,
also Sunday afternoons; closed Jewish holidays.

Utica Square

21st and Utica Streets, Tulsa,
918-742-5531; www.uticasquare.com

This upscale shopping district includes
Saks Fifth Avenue, Coach and Williams-
Sonoma. Set in a peaceful landscape that
features manicured gardens, the area features many restaurants and cafes.

SPECIAL EVENTS

Discoveryland! Outdoor Theater

19501 W. 41st St., Tulsa, 918-742-5255

This theater presents Rodgers and Hammerstein's *Oklahoma!* in a 2,000-seat outdoor
theater complex with a Western theme.
Authentic Native American dancing, Western musical revue and barbecue dinner prior
to performance. Monday-Friday. Mid-June-
late August.

HOTELS

★★Best Western Trade Winds Central Inn

3141 E. Skelly Dr., Tulsa,
918-749-5561, 800-780-7234.;
www.bestwestern.com

164 rooms. Pets accepted; fee. Complimentary continental breakfast. High-speed, wireless Internet access. Restaurant, bar. Fitness
room. Outdoor pool. Airport transportation
available. Business center. $

★★★Crowne Plaza

100 E. Second St., Tulsa,
918-582-9000, 800-227-6963;
www.crowneplaza.com

This hotel caters to business travelers and
has a central Tulsa location. A full-service
spa, restaurant, lounge, business center,
indoor and outdoor pools, fitness room,
and conference facilities are among the
services.

462 rooms. Pets accepted; fee. High-speed,
wireless Internet access. Restaurant, bar.
Fitness room, spa. Indoor pool, outdoor
pool. Airport transportation available. Business center. $

★★Doubletree Hotel

616 W. 7th St., Tulsa,
918-587-8000, 800-222-8733;
www.doubletree.com

169

OKLAHOMA

★
★
★
★
★

417 rooms. Pets accepted; fee. Wireless Internet access. Restaurant, bar. Fitness room. Indoor pool, whirlpool. Airport transportation available. Business center. **$**

★★Embassy Suites
3332 S. 79th E. Ave., Tulsa,
918-622-4000, 800-362-2779;
www.embassysuites.com
244 rooms, all suites. Pets accepted; fee. Complimentary full breakfast. Wireless Internet access. Restaurant, bar. Fitness room. Indoor pool, whirlpool. Airport transportation available. Business center. **$**

★Hampton Inn
3209 S. 79th E. Ave., Tulsa,
918-663-1000, 800-426-7866;
www.hamptoninn.com
148 rooms. Pets accepted; fee. Complimentary continental breakfast. High-speed, wireless Internet access. Outdoor pool. Airport transportation available. Business center. **$**

★

★

★

★

★

★★★Hilton Tulsa Southern Hills
7902 S. Lewis St., Tulsa,
918-492-5000, 800-774-1500;
www.hilton.com
Located in the Southern Hills area of Tulsa and across the street from Oral Roberts University, this hotel features spacious guest rooms with plush beds and Crabtree and Evelyn bath products. There's also complimentary high-speed wireless Internet access and a full fitness center.
282 rooms. Pets accepted, some restrictions; fee. High-speed Internet access. Restaurant, bar. Fitness room. Outdoor pool. Airport transportation available. Business center. **$**

★★★The Inn At Jarrett Farm
38009 Hwy. 75 N., Ramona,
918-371-1200, 877-371-1200;
www.jarrettfarm.com
Perched on a hilltop 20 miles north of Tulsa, this 115-acre countryside bed-and-breakfast offers plenty of space and beautiful views. One 1,100-square-foot master suite is located in the ranch-style main house while the other 10 suites are in yellow cottages

dotting the property. American-continental cuisine is served at the inn's dining room. 11 rooms. Complimentary full breakfast. Restaurant. Outdoor pool, whirlpool. **$$**

★La Quinta Inn
6030 E. Skelly Dr., Tulsa,
918-665-2630, 800-447-0600;
www.laquinta.com
105 rooms. Complimentary continental breakfast. High-speed, wireless Internet access. Fitness room. Outdoor pool. Business center. **$**

★★★Marriott Tulsa Southern Hills
1902 E. 71st St., Tulsa, 918-493-7000,
800-228-9290; www.marriott.com
Rising 11 stories in two connected wings, the Marriott Tulsa Southern Hills offers well-appointed guest rooms with full amenities. It is located near golf courses, tennis facilities, the Tulsa Zoo and other area attractions.
383 rooms. High-speed, wireless Internet access. Restaurant, bar. Fitness room, spa. Indoor pool, whirlpool. Airport transportation available. Business center. **$**

★Presidential Suites Tulsa
8338 E. 61St. S., Tulsa,
918-254-0088, 888-627-1155;
www.presidentialsuitestulsa.com
52 rooms. Pets accepted; fee. Complimentary full breakfast. Wireless Internet access. Bar. Outdoor pool. Airport transportation available. Business center. **$**

★★★Radisson Hotel Tulsa
10918 E. 41st St., Tulsa, 918-627-5000,
800-325-3535; www.radissontulsa.com
This hotel features an indoor water park. Located in the heart of southeast Tulsa, near the Tulsa International Airport and the Philbrook Museum, rooms are comfortable and spacious.
325 rooms. Pets accepted, some restrictions. High-speed, wireless Internet access. Two restaurants, bar. Children's activity center. Fitness room. Indoor pool, outdoor pool, whirlpool. Airport transportation available. Business center. **$**

RESTAURANTS

★★★Atlantic Sea Grill
8321-A E. 61st St., Tulsa, 918-252-7966
This seafood house prides itself on personalized service and good food. The menu features classics like shrimp cocktail, crabcakes and grilled salmon.
Seafood menu. Lunch, dinner. Bar. Business casual attire. Outdoor seating. **$$**

★Baxter's Interurban Grill
717 S. Houston, Tulsa,
918-585-3134; www.baxtersgrill.com
American menu. Lunch, dinner. Closed Sunday; holidays. Bar. Children's menu. Business casual attire. Outdoor seating. **$$**

★★★Bodean Seafood
3323 E. 51st St., Tulsa,
918-743-3861; www.bodean.net
This popular restaurant serves creative seafood dishes—items are flown in twice daily—in a comfortable atmosphere that includes white linen-topped tables. A three-course prix fixe menu is available, and Tuesdays feature a four-course menu with three wines to match.
Seafood menu. Lunch, dinner. Bar. Casual attire. **$$**

★★Cammerelli's
1536 E. 15th St., Tulsa, 918-582-8900
Italian menu. Lunch, dinner, brunch. Bar. Casual attire. Reservations recommended. **$$$**

★★★Fountains
6540 S. Lewis Ave., Tulsa, 918-749-9916;
www.fountainsrestaurant.com
For more than 25 years, this restaurant has served American classics to a loyal following. Old-fashioned, tableside preparations of Bananas Foster add some entertainment to the meal.
Lunch, dinner, Sunday brunch. Bar. Children's menu. **$$**

★Jamil's
2833 E. 51st., Tulsa, 918-742-9097
Seafood menu, Steak menu. Dinner. Casual attire. **$$**

★Metro Diner
3001 E 11th, Tulsa, 918-592-2616
American menu. Breakfast, lunch, dinner. Children's menu. Casual attire. **$**

★★★Polo Grill
2038 Utica Square, Tulsa, 918-744-4280;
www.pologrill.com
The creative American cuisine served at this restaurant features French, Southern and Southwest influences. Signature dishes include oven-roasted tomato bisque, tender leaf spinach and strawberry salad, crispy grit cakes, grilled steaks and baked fudge. There is a nine-course prix-fixe tasting menu and an extensive wine list.
American menu. Lunch, dinner. Closed Sunday. Bar. Children's menu. Business casual attire. Reservations recommended. Outdoor seating. **$$$**

★Ricardos
5629 E. 41st., Tulsa, 918-622-2668;
www.ricardostulsa.com
Mexican menu. Lunch, dinner. Closed Sunday. Children's menu. Casual attire. **$**

★★Ti-Amo Italian Ristorante
6024A S. Sheridan, Tulsa, 918-499-1919;
www.tiamotulsa.com
Italian menu. Lunch, dinner. Bar. Business casual attire. **$$**

★★★Warren Duck Club
6110 S. Yale, Tulsa, 918-495-1000;
www.doubletree.com
This fine-dining restaurant is located inside the Doubletree Hotel. The menu features American classics such as grilled steaks, seafood and more.
American menu. Breakfast, lunch, dinner, late-night. Bar. Children's menu. Valet parking. **$$$**

171

OKLAHOMA

★
★
★
★
★

WEATHERFORD

Weatherford is the home of Southwestern Oklahoma State University (1901) as well as *Gemini* and *Apollo* astronaut Thomas P. Stafford.
Information: Chamber of Commerce, 522 W. Rainey, 580-772-7744, 800-725-7744; www.weatherfordchamber.com

WHAT TO SEE AND DO

Red Rock Canyon State Park
Hwy. 281, Weatherford, 405-542-6344
This park covers 310 acres and features a swimming pool and bathhouse. Hiking, picnicking and camping are also available. Daily.

Stafford Air and Space Center
Stafford Field, 3000 E Logan Rd., Weatherford, 580-772-5871;
www.staffordspacecenter.com
This museum houses memorabilia of former astronaut Thomas Stafford, who flew on Gemini VI and IX as well as Apollo 10. Daily.

HOTELS

★Best Western Mark Motor Hotel
525 E. Main St., Weatherford,
580-772-3325, 800-780-7234;
www.bestwestern.com
63 rooms. Pets accepted, some restrictions; fee. Complimentary full breakfast. Checkout noon. Outdoor pool. $

RESTAURANTS

★★T-Bone Steak House
1805 E. Main St., Weatherford,
580-772-6329, www.tbonesteakhouse.com
Steak menu. Dinner. Bar. Children's menu. $$

WOODWARD

A land run community, Woodward grew thanks to its location on the Great Western Cattle Trail. Temple Houston, son of Texas Republic President Sam Houston, lived and worked here as a lawyer and is buried in Elmwood Cemetary.
Information: Chamber of Commerce, 1006 Oklahoma Ave., 580-256-7411, 800-364-5352; www.woodwardok.com

WHAT TO SEE AND DO

Historic Fort Supply
Hwy. 270, Woodward, 580-766-3767
Established as a temporary cavalry supply camp in the late 1800s, the fort endured as a trail stop between Kansas, Texas and Oklahoma. Restored original buildings include the Powder Monkey's House and Teamsters Cabin (circa 1870), the Commanding Officer's Quarters (1878) and the Officer's Quarters (circa mid-1880s). The Guard House (1892) is now a museum. Tours, Monday-Friday.

Plains Indians & Pioneers Museum
2009 Williams Ave., Woodward,
580-256-6136
Changing and permanent displays depict Native American culture and early life on the plains. Pioneer, cowboy and Native American artifacts and clothing; collection of personal belongings of Temple Houston, son of Sam Houston; exhibits from early-day banks; original building from historic Fort Supply; agriculture building; art center with changing exhibits. Tuesday-Saturday.

HOTELS

★★Northwest Inn
3202 First St., Woodward,
580-256-7600, 800-727-7606
124 rooms. Pets accepted, some restrictions; fee. Restaurant, bar. Indoor pool. $

SOUTH DAKOTA

THIS IS THE LAND OF THE PROUD AND MIGHTY SIOUX. IF YOUR ONLY PICTURE OF THIS TRIBE is from the 1990 film *Dances With Wolves*, a visit to South Dakota will reveal much about the fascinating history of this vast nation that ruled the plains, hunting buffalo by horseback. South Dakota Sioux are generally referred to as Lakota, Dakota or Nakota, and today there are more than 62,000 members of the tribes living in the state.

There are museums and monuments throughout the state where visitors can learn more about the Sioux, from the Crazy Horse Memorial and Indian Musuem of North America in Custer, to the Cultural Heritage Center in the state capital of Pierre. Visit a pow wow, or tribal gathering with dancing and contests, during the summer months in towns throughout the state. Or soak in the scenery with a drive along the Native American Scenic Byway, which stretches from Nebraksa north through the center of South Dakota.

Beyond its rich Native American history, South Dakota is a quiet, sparsely filled space teeming with natural beauty. Each year, scores of tourists visit Badlands National Park, or trek a little further west to take a look at one of the country's most recognizable monuments, Mount Rushmore, a granite mountain carved with the visages of George Washington, Thomas Jefferson, Abraham Lincoln and Theodore Roosevelt.

South Dakota offers more than parks and presidential figures. It's one of the nation's richest archaeological dig sites. The largest and most complete *Tyrranosaurus rex* in the world, Sue (who now lives at Chicago's Field Museum) was discovered here, and mammoths, marine life and other creatures from the earth's past are found regularly. Join in an archaological dig during summer months with Rapid City's Archaeological Research Center, or any of the other organziations digging in the state. South Dakota tourism can provide tips on active digs.

Urbanites will find plenty to do in the state's big cities, from captial city Pierre in the center to Sioux Falls in the west.

Americana abounds in South Dakota, with roadside delights like the famously kitschy Corn Palace in Mitchell and more diners serving inexpensive, hearty meals and fantastic slices of fruit pies than any appetite can handle.

Information: www.travelsd.com

★ SPOTLIGHT

★ Mount Rushmore was supposed to depict the full torsos of the four presidents, not just their faces, but insuffcient funds forced the carvings to stop.

★ Laura Ingalls Wilder's book *By the Shores of Silver Lake* is based on her childhood years in DeSmet.

★ Television news anchor Tom Brokaw is from Webster, South Dakota.

ABERDEEN

The roots of Aberdeen's commerce are the three railroads that converge here, giving it the nickname "Hub City." Alexander Mitchell, a railroader of the 19th century, named the town for his Scottish birthplace. German-Russian immigrants arrived in 1884. Hamlin Garland, author of *Son of the Middle Border*, and L. Frank Baum, author of *The Wizard of Oz*, lived here.

Information: Convention & Visitors Bureau, 514-1-2 S. Main St., 605-225-2414, 800-645-3851; www.aberdeencvb.com

HOTELS

★★Best Western Ramkota Hotel

1400 N.W. Eighth Ave., Aberdeen, 605-229-4040, 800-780-7234; www.ramkota.com

154 rooms. Pets accepted. Restaurant, bar. Fitness room. Indoor pool, whirlpool. Airport transportation available. Business center. $

★★Ramada Inn & Convention Center

2727 S.E. Sixth Ave., Aberdeen, 605-225-3600, 800-272-6232; www.ramada.com

152 rooms. Pets accepted. Complimentary continental breakfast. Internet. Restaurant, bar. Indoor pool, whirlpool. Airport transportation available. $

TOURING THE BLACK HILLS

Magnificent forests, mountain scenery, ghost towns, Mount Rushmore National Memorial, Harney Peak (highest mountain east of the Rockies), Crazy Horse Memorial, swimming, horseback riding, rodeos, hiking, skiing, and the Black Hills Passion Play make up only a partial list of the attractions of this area. Memories of Calamity Jane, Wild Bill Hickock and Preacher Smith haunt the old Western towns. Bison, deer, elk, coyotes, mountain goats, bighorn sheep and smaller animals make this area home.

Black Hills National Forest includes 1,247,000 acres—nearly half of the Black Hills. The forest offers 28 campgrounds, 20 picnic grounds and one winter sports area. Two snowmobile trail systems, one in the Bearlodge Mountains and the other in the northern Black Hills, offer 330 miles of some of the best snowmobiling in the nation. There are also 250 miles of hiking, bridle and mountain biking trails.

There is a whimsical story that explains the formation of the Black Hills. Paul Bunyan had a stove so large that boys with hams strapped to their feet skated on the top to grease it for the famous camp flapjacks. One day when the stove was red hot, Babe, Paul's favorite blue ox, swallowed it whole and took off. He died of a combination of indigestion and exhaustion. Paul, weeping so copiously his tears eroded the Badlands, built the Black Hills as a cairn over his old friend.

Geologists say that the Black Hills were formed by a great geologic uplift that pushed a mighty dome of ancient granite up under the sandstone and limestone layers. Water washed away these softer rocks, exposing the granite. This uplift was slow, and it may still be happening. Pactola Visitor Center, on Highway 385 at Pactola Reservoir west of Rapid City, has information and interpretive exhibits on Black Hills history, geology, and ecology. Memorial Day-Labor Day.

Information: www.blackhills.com

RESTAURANTS

★★Flame Restaurant and Lounge
2 S. Main St., Aberdeen, 605-225-2082

American menu. Lunch, dinner. Closed Sunday. Bar. Children's menu. Casual attire. **$$**

BROOKINGS

Research done at South Dakota State University has helped make Brookings the agricultural capital of the state. It has developed diversified farming and the manufacturing industries. Information: Chamber of Commerce-Convention & Visitor Bureau, 2308 E. Sixth St., 605-692-6125, 800-699-6125; www.brookingssd.com

HOTELS

★★Days Inn Brookings
2500 E. Sixth St., Brookings,
605-692-9471, 877-831-1562;
www.daysinn.com
125 rooms. Pets accepted, some restrictions. Complimentary continental breakfast. Restaurant, bar. Fitness room. Indoor pool,

whirlpool. Airport transportation available. Business center. **$**

RESTAURANTS

★★The Ram & O'Hare's
327 Main Ave., Brookings, 605-692-2485
American menu. Lunch, dinner. Closed Sunday. Bar. Children's menu. Casual attire. **$$**

CUSTER

This is where a prospector with Lieutenant Colonel Custer's expedition of 1874 discovered gold, prompting the gold rush of 1875-1876. Main Street was laid out in the 1880s, wide enough for wagons pulled by teams of oxen to make U-turns. Custer is the seat of Custer County, headquarters of the Black Hills National Forest and center of an area of great mineral wealth. Gold, quartz, beryl, mica and gypsum are some of the minerals that are mined here. Custer is a popular area for winter sports activities. Information: Custer County Chamber of Commerce, 615 Washington St., 605-673-2244; 800-992-9818; www.custersd.com

CRAZY HORSE MEMORIAL

This large sculpture, still being carved from the granite of Thunderhead Mountain, was the life work of Korczak Ziolkowski (1908-1982), who briefly assisted Gutzon Borglum on Mount Rushmore. With funds gained solely from admission fees and contributions, Ziolkowski worked alone on the memorial, refusing federal and state funding. The sculptor's wife and several of their children are continuing the work. Crazy Horse—the stalwart Sioux chief who helped defeat Custer and the United States Seventh Cavalry—is depicted astride a magnificent horse in this nine story carving. When completed in the round, the mountain carving will be 563 feet high and 641 feet long—the largest sculpture in the world. To date, 8.4 million tons of granite have been blasted off the mountain. Audiovisual programs and displays show how the mountain is being carved.

The Indian Museum of North America is located here and has almost 20,000 artifacts in three wings. A Native American educational and cultural center opened in 1997. Memorial, dawn-dusk.

Information: Avenue of the Chiefs, Crazy Horse, five miles north off Hwy. 16, 605-673-4681; www.crazyhorse.org

175

SOUTH DAKOTA

★
★
★
★

HOTELS

★Bavarian Inn
Hwy. 16 and 385 N., Custer,
605-673-2802, 800-657-4312;
www.bavarianinnsd.com
65 rooms. Pets accepted; fee. Complimentary continental breakfast. Indoor pool, outdoor pool, whirlpool. Closed December-February. **$**

★★State Game Lodge
Hwy. 16A, Custer,
605-255-4541, 800-658-3530;
www.custerresorts.com
68 rooms. Pets accepted, some restrictions; fee. Restaurant, bar. Closed October-April. **$**

★★Sylvan Lake Resort
Needles Hwy. and Harney Peak, Custer,
605-574-2561, 800-658-3530;
www.custerresorts.com
33 rooms. Pets accepted, some restrictions; fee. Restaurant. Closed November-April. **$**

SPECIALTY LODGINGS

Custer Mansion Bed & Breakfast
35 Centennial Dr., Custer,
605-673-3333, 877-519-4948;
www.custermansionbb.com
6 rooms. Complimentary full breakfast. **$**

RESTAURANT

★Elk Canyon Steakhouse
511 Mount Rushmore Rd., Custer,
605-673-4477
Steak menu. Breakfast, lunch, dinner, brunch. Bar. Children's menu. Casual attire. **$$**

SOUTH DAKOTA

★
★
★
★
★

CUSTER STATE PARK

This is one of the largest state parks in the United States—73,000 acres. A mountain recreation area and game refuge, the park has one of the largest publicly owned herds of bison in the country (more than 1,400), as well as Rocky Mountain bighorn sheep, mountain goats, burros, deer, elk and other wildlife. Four man-made lakes and three streams provide excellent fishing and swimming. Near the park is the site of the original gold strike of 1874 and a replica of the Gordon stockade, built by the first gold rush party in 1874.

The Peter Norbeck Visitor Center (May-October, daily) has information about the park and naturalist programs, which are offered daily (May-September). Paddleboats; horseback riding, hiking, bicycle rentals, Jeep rides, camping, hayrides, chuckwagon cookouts. The Black Hills Playhouse, in the heart of the park, is the scene of productions for 11 weeks (mid-June-late August, schedule varies; 605-255-4141).

Information: Custer, five miles east on Hwy. 16A, 605-255-4515; www.custerstatepark.info

DEADWOOD

This town is best known for gold and the famous Wild West characters such as Calamity Jane, Preacher Smith and Wild Bill Hickock who lived here. The main street runs through Deadwood Gulch. The rest of the town crawls up the steep canyon sides. A bust of Hickock by Korczak Ziolkowski—creator of the Crazy Horse Memorial—stands on Sherman Street. At the height of the 1876 gold rush, 25,000 people swarmed over the hillsides to dig gold. When gold was first struck at Deadwood, nearly the entire population of Custer rushed to here. Predictably, at the height of a newer strike, nearly the entire population of Deadwood rushed to the town of Lead. Recently, legalized gambling has given Deadwood another boom.

Information: Deadwood Area Chamber of Commerce and Visitors Bureau, 735 Main St., 605-578-1876, 800-999-1876; www.deadwood.org

WHAT TO SEE AND DO

Mount Moriah Cemetery
Deadwood
Graves of Wild Bill Hickock, Calamity Jane, Preacher Smith, Seth Bullock, and others.

Old Style Saloon #10
657 Main St., Deadwood,
605-578-3346
Collection of Western artifacts, pictures, guns. This is the saloon in which Wild Bill Hickock was shot. Entertainment (four shows per day, Memorial Day-Labor Day), gambling, refreshments, restaurant. Daily; closed holidays.

HOTEL

★★Bullock Hotel & Casino
633 Main S., Deadwood,
605-578-1745, 800-336-1876;
www.bullockhotel.com
28 rooms. Internet. Restaurant, bar. Fitness room. Casino. $

RESTAURANT

★★★Jake's Atop the Midnight Star
677 Main St., Deadwood,
605-578-1555, 800-999-6482;
www.themidnightstar.com
Located on the top floor of the Midnight Star Casino, this elegant dining room serves American favorites. Piano entertainment is provided five nights a week.
American menu. Dinner. Bar. Children's menu. Casual attire. Reservations recommended. $$

177

HILL CITY

Hill City is a beautiful mountain town in the heart of the Black Hills. The Black Hills Institute of Geological Research and a Ranger District office of the Black Hills National Forest are located here.

Information: Chamber of Commerce, 324 Main St., 605-574-2368, 800-888-1798; www.hillcitysd.com

HOTELS

★★Best Western Golden
Spike Inn & Suites
106 Main St., Hill City,
605-574-2577, 800-780-7234;
www.bestwesterngoldenspike.com
87 rooms. Pets accepted; fee. Restaurant. Fitness room. Indoor pool, outdoor pool, whirlpool. Closed mid-November-mid-March. $

RESTAURANT

★★Alpine Inn
225 Main St., Hill City, 605-574-2749
American, German menu. Lunch, dinner. Closed Sunday. Casual attire. $

HOT SPRINGS

Hot Springs, the seat of Fall River County, is on the southeast edge of the Black Hills National Forest. Many local buildings are made of pink, red and buff sandstone. A Ranger District office of the Nebraska National Forest is located here.

Information: Chamber of Commerce, 801 S. Sixth St., 605-745-4140, 800-325-6991; www.hotsprings-sd.com

WHAT TO SEE AND DO

Black Hills Wild Horse Sanctuary
Rocky Ford Rd., Hot Springs,
605-745-5955, 800-252-6652;
www.gwtc.net/~iram/
Located between the Black Hills and Hell Canyon, the Wild Horse Sanctuary provides a home for wild horses, which were endangered before 1970s protection tactics but then experienced a population boom that pressured the habitat to its limits. Established in 1988 and managed by IRAM (Institute of the Range and the American Mustang), the unspoiled 11,000-acre sanctuary now supports a population of about 400 free-roaming mustangs. April-October: daily; rest of year by reservation only.

Hot Springs Historic District
River Street, Hot Springs
The presence of underground springs catalyzed the development of Hot Springs in the 1880s, with River Street being the epicenter of the boom. The district includes 130 buildings on more than 3,000 acres, including 39 impressive Richardsonian-Romanesque structures made of locally quarried sandstone. Several are occupied by spas fed by the springs, while others house eateries and art galleries.

Mammoth Site of Hot Springs
Hot Springs, 605-745-6017
Excavation of a remarkable concentration of mammoth skeletons; to date the remains of 51 mammoths, a camel and a giant short-faced bear have been unearthed. Daily.

178

SOUTH DAKOTA

HURON

Huron, the seat of Beadle County, is also the administrative center for a number of federal and state agencies. Twelve city parks feature swimming, picnicking, golf, tennis and ballfields. Nearby De Smet is famous for being the home of author Laura Ingalls Wilder.

Information: Huron Convention & Visitors Bureau, 15 Fourth St. S.W., 605-352-0000, 800-487-6673; www.huronsd.com

WHAT TO SEE AND DO

Gladys Pyle Historic Home
376 Idaho Ave. S.E., Huron,
605-352-2528
This Queen Anne-style house, built in 1894, was the residence of the first elected female U.S. senator. Daily, afternoons only.

Hubert H. Humphrey Drugstore
233 Dakota S., Huron,
605-352-4064
Mid-1930s atmosphere; owned by the former senator and vice-president until his death; still owned by Humphrey family. Monday-Saturday.

Laura Ingalls Wilder Home
105 Olivet Ave., De Smet,
605-854-3383;
www.lauraingallswilder.com
Laura Ingalls Wilder and her family lived in these houses from 1887 to 1928, and they figure into her book *Little Town on the Prairie*. Tours are offered of the two houses, and interested visitors can follow a self-guided tour of 16 other De Smet sites mentioned by Ingalls in her books. Daily.

Laura Ingalls Wilder Memorial
105 Olivet Ave., De Smet,
605-854-3383; www.lauraingallswilder.com

Laura Ingalls Wilder wrote a series of children's books based on her childhood experiences in De Smet, on which the *Little House on the Prairie* television series was based. Located here is a restored surveyors' house, the family home from 1879-1880; original family home (1887); replica of a period schoolhouse; memorabilia; and many other sites and buildings mentioned in her books. Guided tours. Open daily.

HOTELS

★★Crossroads Hotel & Convention Center
100 Fourth St. S.W., Huron,
605-352-3204, 800-876-5858;
www.crossroadshotel.com
100 rooms. Pets accepted, some restrictions; fee. Restaurant, bar. Indoor pool, whirlpool. Airport transportation available. $

KEYSTONE

Sculptor Gutzon Borglum began drilling into the 6,200-foot Mount Rushmore in 1927. His carving took 14 years to complete and cost a mere $1 million, though it's now deemed priceless. Keystone is the entrance to Mount Rushmore and Custer State Park. A former mining town supplying miners for the Peerless, Hugo and the Holy Terror Gold Mine, it was also home to Carrie Ingalls (sister of Laura Ingalls Wilder) and the men who carved Mount Rushmore.
Information: Chamber of Commerce, 605-666-4896, 800-456-3345;
www.keystonechamber.com

WHAT TO SEE AND DO

Borglum Historical Center
342 Winter St., Keystone,
605-666-4449, 800-888-4369
Born in Idaho, Gutzon Borglum (1867-1941) won acclaim for his early paintings and was sent by patrons to study in Paris. After he returned to the United States, his lifelike sculptures generated a buzz in the national arts community. Sculpting success led Borglum in 1916 to propose carving the likeness of Robert E. Lee into Stone Mountain in Georgia, a project that he left in 1925 after clashing with financiers. At the age of 60, he embarked on the work that immortalized his fame—carving the presidents' faces on Mount Rushmore. Borglum died just before its completion and his son Lincoln finished the sculpture. The Borglum Historical Center tells the story of Gutzon's remarkable life, focusing on his Mount Rushmore days. The center's exhibits include a full-size replica of Lincolns eye from the monument, assorted artworks by Borglum and a documentary about the Mount Rushmore project, narrated by former U.S. Senator (and South Dakotan) Tom Daschle. May, September:

daily 9 a.m.-5 p.m.; June-August: daily 8 a.m.-6 p.m.

Rushmore Aerial Tramway
203 Cemtery Rd., Keystone,
605-666-4478
This 15-minute ride allows a view of the Black Hills and Mount Rushmore across the valley. May-mid-September: daily.

Rushmore Helicopter Sightseeing Tours
301 Cemetery Rd., Keystone,
605-666-4461
Helicopter rides over Mount Rushmore and nearby points of interest. Mid-May-late September, daily.

HOTELS

★Best Western Four Presidents Lodge
24075 Hwy. 16A, Keystone,
605-666-4472, 800-780-7234;
www.fourpresidents.com
49 rooms. Closed November-March. Complimentary continental breakfast. High-speed Internet access. Fitness room. Indoor pool, whirlpool. $

★
★
★
★
★

LEAD

The chain of gold mines that began in Custer and spread through the Black Hills to Deadwood ended in Lead. The discovery of gold here in 1876 eventually led to the development of the Homestake Mine, one of the largest gold producers in this hemisphere. Lead is located on mountaintops with the Homestake Mine burrowing under the town.

Information: Deadwood Area Chamber of Commerce and Visitors Bureau, 735 Historic Main St., Deadwood, 605-578-1876, 800-999-1876; www.lead.sd.us

HOTEL
★★Golden Hills Resort
900 Miners Ave., Lead,
605-584-1800, 888-465-3080

100 rooms. Pets accepted, some restrictions; fee. Complimentary continental breakfast. Restaurant, bar. $

MITCHELL

This is a tree-shaded town in the James River Valley, where agriculture is celebrated with a colorful nine-day festival each September at the famous Corn Palace, a popular tourist attraction.

Information: Chamber of Commerce, 601 N. Main St., 605-996-6223, 866-273-2676; www.cornpalace.org

WHAT TO SEE AND DO
The Corn Palace
601 N. Main St., Mitchell,
605-996-5031, 866-273-2676;
www.cornpalace.org

Mitchell dubs itself the Corn Capital of the World, a designation backed up by this one-of-a-kind community center. Each year since 1921, locals have decorated the exterior of the turreted, czarist Russia-style palace with different murals, but with a twist— the medium is not paint, but thousands of bushels of corn and other South Dakota grains. The initial intent of the place was to prove the fertility of the South Dakota soil, but it has since evolved into a roadside tourist attraction. The Corn Palace Festival, held annually in September, celebrates the annual fall harvest with concerts, a carnival midway and other festivities. After the harvest, pigeons devour the palace's second skin, leaving the grand facade blank and ready for redecoration the following spring. Daily 8 a.m.-5 p.m., until 9 p.m. in summer.

HOTELS
★Comfort Inn
2020 Highland Way, Mitchell,
605-996-1333, 866-996-1333;

www.comfortinn.com
60 rooms. Complimentary continental breakfast. High-speed Internet access. Indoor pool, whirlpool. Business center. $

★Days Inn
1506 S. Burr St., Mitchell,
605-996-6208; www.daysinn.com
68 rooms. Complimentary continental breakfast. High-speed, wireless Internet access. Indoor pool, children's pool, whirlpool. Business center. $

★★Holiday Inn
1525 W. Havens St., Mitchell,
605-996-6501, 800-888-4702;
www.holiday-inn.com-mitchellsd
153 rooms. Pets accepted, some restrictions; fee. Restaurant, bar. Fitness room. Indoor pool, children's pool, whirlpool. Airport transportation available. $

RESTAURANTS
★★Chef Louie's
601 E. Havens., Mitchell, 605-996-7565
Steak menu. Dinner. Closed Sunday. Bar. Children's menu. Casual attire. $$

★
★
★
★
★

MOBRIDGE

The Milwaukee Railroad built a bridge across the Missouri River in 1906 at what was once the site of an Arikara and Sioux village. A telegraph operator used the contraction "Mobridge" to indicate his location. The name has remained the same. Today, Mobridge is centered in farm and ranch country and is still home for a large Native American population. Located on the Oahe Reservoir, Mobridge is noted for its superb fishing.

Information: Chamber of Commerce, 605-669-3333; www.murdosd.com

WHAT TO SEE AND DO

Sitting Bull Monument

County 1806, off Hwy. 12, Mobridge
Korczak Ziolkowski sculpted the bust for this monument to the legendary Lakota Sioux chief Sitting Bull. The burial ground on the hill affords a beautiful view of the Missouri River and surrounding country.

HOTELS

★★Best Value Wrangler Inn

820 W. Grand Crossing, Mobridge, 605-845-3641, 888-884-3641; www.wranglerinn.com
60 rooms. High-speed Internet access. Restaurant, bar. Indoor pool, whirlpool. Business center. $

PIERRE

Pierre is the capital of South Dakota, an honor for which it campaigned hard and won because of its central location—the geographic center of the state. The town grew thanks to cattle ranchers from the west, farmers from the east, local businesspeople and government officials.

Information: Chamber of Commerce, 800 W., Dakota, 605-224-7361, 800-962-2034; www.pierre.org

181

SOUTH DAKOTA

WHAT TO SEE AND DO

Cultural Heritage Center

900 Governors Dr., Pierre, 605-773-3458
This historical museum north of the South Dakota State Capitol is home to collections of artifacts used by ranchers, miners and Native Americans of the state's past.

On display is the Verendrye Plate, buried by French brothers who explored this area in 1743 (making them the first Europeans to visit South Dakota), and more than 1,300 artifacts depicting the history of the Sioux tribes. Monday-Friday 9 a.m.-4:30 p.m., Saturday-Sunday 1-4:30 p.m.

South Dakota Discovery Center and Aquarium

805 W. Sioux Ave., Pierre,
605-224-8295; www.sd-discovery.com

Visitors of all ages can encase themselves in a Body Bubble, explore a maze laden with displays about the lifestyles of wild animals, or dismantle retired appliances at the Take Apart Table. The modest aquarium houses fish native to South Dakota. Summer workshops allow kids to dig deeper into a science of their choosing. Daily until 5 p.m.; opening time varies by season.

HOTELS

★★Best Western Ramkota Hotel

920 W. Sioux Ave., Pierre,
605-224-6877, 800-780-7234;
www.ramkotahotels.com

151 rooms. Pets accepted. High-speed Internet access. Restaurant, bar. Fitness room. Indoor pool, outdoor pool, whirlpool.

Airport transportation available. Business center. **$**

★Days Inn

520 W. Sioux Blvd., Pierre,
605-224-0411, 800-329-7466;
www.daysinn.com

79 rooms. Fitness room. **$**

RESTAURANTS

★★★La Minestra

106 E. Dakota Ave., Pierre,
605-224-8090; www.laminestra.com

Set in Pierre's historic downtown in an 1896 building, the restaurant's dining room features original wainscoting and tin walls and ceilings. Upscale Italian is served here, including lobster tortellini and eggplant parmesan.

Lunch Monday-Friday, dinner. Closed Sunday. Bar. Reservations not accepted. **$$$**

RAPID CITY

SOUTH DAKOTA

★
★
★
★
★

In the last few decades, tourism has replaced gold mining as the main industry of Rapid City. Visitors come here to visit nearby Mount Rushmore, or to learn about the many dinosaurs that once roamed the area (and even participate in dinosaur digs). Founded only two years after gold was discovered in the Black Hills, Rapid City is a boomtown that persevered. It is the seat of Pennington County, second-largest city in South Dakota, and home of Ellsworth Air Force Base.

Information: Convention and Visitors Bureau, 444 Mount Rushmore Rd. N.,
605-343-1744, 800-487-3223;
www.rapidcitycvb.com

WHAT TO SEE AND DO

Black Hills Petrified Forest
8228 Elk Creek Rd., Rapid City,
605-787-4560
Includes interpretive film on the Black Hills geology and petrifaction process; five-block walk-through area of logs ranging from 5-100 feet in length and up to 3-5 feet in diameter and stumps 3-5 feet in height. Self-guided tours. Rock, fossil and mineral museum; gift and rock-lapidary shops. Memorial Day-Labor Day: daily; weather permitting.

Dinosaur Park
940 Skyline Dr., Rapid City,
605-343-8687
This park has life-size steel and cement models of the dinosaurs once numerous in the area. Daily.

Museum of Geology
O'Harra Memorial Building, 501 E. St. Joseph, Rapid City,
605-394-2467
Exceptional display of minerals, fossils, gold samples and other geological material; first *Tyrannosaurus rex* skull found in South Dakota. Monday-Saturday, Sunday afternoons.

Thunderhead Underground Falls
10940 W. Hwy. 44, Rapid City,
605-343-0081
This tunnel, which dates to 1878, is one of the oldest gold mining tunnels in the Black Hills area. Stalactites and gold-bearing granite formations. Falls are 600 feet inside the mine. May-October: daily.

HOTELS

★★Alex Johnson
523 Sixth St., Rapid City,
605-342-1210, 800-888-2539;
www.alexjohnson.com
143 rooms. Pets accepted; fee. Restaurant, bar. Airport transportation available. Business center. $

★Americinn Rapid City
1632 Rapp St., Rapid City,
605-343-8424, 800-634-3444;
www.americinn.com
64 rooms. High-speed Internet access. Fitness room. Indoor pool, whirlpool. $

MOUNT RUSHMORE NATIONAL MEMORIAL

The faces of four great American presidents—Washington, Jefferson, Lincoln and Theodore Roosevelt—are carved onto a 5,675-foot mountain in the Black Hills of South Dakota, as grand and enduring as the contributions of the men they represent. Senator Peter Norbeck was instrumental in the realization of the monument. The original plan called for the presidents to be sculpted to the waist. It was a controversial project when sculptor Gutzon Borglum began his work on the carving in 1927. With crews often numbering 30 workers, he continued through 14 years of crisis and heartbreak and had almost finished by March, 1941, when he died. Lincoln Borglum, his son, brought the project to a close in October of that year. Today, the memorial is host to almost three million visitors a year. An orientation center, administrative and information headquarters and a snack bar (daily) are on the grounds. Evening program followed by sculpture lighting and other interpretive programs; mid-May-mid-September, daily. Sculptor's studio museum.

Information: Custer, 25 miles southwest of Rapid City off Hwy. 16A and Hwy. 244, 605-574-2523; www.nps.gov/moru

BADLANDS NATIONAL PARK

This fantastic, painted landscape of steep canyons, spires and razor-edged ridges was made a national monument by President Franklin D. Roosevelt in 1939 and became a national park in 1978. Its stark and simple demonstration of geologic processes has an unusual beauty. Soft clays and sandstones deposited as sediments 26 to 37 million years ago by streams from the Black Hills created vast plains, which were inhabited by the saber-toothed cat, the rhinoceros-like brontothere, and ancestors of the present-day camel and horse. Their fossilized bones make the area an enormous prehistoric graveyard. Herds of bison roam the area again. Pronghorn antelope, mule deer, prairie dogs and Rocky Mountain bighorn sheep can also be seen.

The Ben Reifel Visitor Center, with exhibits and an audiovisual program, is open all year at Cedar Pass (daily). Evening programs and activities conducted by ranger-naturalists are offered during the summer. Camping is available at Cedar Pass and Sage Creek. The White River Visitor Center, 60 miles southwest of the Ben Reifel Visitor Center, features colorful displays on the history and culture of the Oglala Sioux.
Information: Hwy. 44, 605-433-5361; www.nps.gov-badl

SOUTH DAKOTA

★★**Best Western Ramkota Hotel**
2111 N. Lacrosse St., Rapid City,
605-343-8550, 800-780-7234;
www.ramkota.com
267 rooms. Pets accepted, some restrictions. High-speed, wireless Internet access. Restaurant, bar. Fitness room. Indoor pool, whirlpool. Airport transportation available. $

★**Best Western Town 'N Country**
2505 Mount Rushmore Rd., Rapid City,
605-343-5383, 877-666-5383;
www.bestwestern.com
99 rooms. Complimentary continental breakfast. High-speed Internet access. Outdoor pool, whirlpool. Airport transportation available. $

★**Days Inn**
1570 Rapp St., Rapid City,
605-348-8410, 800-329-7466;
www.daysinnrapidcity.com
77 rooms. Complimentary continental breakfast. Fitness room. Indoor pool, whirlpool. Airport transportation available. $

★★**Holiday Inn**
505 N. Fifth St., Rapid City,
605-348-4000, 800-465-4329;
www.holidayinnrapidcity.com
205 rooms. Pets accepted; fee. High-speed Internet access. Restaurant, bar. Fitness room. Indoor pool, whirlpool. Airport transportation available. Business center. $

★★**Ramada Inn**
1721 N. Lacrosse St., Rapid City,
605-342-1300; www.ramadamtrushmore.com
139 rooms. Pets accepted; fee. Restaurant, bar. Fitness room. Indoor pool, whirlpool. Airport transportation available. Business center. $

SPECIALTY LODGINGS

Abend Haus Cottages & Audrie's Bed & Breakfast
23029 Thunderhead Falls Rd., Rapid City,
605-342-7788; www.audriesbb.com
10 rooms. No children allowed. Complimentary full breakfast. $

RESTAURANTS

★Firehouse Brewing Co.
610 Main St., Rapid City, 605-348-1915; www.firehousebrewing.com
American menu. Lunch, dinner. Bar. Children's menu. Casual attire. Outdoor seating. **$$**

★Flying T. Chuckwagon Supper & Show
8971 S. Hwy. 16, Rapid City, 605-342-1905; www.flyingt.com
American menu. Dinner. Closed mid-September-late May. **$**

★★Great Wall
315 E. North St., Rapid City, 605-348-1060; www.greatwalltogo.com
Chinese menu. Lunch, dinner. Children's menu. Casual attire. **$$**

★★Imperial
702 E. North St., Rapid City, 605-394-8888
Chinese menu. Lunch, dinner. Children's menu. Casual attire. **$$**

SIOUX FALLS

At the falls of the Sioux River, this city has developed at a constant pace since it was reestablished in 1865 (after being abandoned in 1862 following threats of a Lakota attack). Cattle are shipped from a three-state area, slaughtered and packed here, then shipped east. Manufactured goods from the East are distributed throughout much of South Dakota from Sioux Falls.

Sioux Falls is the center for EROS (Earth Resources Observation Systems), an international center for space and aircraft photography of the Earth.

Information: Chamber of Commerce and Convention and Visitors Bureau, 200 N. Phillips Ave., 605-336-1620, 800-333-2072; www.siouxfallscvb.com

SPOT★LIGHT

★TV ENTERTAINMENT REPORTERS PAT O'BRIEN AND MARY HART BOTH HAIL FROM SIOUX FALLS.

★THE FALLS OF THE BIG SIOUX RIVER RUSH OVER PINK QUARTZITE ROCK.

WHAT TO SEE AND DO

Great Plains Zoo
805 S. Kiwanis Ave., Sioux Falls, 605-367-7003; www.gpzoo.org
The centerpiece of Sherman Park, the Great Plains Zoo focuses on animals native to places outside of South Dakota: black rhinos, red pandas and Galapagos tortoises are among the 400 residents (representing 100 species in all). The zoo replicates a variety of ecosystems, including the Australian Outback and the banks of the Nile River, to

give visitors a better understanding of how the animals live in the wild. A seasonal train takes riders on a behind-the-scenes look at the African Savannah exhibit, and summertime shows give kids a closer look at some of the animals. Daily; hours vary by season.

Old Courthouse Museum
200 W. Sixth St., Sioux Falls,
605-367-4210
Restored Richardsonian-Romanesque quartzite stone courthouse (1890) contains exhibits of Siouxland history, special exhibits on local culture. Daily.

Pettigrew Home and Museum
131 N. Duluth Ave., Sioux Falls,
605-367-7097
This restored Queen Anne house (1889) is furnished to show the life of state's first senator. The house features galleries of Native American items and the cultural history of the Sioux. Daily.

USS *South Dakota* Battleship Memorial
W. 12th St., Sioux Falls, 605-367-7060
The USS *South Dakota* was the first ship to fire on Japanese enemies in World War II and played a role in every major Pacific battle between 1942 and 1945. Located in Sherman Park, the memorial pays honor to the crew that served on the *South Dakota* and has the same dimensions as the ship, which was sold by the Navy in 1962, and features many items that were once onboard. A small museum is also on-site. Memorial Day-Labor Day: daily.

★
★
★
★
★

HOTELS

★AmericInn
3508 S. Gateway Blvd., Sioux Falls,
605-361-3538, 800-634-3444;
www.americinn.com
65 rooms. Complimentary continental breakfast. High-speed Internet access. Indoor pool, whirlpool. $

★Baymont Inn
3200 S. Meadow Ave., Sioux Falls,
605-362-0835, 877-229-6668;
www.baymontinns.com
78 rooms. Pets accepted; fee. Complimentary continental breakfast. High-speed, wireless Internet access. Indoor pool, whirlpool. $

★★Best Western Ramkota Hotel
2400 N. Louise Ave., Sioux Falls,
605-336-0650, 800-780-7234;
www.ramkota.com
226 rooms. Pets accepted, some restrictions. Restaurant, bar. Indoor waterpark, outdoor pool, whirlpool. Airport transportation available. $

★Comfort Inn
3216 S. Carolyn Ave., Sioux Falls,
605-361-2822, 800-252-7466;
www.comfortinn.com
65 rooms. Pets accepted; fee. Complimentary continental breakfast. Indoor pool, whirlpool. $

★Comfort Suites
3208 Carolyn Ave., Sioux Falls,
605-362-9711, 800-424-6423;
www.comfortsuites.com
61 rooms. Pets accepted; fee. Complimentary continental breakfast. High-speed, wireless Internet access. Indoor pool, whirlpool. $

★Days Inn
3401 Gateway Blvd., Sioux Falls,
605-361-9240;
www.siouxfallsdaysinnempire.com
80 rooms. Complimentary continental breakfast. Airport transportation available. $

★★Holiday Inn
100 W. Eighth St., Sioux Falls,
605-339-2000, 800-465-4329;
www.holiday-inn.com-fsd-cityctr
299 rooms. High-speed Internet access. Restaurant, bar. Fitness room. Indoor pool, whirlpool. Airport transportation available. Business center. $

★Kelly Inn - Sioux Falls
3101 W. Russell, Sioux Falls,
605-338-6242, 800-635-3559;
www.kellyinnsiouxfalls.com
43 rooms. Pets accepted. Complimentary continental breakfast. High-speed, wireless Internet access. Whirlpool. Airport transportation available. **$**

★★Ramada Inn and Suites Airport
1301 W. Russell St., Sioux Falls,
605-336-1020, 866-336-1020;
www.ramada.com
153 rooms. Pets accepted, some restrictions; fee. Restaurant, bar. Fitness room. Indoor pool, whirlpool. Airport transportation available. **$**

★★★Sheraton Sioux Falls and Convention Center
1211 N. West Ave., Sioux Falls,
605-331-0100, 800-325-3535;
www.starwoodhotels.com-sheraton-siouxfalls
The Sioux Falls Convention Center is attached to this hotel by an indoor walkway, while the hotel itself offers 97,400 square-feet of meeting space. Rooms cater to the business travelers with amenities like oversized desks, data ports and voicemail as well as plasma TVs and plush beds. The hotel has an indoor heated pool, whirlpool, sauna, fitness room and sun deck. The Falling Waters Grille offers a menu of traditional American fare for breakfast, lunch, and dinner, while the Waters Edge Lounge is a popular stop for cocktails. 184 rooms. Pets accepted, some restrictions. High-speed, wireless Internet access. Restaurant, bar. Fitness room. Indoor pool, whirlpool. Airport transportation available. Business center. **$**

RESTAURANTS
★★★C.J. Callaway's
500 E. 69th St., Sioux Falls,
605-334-8888; www.cjcallaways.com
Overlooking Prairie Green Golf Course, this handsome, country-club-style restaurant offers creatively prepared regional fare. American menu. Dinner. Closed Sunday. Bar. Children's menu. Casual attire. Reservations recommended. Outdoor seating. **$$**

SPEARFISH
The fertile valley in which Spearfish lies is at the mouth of Spearfish Canyon, famous for its scenery and fishing. A Ranger District office of the Black Hills National Forest is located here.
Information: Chamber of Commerce, 106 W. Kansas, 605-642-2626, 800-626-8013; www.spearfish.sd.us

WHAT TO SEE AND DO
High Plains Western Heritage Center
825 Heritage Dr., Spearfish, 605-642-9378;
www.westernheritagecenter.com
Covering pioneer life in the Dakotas, Montana, Wyoming and Nebraska, this history museum includes artwork, artifacts and snazzy custom saddles and Western furnishings. Among the exhibits is the original stagecoach that ran the Deadwood-to-Spearfish route and displays covering mining, forestry and rodeo. Outside, there is a furnished log cabin, a one-room schoolhouse, a seasonal farm with small animals and pastures populated by bison and longhorn cattle year-round. Daily 9 a.m.-5 p.m.

HOTELS
★Best Western Black Hills Lodge
540 E. Jackson, Spearfish,
605-642-7795, 800-780-7234;
www.bestwestern.com
49 rooms. Pets accepted; fee. Complimentary continental breakfast. High-speed Internet access. Outdoor pool, two whirlpools. **$**

★Fairfield Inn
2720 E. First Ave., Spearfish,
605-642-3500, 800-450-4442;

www.fairfieldinn.com
57 rooms. Complimentary continental breakfast. Indoor pool, whirlpool. **$**

★★**Holiday Inn**
305 N. 27th St., Spearfish,
605-642-4683, 800-999-3541;
www.holidayinn-spearfish.com
145 rooms. Pets accepted; fee. High-speed Internet access. Restaurant, bar. Fitness

room. Indoor pool, whirlpool. Airport transportation available. **$**

★★**Spearfish Canyon Resort**
10619 Roughlock Falls Rd., Spearfish,
605-584-3435, 877-975-6343;
www.spfcanyon.com
54 rooms. Pets accepted; fee. Bar. Whirlpool.
$

STURGIS

Originally a "bullwhackers" (wagon drivers) stop on the way to Fort Meade, this was once known as "Scooptown" because soldiers who came in were "scooped" (cleaned out) by such characters as Poker Alice, a famed cigar-smoking scoop-expert. Now Sturgis is a busy Black Hills trade center.
Information: Chamber of Commerce, 2040 Junction Ave., 605-347-2556;
www.sturgis-sd.org

WHAT TO SEE AND DO

Bear Butte State Park
N. Hwy. 79, Sturgis, 605-347-5240;
www.state.sd.us-gfp-sdparks-bearbutt-
bearbutt.htm
Called Mato Paha (or Bear Mountain) by the Lakota people, the defining feature at this park is not actually a flat-topped butte, but a singular mountain (4,422 feet above sea level) rising from the plains. For generations, the mountain has been a spiritually significant site for the Lakota and Cheyenne people, and thousands of worshippers continue to visit the ceremonial area at its base every year. The 1.7-mile Summit Trail takes hikers on a steep path (gaining 1,253 feet) to the peak, where four states can be seen. The park also serves as the northern trailhead for the 111-mile Centennial Trail into the Black Hills. Bison roam free within the parks boundaries. The visitor center features displays on the area's ecology and history and there is a small campground and a lake with a boat ramp in the park. Visitor center, May-early September: daily 8 a.m.-6 p.m. Park, daily 8 a.m.-7 p.m.

Motorcycle Museum and Hall of Fame
2438 Junction Ave., Sturgis,
605-347-4875
Vintage motorcycles; gift shop. Daily.

SPECIAL EVENTS

Sturgis Rally
Sturgis; www.sturgis-rally.com
The biggest motorcycle rally in the country isn't just for bikers anymore—it attracts lawyers, doctors and virtually everybody else who's ever revved a bike. The inaugural rally was held by the local motorcycle club, the Jackpine Gypsies, in 1938, and was quite modest: nine racers riding in front of a small audience. The annual August event has since snowballed into an extravaganza that draws in a crowd of more than 450,000. (More than 100 marriage licenses have been issued to attending couples in recent years.) During the rally, five blocks of Sturgis's historic Main Street are open to motorcycle traffic only, creating a wild atmosphere of wall-to-wall bikes and people. The schedule includes motorcycle races and tours, and there are hundreds of vendors selling everything from leather of all descriptions to exotic foods. Hotels, campgrounds and restaurants in Sturgis book up months before the bikes roar into town. Mid-August.

HOTELS

★**Days Inn**
2630 Lazelle St., Sturgis,
605-347-3027, 800-329-7466;

53 rooms. Pets accepted, some restrictions; fee. Complimentary continental breakfast. Whirlpool. **$**

VERMILLION

Vermillion, the seat of Clay County, was located below the bluffs of the Missouri River until the flood of 1881 changed the river's course, forcing residents to higher ground. Located in a portion of the state that was claimed twice by France and once by Spain before being sold to the United States, Vermillion now prides itself on its rich farmland, good industrial climate and the University of South Dakota, which is located here.

Information: Chamber of Commerce, 906 E. Cherry St., 605-624-5571, 800-809-2071; www.vermillionchamber.com

WHAT TO SEE AND DO
University of South Dakota
Dakota St., Vermillion,
605-677-5326, 877-269-6837;
www.usd.com

On campus is the DakotaDome, a physical education, recreation and athletic facility with an air-supported roof. Art galleries and theaters are located in the Warren M. Lee Center for the Fine Arts and Coyote Student Center.

HOTELS
★Comfort Inn
701 W. Cherry St., Vermillion,
605-624-8333, 800-228-5150;
www.choicehotels.com

46 rooms. Pets accepted; fee. Complimentary continental breakfast. High-speed Internet access. Fitness room. Indoor pool, whirlpool. **$**

RESTAURANTS
★Silver Dollar
1216 E. Cherry St., Vermillion,
605-624-4830

American menu. Lunch, dinner, brunch. Bar. Children's menu. Casual attire. **$$**

189

SOUTH DAKOTA

★
★
★
★
★
★

WALL

Established as a station on the Chicago & North Western Railroad in 1907, Wall is a gateway to Badlands National Park. The town is a trading center for local farmers and ranchers and is noted for its pure water, which is brought up from wells 3,200 feet deep. A Ranger District office of the Nebraska National Forest is located here.

Information: www.wall-badlands.com

WHAT TO SEE AND DO
Wall Drug Store
510 Main St., Wall, 605-279-2175;
www.walldrug.com

Ted and Dorothy Hustead bought the Wall Drug pharmacy in 1931 during the Great Depression. Business was lukewarm for five years until Ted put up signs around town advertising free ice water. It worked and business boomed. Now in the hands of a third Hustead generation, Wall Drug is a sprawling tourist outpost that attracts nearly 20,000 visitors on hot summer days, pouring some 5,000 glasses of ice cold water in the process. The signs remain integral and thousands are in existence along I-90, in European cities like Amsterdam and London, and even in local homes. All this advertising has helped the Husteads build an empire that includes not just a drugstore, but also a shopping mall and a 500-seat restaurant. Studies have shown that about three-quarters of I-90s traffic exits at Wall, South Dakota. Daily 6:30 a.m.-6 p.m.

HOTELS

★Days Inn
210 10th Ave., Wall,
605-279-2000, 800-329-7466;
www.daysinn.com
32 rooms. Pets accepted, some restrictions;
fee. Complimentary continental breakfast.
Whirlpool. $

RESTAURANTS

★Wall Drug
510 Main St., Wall, 605-279-2175;
www.walldrug.com
American menu. Breakfast, lunch, dinner.
Children's menu. Casual attire. $

WATERTOWN

Originally called Waterville, this settlement owed its boom to the railroads. Two large lakes, Kampeska and Pelican, are on the edges of town.
Information: Convention & Visitors Bureau, 1200 33 St. S.E., 605-886-5814, 800-658-4505; www.watertownsd.com

WHAT TO SEE AND DO

Mellette House
421 Fifth Ave. N.W., Watertown,
605-886-4730
This house was built in 1883 by Arthur C. Mellette, the last territorial and the first state governor of South Dakota. Original Victorian furnishings, heirlooms, family portraits. May-September: Tuesday-Sunday, afternoons.

Redlin Art Center
1200 33rd St. S.E., Watertown
605-882-3877
Houses more than 100 of artist Terry Redlin's original oil paintings. Center also includes the only planetarium in the state, an amphitheater, gift shop and Glacial Lakes and Prairie Tourism Association. Daily; seasonal schedule.

HOTELS

★★Best Western Ramkota Hotel
1901 S.W. Ninth Ave., Watertown,
605-886-8011, 800-780-7234;
www.ramkota.com
101 rooms. Pets accepted, some restrictions. High-speed Internet access. Restaurant, bar. Indoor pool, whirlpool. Airport transportation available. $

190

SOUTH DAKOTA

WIND CAVE NATIONAL PARK

Wind Cave, one of many caves in the ring of limestone surrounding the Black Hills, is a maze of subterranean passages known to extend more than 79 miles. It's named for the strong currents of wind that blow in and out of its entrance according to the atmospheric pressure. (When the pressure decreases, the wind blows outward; when it increases, wind blows in.) It was the rushing sound of air coming out of the entrance that led to its discovery in 1881. The cave and surrounding area became a national park in 1903.

The temperature inside Wind Cave is a constant 53 Fahrenheit. Various one- to two-hour guided tours (daily) and four-hour tours (June-mid-August, daily). Tours are moderately strenuous.

On the surface are prairie grasslands, forests and a wildlife preserve the home of bison, pronghorn elk, deer, prairie dogs and other animals. The Centennial Trail, a 111-mile, multi-use trail, takes visitors from one end of the Black Hills to the other. The trail begins here and ends at Bear Butte State Park. Visitor center (daily). Hours may vary throughout the year. Park (daily). 605-745-4600.

Information: Hwy. 385, Hot Springs, 605-745-4600; www.nps.gov-wica

SOUTH DAKOTA

★
★
★
★
★

INDEX

194

INDEX

★
★
★
★
★

197

INDEX

★
★
★
★
★

199

INDEX

★
★
★
☆
☆

200

INDEX

★
★
★
★
★

203

INDEX

★

★

★

★

★

204

INDEX

205

INDEX

★
★
★
★
★

206

INDEX

★
★
★
☆
☆

Y

Yacovelli's (Florissant, MO), *106*
Yahooz (Leawood, KS), *44*
Yellow Smoke Park (Denison, IA), *18*
Yemanja Brasil (St. Louis, MO), *106*
Yen Ching (Dubuque, IA), *26*
Yia Yia (Lincoln, NE), *120*
Yia Yia's Eurobistro (Overland Park, KS), *49*

Z

Zeno's Motel and Steak House (Rolla, MO), *87*
Zia's (St. Louis, MO), *106*
Zinnia (Webster Groves, MO), *106*
Zuber's (Amana Colonies, IA), *4*

207

INDEX

NOTES

★

★

★

★

★

NOTES

★
★
★
★
★

NOTES

★
★
★
★
★

NOTES

★
★
★
★
★

NOTES

★
★
★
★
★

NOTES

★
★
★
★
★

NOTES

★
★
★
★
★

NOTES

★
★
★
★
★

NOTES

★
★
★
★
★

NOTES

★
★
★
★
★

NOTES

★

★

★

★

★

NOTES

★
★
★
★
★

NOTES

INDEX

★
★
★
★
★

NOTES

★
★
★
★
★

NOTES

INDEX

★
★
★
★
★

NOTES

223

INDEX

★
★
★
★
★

NOTES

★
★
★
★
★